EMBRACING disABILITIES in the CLASSROOM

Strategies to **MAXIMIZE** Students' Assets

Toby J. Karten

CORWIN PRESS
A SAGE Company
Thousand Oaks, CA 91320

For information:

Corwin Press
A SAGE Company
2455 Teller Road
Thousand Oaks, California 91320
www.corwinpress.com

SAGE Ltd.
1 Oliver's Yard
55 City Road
London EC1Y 1SP
United Kingdom

SAGE India Pvt. Ltd.
B 1/I 1 Mohan Cooperative
    Industrial Area
Mathura Road, New Delhi 110 044
India

SAGE Asia-Pacific Pte. Ltd.
33 Pekin Street #02–01
Far East Square
Singapore 048763

Printed in the United States of America.

Library of Congress Cataloging-in-Publication Data

Karten, Toby J.
Embracing disabilities in the classroom: strategies to maximize students' assets / Toby J. Karten.
    p. cm.
Includes bibliographical references and index.
ISBN 978-1-4129-5769-4 (cloth)
ISBN 978-1-4129-5770-0 (pbk.)

    1. Children with disabilities—Education—United States. 2. Inclusive education—United States.
I. Title.

LC4031.K358 2008
371.91—dc22   2007049091

This book is printed on acid-free paper.

08   09   10   11   12   10   9   8   7   6   5   4   3   2   1

Acquisitions Editor:	David Chao
Editorial Assistant:	Mary Dang
Production Editor:	Libby Larson
Copy Editor:	Teresa Herlinger
Typesetter:	C&M Digitals (P) Ltd.
Proofreader:	Carole Quandt
Indexer:	Michael Ferreira
Cover Designer:	Scott Van Atta

Contents

PART I: INTRODUCING DISABILITIES

Chapter 1

Historical Background of Disabilities

Chapter 2

How Others Interact With & Acknowledge Disabilities & Differences

PART II: CLASSROOM IMPLICATIONS

Chapter 3

Entering the Inclusive Classroom

Chapter 4

Mastering the Curriculum

Chapter 5

Content-Related Strategies & Lessons

Chapter 6

Instructional Differentiation & Sensitivities That Respond to Students' Behavioral, Social, Emotional, & Perceptual Needs

PART III: SCHOOLS, FAMILIES, AND THE FUTURE

Chapter 7

Increasing Disability Awareness: Promoting Positive Attitudes for Families & All Communities

Chapter 8

Future Horizons for People With Disabilities

APPENDIXES

Appendix A

Differentiating & Assessing Attitudes With Ability Awareness Rubrics

Appendix B

Enabling Versus Challenging Your Students

Appendix C

Student Data Documentation

Appendix D

Increasing Communication & Collaboration

Preface

All students are able. Students are able to achieve, and able to maximize their abilities, given the appropriate guidelines and accepting environments. Disability awareness is not an isolated subject to be taught, but a prevailing level of acceptance that must be shared and practiced by all students and adults. This includes using effective instructional strategies for curriculum delivery and promoting positive attitudes about disabilities for peers, colleagues, and families in schools, homes, and communities.

Teachers modeling *disability etiquette* treat all students as capable individuals, regardless of their weaknesses or differences, be they cognitive, physical, cultural, social, behavioral, perceptual, or sensory. Maximizing students' assets translates to each educator maximizing his or her own assets, as well, to reach each and every student. An ideal societal attitude toward those with differences involves inclusive mindsets both inside and outside of the classroom. *Embracing Disabilities in the Classroom: Strategies to Maximize Students' Assets* illustrates how literature, role-playing, interdisciplinary lessons, teachers, students, administrators, families, legislators, and community members can all act as conduits to maintain, promote, and foster the equal participation of students of all abilities.

We cannot judge a person's worth based upon what we see or think we know about an individual. Some disabilities or differences are hidden, while others are more visible. Is it the disability or difference that disables a student from achieving his or her potential, or is it the reaction of others that is more disabling or isolating? How we treat others in society very often influences how individuals feel about themselves. The media sends out messages that influence both the young and old, in both overt and subliminal ways. Some disabilities or differences even have their own cultures or viewpoints. Others were and may still be subjective recipients of skewed viewpoints held by some people in society. Classrooms are communities of young learners who create our future. Educators can effectively model and establish positive attitudes about disabilities in an *accepting*—not *excepting*—way!

Embracing Disabilities in the Classroom gives the historical background of some past exclusive attitudes toward students with disabilities, compared to today's increasingly more sensitive and inclusive practices. In addition, the book delineates classroom interventions and lessons to promote and propagate societal inclusion to differentiate attitudes and expand opportunities. To counteract any existing negativities, everyone needs to get on board and act as a crew who wants to cheer and celebrate the achievements and possibilities of others. How do we know what lies beyond a disability, if we never stretch our mindsets to realize that differences are not only okay, but welcomed? Throughout

Embracing Disabilities in the Classroom there are numerous curriculum connections and lessons to teach about differences. Educators can concretely connect the idea of differences to successes when the focus is on strengths and potentials. When appropriate accommodations are applied in school settings, individual student profiles are maximized. The purpose of the lessons, tables, rubrics, and charts in the chapters of this book and the appendix is to increase and improve interactions, information, and introspection about disabilities in school settings and beyond. When a student with a disability enters a classroom, he or she will succeed if the best instructional designs, programs, support, and attitudes are in place. These classroom designs include collaboration among planning teams with accommodations and modifications that are intended to recognize a student's level. The preplanning, interplanning, and postplanning are ongoing! Educators who proceed forward with a positive attitude say to their students, *"Yes, you can, and we'll figure out how!"*

Maximizing the potentials for students with disabilities means that everyone else who comes into contact with these students is maximizing their potentials, too! This type of differentiation of attitudes does not let a disability define a person, nor a school program. Strengths exist in all of us. Our assets can yield a future filled with bright horizons. Empower students with and without disabilities to sail into the sunset, charting their own course of destiny, with abilities that match their own possibilities and strengths, not the limitations or anchors imposed by others. So what if a student cannot do something in the same way as others. Maybe a different way is even better! Differentiate the student from the disability. Differentiate attitudes, too! Remove the prefix, and focus on the ability!

Disability

Is

Sometimes

Adjusted

Because

Individuals

Learn

It's

Time to

Incorporate

Everyone's

Strengths!

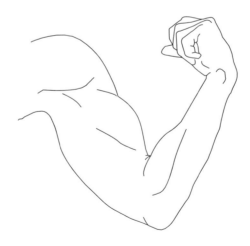

ACKNOWLEDGMENTS

Thank you to my family and friends for your understanding when I sometimes enter that *writing cocoon,* the one with my laptop attached to my hip! Marc and Adam, as always, I couldn't be me without us.

Thank you to those colleagues of mine who consistently include students with differing strengths in their classrooms and then welcomingly discover new ways to reach and teach. Smiles to those educators and administrators who are always on the right page, the ones that talk about caring and learning. To my students throughout the years, continue with your perseverance to succeed; the world awaits your brilliance!

To all at Corwin Press involved with this book, many kudos for your constant dedication in producing the best product possible. That list of professionals at Corwin includes Allyson Sharp, David Chao, Mary Dang, Teresa Herlinger, and many more.

To those individuals who embrace disabilities within themselves and others, you are creating a stronger world for all!

Corwin Press would also like to thank the following for their contributions to this book:

Anne Beveridge
Assistant Head Coordinator,
  Primary Years Programme
Special Education/Literacy Consultant
Branksome Hall, K–12
Toronto, Ontario

Cara Convery
Special Education Teacher
Clayton Elementary School
Englewood, Colorado

Vicki McFarland
Special Education Director
Learning Matters Educational Group
Glendale, Arizona

Kathy Sessions
Teacher, Emotion Behavioral Disorder (EBD)
Cannon Falls Elementary School
Cannon Falls, Minnesota

Leslie Hitchens
Special Education Teacher
Crossroads Elementary
St. Paul, Minnesota

About the Author

 **Toby Karten** is an experienced educator who has worked in the field of special education since 1976. She has an undergraduate degree in special education from Brooklyn College, a master of science in special education from the College of Staten Island, and a supervisory degree from Georgian Court University. Along with being a mentor and resource center teacher in New Jersey, Ms. Karten designed a graduate course entitled Skills and Strategies for Inclusion and disABILITY Awareness and has trained other instructors to teach her course. She is an adjunct professor at the College of New Jersey, Gratz College in Pennsylvania, and Washington College in Maryland. Ms. Karten has presented at local, state, and international staff development workshops and conferences. She has been recognized by both the Council for Exceptional Children and the New Jersey Department of Education as an exemplary educator, receiving two "Teacher of the Year" awards. Ms. Karten has authored several books for Corwin Press about inclusion practices, which are currently used for instruction on many college and university campuses and in schools throughout the world. Ms. Karten believes that once we place the adjective *special* in front of the noun *education*, every classroom student is a winner, receiving the best instructional strategies from a highly trained and prepared staff. She currently resides in New Jersey and Vermont, spending time with her husband, son, and two dogs. She loves her family, teaching, art, and discovering the beauty and the upside to all!

This book is dedicated to Adam Karten, my son,
who taught me the most I've ever learned in life.

PART I

Introducing Disabilities

1

Historical Background of Disabilities

> **Chapter Highlights:** This chapter highlights the historical background of disabilities along with past and current legislation about the Americans with Disabilities Act (ADA), the Individuals with Disabilities Education Act (IDEA), and individualized education programs (IEPs). Disability statistics and vocabulary are outlined along with an introduction to response to intervention (RTI) and universal design.
>
> **Classroom Connections:** Hypothetical scenarios and analogies in this chapter outline the many learning, behavioral, and social concerns that currently exist in inclusive classrooms, communities, homes, and other environments.
>
> **Ways to Differentiate Attitudes:** Perspectives are given about both visible and unseen disabilities. This chapter addresses how barriers can be removed by focusing on strategies that match and maximize individual students' strengths and needs.

THEN AND NOW

Sometimes we need to know where we have been to figure out where we are now, and what the future may hold. The following historical perspectives and quotes shed light on past, present, and future perspectives about disabilities.

> The hard reality is this. Society in every nation is still infected by the ancient assumption that people with disabilities are less than fully human and therefore, are not fully eligible for the opportunities which

are available to other people as a matter of right. (Justin Dart, disability rights activist, 1992, quoted in DEMOS, 2002)

Throughout history, people with disabilities have been treated differently from those who conform to or *fit* societal *norms*. The following bulleted list outlines some of those unfair treatments that were acceptable by different societies in given time periods.

- Killed or abandoned in the woods in ancient Greece
- Kept as jesters for nobility in the Roman Empire courts
- Experienced acts of infanticide during the Renaissance
- Drowned and burned during the Spanish Inquisition
- In 1601, Queen Elizabeth's government divided the poor into three groups. The disabled poor were placed in the group labeled "helpless poor."
- Kept in cellars in correctional institutions in early colonial America if family support was not available; people then paid admission to *gawk at the oddities.*
- Dehumanization in orphanages and asylums in nineteenth-century Europe
- Primary care given by the family at home in the early history of the United States instead of children being allowed out in public, e.g., home-schooled and excluded from community activities
- "Institution for Idiots" founded in Massachusetts in 1848
- Shackled to their beds in U.S. institutions because there was an insufficient number of staff members to care for residents
- Involuntary sterilization of people with developmental disabilities in the United States, beginning in 1907, to prevent the passing on of *inferior* traits
- Considered by eugenicists as defective and an interference with the process of "natural selection"
- Gassed, drugged, blood let, and euthanized in Nazi Germany
- Institutionalized regardless of needs, e.g., person with cerebral palsy was considered mentally retarded
- Housed in separate institutions throughout the world
- Not allowed to attend neighborhood schools
- Aversion techniques used
- Seclusion policies applied
- Restraint applied
- Abuse prevalent (physical, mental, sexual, financial)
- Victimized with inhumane treatments
- Lives devalued
- Stigmatized as criminals
- Viewed as *sickly*
- Inaccurately tested
- Inappropriate labels and services rendered

During World War II, when many jobs were left vacant in the United States, adults with disabilities joined the workforce, showing their competencies, until returning soldiers replaced them in the years following the war. Thankfully, during the 1960s and 1970s, the civil rights movement began and created an even more favorable climate for people with disabilities to continue to enter and succeed in the workforce and beyond. When the inhumane treatment of people with disabilities in institutions in the United States was exposed, this laid down a supportive stage for improving conditions inside and outside of schools for people with disabilities. Eventually, more civil rights and educational laws were passed that consequently changed and expanded services for students and adults with disabilities. This led to the deinstitutionalization of people with disabilities and altered the way society viewed disabilities in general. Group homes became the norm rather than the exception, and more community integration came to be afforded to people with disabilities, with settings that promote independent living. Appropriate education was advocated by U.S. presidents such as Harry Truman, John F. Kennedy, Lyndon Johnson, Ronald Reagan, Gerald Ford, George H. W. Bush, Bill Clinton, and George W. Bush. The table on the next page gives some of these directives, implications, and the beneficial results for people with disabilities in the United States.

Legislation today is continually replacing skewed views with ones that allow students of all ages and abilities to maximize their potential. Limitations may exist for those with disabilities, but many of the additional *imposed anchors* have been removed and replaced with not only *life preservers to stay afloat*, but also the opportunity for *smooth and pleasurable sailing.*

Public Law 94-142 (the Education for All Handicapped Children Act of 1975) introduced a piece of legislation that drastically improved the way students with disabilities were treated in school settings. Consequently, through the decades that followed, peoples' attitudes toward children and adults with disabilities have become more accepting. The earlier subhuman institutions were replaced with mindsets that advocated community integration. Each decade that followed P.L. 94-142 has added more provisions and continues to recognize future possibilities by not only leaving the *educational door ajar,* but also placing a *welcome mat* outside every classroom!

Services now include recognizing students and those of all ages as individuals who have the same basic needs and desires. Equal treatment in schools, private and government facilities, and community activities eventually translates to students with disabilities succeeding in life. With positive educational and social experiences, people with differing cognitive, physical, and social abilities and levels are primed to become happy and productive citizens and adults.

> So why can't we see students' difficulties as human variation rather than pathology? (Reid & Valle, 2004)

Maybe one day we will!

OUT AND ABOUT

> Increased visibility of persons with *disabilities* came about as the logical extension of the independent living, normalization, and self-advocacy movements of recent decades. (Ward, 1996)

Unfortunately, this visibility did not automatically translate into acceptance by school personnel, community, and other students. The way someone views another person is dependent upon factors such as his or her comfort level; prior background and experiences, be they positive or negative; cognitive levels; social skills; and feelings of self-esteem. This complicates issues about how a student with a difference is viewed.

Quite often, students try to "overcome" or hide their disability and don't even ask for help because they are afraid of being seen as more disabled. In addition, relationships and viewpoints of others at times influence individual successes and failures of students with disabilities in school settings, communities, and in their adult lives.

Table 1.1   Legislative Accomplishments and Disability Directives

Legislative Accomplishments and Disability Directives	Implications and Results
In 1947, the President's Committee on National Employ the Physically Handicapped Week was established by President Truman.	Today that week is now expanded to a month in October, *National Disability Employment Awareness Month*, to increase public awareness and job opportunities for individuals with disabilities.
In the 1950s, Vocational Rehabilitative Amendments along with U.S. Civil Service Commission directives were passed. In 1954, *Brown v. Topeka Board of Education* had a major impact upon integration and other civil rights movements in education and beyond.	More people with disabilities were given opportunities to become gainfully employed to maximize their independence. Two court cases, *PARC v. Pennsylvania* (1972) and *Mills v. D.C. Board of Education* (1972), used the precedent of *Brown v. Topeka* to argue that students with disabilities also deserve protective equal educational rights. Later on, this opened the door for EHA, ESEA, and IDEA.
In 1962, Executive Order 10994 by President John F. Kennedy removed the word "physically" from the President's Committee's name.	This recognized that there were other disabilities besides physical ones that would be addressed in legislation and beyond. This now expanded society's need to include and protect people with developmental, psychiatric, and intellectual disabilities in the workforce and more, leading to increased acceptance and fewer stigmas.
In 1965, President Lyndon Johnson signed the Elementary and Secondary Education Act (ESEA). This federal education law applied to funding K–12 grades for professional development, instruction, educational resources, and parental participation.	In 1967, Congress added Title VI to the Elementary and Secondary Education Act of 1965, creating a Bureau of Education for the Handicapped (BEH). Then, in 1983, this bureau was replaced by the Office of Special Education Programs (OSEP). ESEA was influential in the development of IDEA, the Bilingual Education Act, and Goals 2000: Educate America Act. In the years 2001–2002, President George W. Bush renamed ESEA the No Child Left Behind Act (NCLB).
The 1973 Rehabilitation Act prohibited businesses with federal contracts to discriminate in employment or services on the basis of disability, allowing for affirmative action programs for hiring people with disabilities. Section 504 referred to qualified *handicapped individuals* not being excluded from participation in programs or activities that receive federal financial assistance, e.g., school district, state education agency.	Through the following decades, this law was extended and applied to school settings to include those students with a "record" of a disability or "regarded as" having a disability. Eligibility pertains to children who currently suffer from an impairment substantially limiting learning or another major life activity, allowing them to receive referral, evaluation, and educational services. It stops discrimination and prejudicial treatments against students in academic and extracurricular activities.
P.L. 93-380, The Family Education Rights and Privacy Act (FERPA) of 1974.	Allows parents of students under the age of 18, and students age 18 and over, the right to examine records kept in the student's personal file.

(Continued)

Table 1.1 (Continued)

Legislative Accomplishments and Disability Directives	Implications and Results
In 1974, EHA was enacted. In 1975, the Education for All Handicapped Children Act (P.L. 94-142) mandated that all children with disabilities be granted a free, appropriate public education (FAPE) in the least restrictive environment possible.	Signed by President Gerald Ford in 1975 and went into effect in October of 1977 when the regulations were finalized. Expanded to include preschool special education programs, early intervention, and transition programs in 1983. In 1986, age of eligibility was lowered to age 3 and early intervention services (birth–3) were made available. In 1990, it was changed to the Individuals with Disabilities Education Act or IDEA (P.L. 101-476). Services were made available to students with autism or traumatic brain injury as well as those needing transition services, social services, and more. Changed again to IDEIA in 2004. EHA is considered to be the grandparent of IDEA.
P.L. 98-524, The Vocational Education Act of 1984.	Required that vocational education be provided for students with disabilities. In 1988, President Ronald Reagan established by executive order the current name of the President's Committee on Employment of People with Disabilities. In 1990 and 1991, Congress passed P.L. 101-392 and P.L. 102-103, respectively. The name was changed to the Carl D. Perkins Vocational and Applied Technology Education Act and its goal was to improve academic and occupational skill competencies and programs.
Americans with Disabilities Act of 1990 (ADA).	President George H. W. Bush signed this civil rights law that guarantees equal opportunity for individuals with disabilities in employment, public accommodation, transportation, state and local government services, and telecommunications.
In 2002, NCLB was signed and renamed from ESEA, by President George W. Bush. It included increased accountability for students and teachers and more effective teaching methods.	Includes additional parental options to send their children to an alternate school, have state-administered standardized testing, flexibility with school budget (allocation of funds to various NCLB programs), and professional development (e.g., reading programs). Its goal is to allow all students access to promising futures with educational improvements across socioeconomic levels.
IDEIA, Individuals with Disabilities Education Improvement Act of 2004.	Functional or nonacademic goals now included, meaning those regarding getting along in the real world. This includes a statement of academic achievement and functional performance. Other highlights include more parental participation in the IEP, periodic or quarterly progress reports of goals, and using the response to scientifically based instructional practices instead of only the discrepancy model as criteria for identification of students with learning needs (RTI). Advocates more preparation, knowledge, and skills for teachers. Students with disabilities are now receiving many more school opportunities with focus on outcomes rather than compliance.

Whose Perspective?

A student with a disability is viewed differently by

1. Other students in the class
2. The community
3. Families/caregivers
4. Siblings
5. General education teachers
6. Special education teachers
7. Parents of other students in the class
8. Administration
9. Bus drivers
10. Cafeteria workers
11. Specialists: art, gym, or music teachers; speech pathologists
12. Other students with disabilities

The following excerpt tries to examine the complexities of including a hypothetical student with a disability, Sam, in a school setting. Being with the general education population, interacting with the "regular" kids, is sometimes tough! Although educational legislation has now guaranteed students with disabilities the right to a physical space in the classroom, not all student and adult attitudes are accepting ones. Other people are still sometimes frustrated or confused by differences. Thank goodness many educators, school personnel, peers, and families are coming to be on the same academic, social, and behavioral learning page—one that allows students with differences and disabilities to maximize their assets.

"Presenting Sam" is a hypothetical classroom situation that delineates possible reactions, perspectives, and complex attitudes and sentiments various stakeholders may possess when students with disabilities are educated in school settings. The two scenarios depict different attitudes, which then result in different outcomes. Although these statements are hypothetical ones, some of them may be recognizable to you.

Presenting Sam

From Sam (the student)

<u>1st Scenario</u>: I want to be normal, but how? Those special classes are the worst. I hate the short lines and those stares. Everyone is looking at us. Yuck! *Why*? we wonder. When will our wishes win? Where are the welcoming words? Why do they think we are weirdos?

<u>2nd Scenario</u>: I'm so glad that I'm in the same class as the kids I go on the school bus with! I don't always understand the lesson the first time, but since there are two teachers in the room, I can always go to one of them for extra help. Everybody else does, too, even the kids who aren't supposed to! Wow! Wisdom's wonderful!

From Sam's mom:

1st Scenario: Well, he's my son and no one is going to tell me that he's not like the other kids. What do they know? It's the teacher's fault. She never liked my son and she wants him out of the class. She shuns. She shoos. She stigmatizes Sam.

2nd Scenario: I realize that Sam learns differently and needs some extra help. It's no big deal if he receives his reading instruction and study skills support in the resource room. At least he'll be getting the direct skill instruction he needs there. Then, maybe he'll be able to be in his classroom full time, once progress has been achieved. I think that the teachers know what they're doing here. Sam smiles. Sam sees some support. Sam shines!

From Sam's dad:

1st Scenario: Sam is my boy, my own flesh and blood. He has my genes and they're strong ones. No one in my family ever had Sam's problems. He'll outgrow it and get smarter. I'm going to tell the teacher to try teaching to take away Sam's troubles.

2nd Scenario: Okay, so what if Sam needs some extra help! No one is to blame; everybody needs help sometimes. I remember I never really loved school, but now Sam is able to reach out and be taught in a way that helps him to understand more. They use pictures to help Sam understand the words, and sometimes the class even sings songs about what they are learning! Tell the terrific teacher, thanks! Time to try tolerance!

From Sam's sibling:

1st Scenario: Sam, this, Sam, that! What about me? What about my feelings? Don't I count, too? Please, parents. I hate my pouts. Plus, I have no more prayers and even less patience. Please end this pandemonium!

2nd Scenario: Sam, Sam, my sweet brother! How can I help you? I don't think that this is a time to say who is more important. We all count and can lean on each other! Progress prevails!

From Sam's peer:

1st Scenario: Can't believe that Sam is in the same school as I am! He travels on the bus with me and he's even in my gym class! Sam acts strangely and is always jumping out of his seat. He can't even sit still long enough to listen. Definitely a dork! He's different, and distracting!

2nd Scenario: Sam sure is different, but I like him! He has a unique way of seeing the world. Wish I sometimes was a little more like Sam. Defend differences!

From a parent of a student in the general education class who is not receiving services:

1st Scenario: Just what do they think they are doing by placing a kid like Sam in the same class as my daughter, Angel! Angel is much brighter than Sam and shouldn't be held back while those two teachers are slowing down the pace for the other kids. Besides, Sam does weird flapping things with his hands. Sometimes the teachers ask my Angel to help him! It's insulting! I'm incensed!

2nd Scenario: Angel acts differently this year. She seems more mature and has become even nicer now that she has become friends with Sam. Sam needs a little extra help, and my Angel sometimes tutors him. It's a great lesson in character education. During classroom visitation week, I saw those two teachers in action. It's amazing how they set up the class to reach all of the students through those cooperative projects. My Angel even gets to complete some independent research assignments as the teachers drift around the classroom, helping all. I'm immensely impressed! Individualized instruction is interesting!

From Sam's General Education teacher:

1st Scenario: How can I reach Sam? How can I teach him? How can I…? Am I prepared to work with Sam? He needs nurturing. No nonsense. Necessary knowledge, now!

2nd Scenario: I'll figure out a way to reach Sam. I have all this literature that can help. I think that I'll attend a workshop on my professional development day that will help me apply some appropriate strategies to address Sam's IEP goals. I won't blame other teachers or the administration for placing Sam in my class. I'll be more prepared and try to differentiate my instruction to meet Sam's academic, behavioral, emotional, and social needs. So much has to do with my attitude and the attitudes of the students in the class. I'll maximize Sam's assets! No need for negativism!

From Sam's Special Education teacher:

1st Scenario: How can I get the other teachers to accept Sam in their class and have high expectations for him, too? When will the teachers realize that Sam does belong here? How will I make accommodations, without the other kids wondering why they aren't getting the same special treatment? When will I have planning time to collaborate with all of Sam's other teachers? Big burdens. Bury the blame. Believing in the best outcome is the basic building block for inclusive successes.

2nd Scenario: Wow! I thought that this would be harder than it really is! Coteaching is awesome! I get to help Sam and no one even realizes that's why I'm here. My views are less skewed since I am able to align Sam's strides to the curriculum and see how his progress compares to some of the work produced by the other students. I even help everyone pay attention! The GE teacher is terrific! He lets me offer strategies and we trade off teaching the lesson. I'm glad that I took my math praxis and brushed up on my calculus skills! Sam definitely needs two strong teachers! Big bonds built between both!

From the administrator at Sam's school:

1st Scenario: The teachers need to raise Sam's test grades. Where's the yearly progress? Everyone should follow the school's program and rules. It's about answers! Accommodate and appropriately approach all as adults.

2nd Scenario: Sam will be placed where he belongs. We'll monitor his progress and definitely not teach to the test, but teach to Sam's needs within his classroom. I'll support my teachers and offer them my resources and assistance in their efforts to reach and teach everyone the skills they need. Answers await as all allow alternate avenues. Achieving awesome advances!

Read more about ways to address Sam's concerns as expressed in each of the first scenarios above:

Helping and Supporting Sam, His Family, Teachers, Peers, and Others

<u>For Sam</u> (the student): Depending upon his age and cognitive, behavioral, and social levels, Sam needs to be taught the *hidden curriculum.* This means that he has to learn how to fit in with the school culture. If he does, then the unwanted stares, negative comments, and exclusion from other students will diminish. The hidden curriculum is also about learning how to learn. That sometimes includes what the teacher is not directly teaching, but what the students need to know about the teacher, other students, or even the way the school is organized. This will help Sam to make generalizations and apply the learning. Sam also has to learn that *it's okay to be different* and that everyone has varying strengths and weaknesses. If Sam needs extra help, he has to understand that it's not something to hide or be ashamed of. Allowing his needs to be known will make him stronger. Younger students can read picture books about characters who overcome obstacles. Older students can read about protagonists who have disabilities in fiction genres. Another option is to learn about and from real people with disabilities who turned things around by maximizing their potential and maintaining positive attitudes. The goal is to increase self-advocacy, self-image, and self-determination to succeed. When Sam is aware of his own levels and needs, he will then realize that asking for help is an avenue to continually explore.

<u>For Sam's mom</u>: Sam's mom needs to know that no one is to blame for Sam's difficulties. If she thinks that Sam's teacher does not treat Sam fairly, then she can schedule a meeting to open up the dialogue and include other staff members who know Sam, e.g., case managers, prior teachers, and Sam, if he is of the appropriate age and possesses the maturity to attend.

<u>For Sam's dad</u>: Sam's father needs a realistic view of his son, understanding that Sam will not outgrow his disability, but rather will learn strategies to maximize his strengths. It's possible that Sam's dad could benefit from joining a parent support group to discuss his emotions about Sam and hear thoughts from other families. It might be a group that his son, his wife, and their other children could attend together as a family.

<u>For Sam's sibling</u>: Sam's sibling desperately needs attention, too! Raising a child with a disability can be taxing on the whole family, creating undue tensions for all members. Maybe Sam's dad and mom can schedule quality time individually or together with Sam's sibling, letting him or her know that they have enough love for Sam and his brother and/or sister, too! The family also needs to spend time together as a unit to bond, rather than letting jealousies brew and fester. Just reading a book, going for a walk, or watching a movie or television show together might be all that's needed to reassure Sam's sibling that he or she is loved, too!

<u>For Sam's peers</u>: If possible, educators, families, guest speakers, or students with disabilities can conduct disability sensitivity activities that outline specific characteristics students with differing abilities might display in the classroom. In addition, guided character-building lessons can raise peers' self-esteem, so they will not need to *pick on* other students they perceive to be inferior to feel better about themselves.

<u>For Sam's General Education teacher</u>: Available and frequent training sessions and workshops with agendas that teach about disabilities and appropriate instructional strategies will help teachers implement lessons, adapt strategies, and assess Sam's varying needs while delivering the curriculum. In addition, allotting planning time for meeting with Sam's coteachers, other colleagues, parents, and guardians to gain more insights, open up communication, and review Sam's assessments and progress gives everyone a chance to collaborate. Information regarding Sam's past needs and performance must be available to bridge the knowledge and share effective strategies implemented by former teachers. Transitional conferences to discuss the transition between grades can be scheduled on staff development workshop days at the beginning of the year.

<u>For Sam's Special Education teacher</u>: Again, allot common planning time in teachers' schedules to meet and discuss Sam's ongoing needs and progress. Respect from the administration for teachers' efforts with Sam is the encouraging pat on the back some educators need. It is important for principals and other administrators to acknowledge Sam's partial achievements. Include Sam's special education teacher in general education curriculum meetings, too.

<u>For the administrator at Sam's school</u>: Realize and honor everyone's efforts in helping Sam work toward his individual educational goals. Listen to teachers' feedback regarding workshops needed to obtain more strategies to maximize Sam's strengths. Honor and respect the people who know Sam. Be Sam's administrator and his advocate, too!

These two quotes relate to Sam and many other students who are the recipients of special services in school settings:

When you start to understand how he sees the world, you will learn that seeing things differently from others is not such a bad thing. (Hoopman, 2001, p. 69)

I don't think it's an exaggeration to say that special education saved my life. (Abeel, 2003, p. 100)

BEYOND THE TERMINOLOGY

So What Exactly Is a Disability?

Most instructors and students do not have 100% of their faculties working at 100% capacity for 100% of the time; disability is pretty much a relative term. (Miller, 2004)

People with disabilities should not be viewed as being in the "sick" role.... [It is] not a health issue...not a medical question....A person with a disability is not "sick" because of a disability. (Pfeiffer, 1996)

It's easier for visitors to *The Land of Disability* to pass a multiple-choice test about disabilities than it is for them to be comfortable with an authentic, genuine, disabled person. (Brightman, 2006)

I don't see disability as a tragedy. People have various forms of disabilities and some of those are acquired through age, and some are acquired because of poverty, and some are the result of being young—car crashes and wars and things of that nature. I see disability as a normal part of life. I look at it like, *What do people need in order to be able to live their life like anybody else?* (Judith Heumann, quoted in Montes, 2007)

 Each child has his or her own set of fingerprints. Children have their own likes and dislikes. A child with a disability must be seen as a child first. (Karten, 2005)

Society sometimes determines the extent of someone's disability by its reaction to and treatment of that person. For example, a person in a wheelchair or someone who is blind may receive more attention for being disabled than a person who has a learning difference, hearing loss, or emotional issues. Some disabilities are structural, while others are internal, not as apparent or visible as others. An analogous classroom situation would be when teachers try to instruct students with concrete facts vs. abstract learning. Many students understand things that are spelled out and visible, while the connections that are required to understand what is not seen or the abstract may be more difficult. Both the concrete and abstract must be comprehended, however. The same holds true about disabilities: both the visible and the *unseen* need to be understood and *accepted* by all, *no exceptions!*

Visible Versus Unseen Disabilities

(How would you categorize these?)

- Dyslexia
- Depression
- Diabetes
- Language disorder
- Hearing impairment

- Cerebral palsy
- Down syndrome
- Speech impediment
- Asperger syndrome
- Autism

He Won't Always Be *Retarded!*

While off to present a workshop entitled *Celebrating the Challenges!* I met a wonderful mom who raised a son with *developmental issues.* While conversing with me as she was traveling on a plane with her 44-year-old son to visit relatives, she shared a very poignant viewpoint. She mentioned that when her son was younger, she was told that he wouldn't always be retarded. She then explained how a woman told her that the term *retarded* would not always be politically correct. Sure enough, she remarked, when he was a teenager, she attended a meeting and was told that her son was now *developmentally disabled.* "Wow, now isn't that a mouthful!" she said.

The term mental retardation is still in use in federal statutes as a diagnostic term in determining eligibility for public benefit programs ("How should the disabled be described?" 2006). The nonprofit organization called the Arc, though its acronym stands for the Association for Retarded Citizens, no longer uses the term *mental retardation,* but in its mission statement says that it works to include children and adults with cognitive, intellectual, and developmental disabilities in every community. The term *mental retardation* was offensive to many people, so the Arc decided to keep the acronym, but changed their language, though certainly not their commitment to the people they serve (www.thearc.org).

However, many labels today still stigmatize students before they even set foot in a classroom. Regardless of the name or diagnosis, whether it is mental retardation, intellectual disability, cognitive challenge, or a developmental disability, the needs of these students remain the same. The utmost necessity is for students with disabilities to be treated with respect by adults, students, and peers in school, community, and home settings. Relating learning to students' lives is important for those whose measured aptitudes may seem limited or deficient, but are in fact capable of achieving strides in different ways. If the goal is to have students lead productive, independent lives, then all role models must *treat the student, not the label!*

This includes training for not only the teachers and families, but also the bus drivers, instructional assistants, lunchroom aides, and more! In addition, when the music, art, physical education, world language, speech, and other staff know what topics and concepts are being taught, they can plan and incorporate appropriate lessons that mirror the classroom's concept, e.g., singing ballads from the Civil War, or learning about art from the Renaissance period. More strides are reached when social, cognitive, communication, and self-help skills are directly modeled, taught, reinforced, and broken down into their components in all settings.

The following tables include how to monitor and escalate *inclusion* across settings.

Table 1.2   Monitoring Students' Behaviors in All Settings

Feedback from a bus driver, lunchroom aide, special subject teacher, or instructional assistant	*Yes or No*	*Additional observations, comments, or concerns about behavior or performance*
1. Student behaves appropriately on the bus, in the lunchroom, in the classroom, or other setting.		
2. Other students or families are displeased with this student's actions.		
3. This student needs extra attention on the bus, in the lunchroom, or in the classroom.		
4. Other students are eager to sit near this student and help.		
5. Student listens and follows directions.		
6. Student exhibits self-control with improvements noted.		
7. Additional monitoring is needed.		
8. Glad to have this student included!		
Report by: _____ Student: _____ Date: _____	Class/Room/Bus: _____	

Table 1.3 Collaboration and Communication With All Teachers and Staff

Collaboration and Communication With All Teachers and Staff to Promote Academics in Other Settings		
From: _____ To: _____		
	Topic	*Concept*
This Week's Lessons		
Next Week's Lessons		
Projects We're Doing		
Future Lessons		

The following similes and metaphors relate disabilities to the curriculum in a positive way. Unintentionally, people's perspectives and descriptions of disabilities can at times be the unnecessary stumbling blocks in *unfair obstacle courses!* Life has enough everyday challenges without superimposed prejudicial attitudes blocking goals for students. Labels are intended to reveal the contents, yet somehow they never do justice to the real flavor!

Disability–Curriculum Analogies

Read these similes and metaphors, and then try to write your own subjective, yet objective ones.

Table 1.4

Subject	Metaphor	Simile
Math	A disability is a decimal that is sometimes regarded by others as less worthy than a whole number.	A disability is like a decimal, seeking the same *points* in life.
Science	A disability is a telescope trying to grasp shining stars.	A disability is sometimes like a microscopic slide that has its traits magnified for others to view.
Social Studies	A disability is often a map without a legend.	A disability is like a map that represents more than what is seen.
Reading	A disability is a book that reveals itself, page by page.	A disability is as varied as the genres in a library.
Writing	A disability is an epic poem.	A disability is like a novel, revealing its plot.
Languages	A disability is a story that sometimes requires subtitles for others to understand.	A disability is as beautiful as a romance language.
Art/Music	A disability is a picture with elements in the foreground and background.	A disability is as joyous and as talent-filled as a Broadway musical!

Educational Stops

 Special education (SE) was always the *first stop* along the *educational train* if students were not achieving classroom strides. Students who did not respond to the learning in the same way and had diverse abilities were sometimes unnecessarily *tracked* under the SE label for the rest of their schooling. This exclusion from their age-appropriate peers denied many students the opportunities to maximize their abilities.

Academic and social interactions with peers were limited. Quite often, the curriculum delivered in self-contained classes deleted and diluted many concepts. Aside from limited academics, not being with the general education population did not afford students with and without disabilities the opportunity to develop friendships with each other.

SE labels are complex. Unnecessary labeling can be injurious, but at the same time it directs school personnel to the need to provide appropriate resources and supports. Labels may offer common characteristics of some disabilities, but they do not define students since diversities exist within each disability category. It's the student who should be seen first, not the label. Basically, schools should be more about outcomes and delivering services, rather than assigning labels or *tracking* students.

The train is gaining momentum for students with disabilities, now in the classroom, who are on board for the *curriculum stops* and hopefully a

Table 1.5

Positive Traits	Strengths
interests	likes
capabilities	competencies
strategies	interventions
appropriate	fitting
collaboration	coplanning
goals	objectives
success	achievements
response	progress
confidence	optimism
choices	options

life filled with diverse possibilities. This is evidenced in higher graduation rates, lower dropout rates, more inclusion with assessments and accountabilities, and RTI. Improved postsecondary outcomes, which are not limited to college attendance, are now more possible for students with disabilities. Apprenticeship opportunities and vocational/career education programs exist, but still more are needed to better allow students to maximize their strengths and interests to become contributing members of society. Schools that offer a combination of programs, not strictly academic ones, allow all students, not just those with disabilities, to have options concerning postsecondary programs. The best approach is to give students the opportunity to master the curriculum and honor their positive traits and strengths. Education is the ticket that will allow students to make choices with strategies and concepts learned in school that will hopefully be productively transferred and transitioned into adulthood. Education for students with and without disabilities needs to concentrate on their strengths as shown in the table with synonyms about abilities and possibilities. As Samuels (2007) poignantly states, "It's not a special ed issue, it's an every ed issue."

WHO IS CONSIDERED TO BE A PERSON WITH A DISABILITY?

These collective quotes offer some insights about students with special needs. Some of the following statistics by themselves can be misleading since many factors influence the numbers. Equally important are socioeconomic factors, and how children's schooling, work ethic, and progress are influenced by where they live; who's home to support them; what resources are in the home; and, if they are a member of a minority, how that minority group is viewed by others. How much money is earned in the home can influence a family's views on education. Students living in poverty unfortunately sometimes have impoverished educations, if steps are not taken to circumvent monetary factors and abysmal outlooks. A student with a disability who is born into a family with more money and resources may have more chances to excel than a student whose family is also worried about where the next plate of food is coming from. Our awareness—including acceptance of differences, diagnostic tools, and medical acumen—has increased, while much of the shunning and stigmas have decreased. There are a multitude of factors underlying these statistics across geographic regions of our country, as well.

Some statistics:

Approximately 6.5 million children ages 3 to 21 have been diagnosed with special needs, up nearly 40% in eight years. (Gutner, 2004, quoting statistics from the U.S. Department of Education)

In 1976–77, about 3.7 million youth were receiving special education services, which was about 8% of the total enrollment in public schools. Then in 2005–2006, about 6.7 million students were receiving services under IDEA, which was about 14% of the public school enrollment. (U.S. Department of Education, 2007)

More than 10% of U.S. households have offspring (adult children included) with special needs. (Gutner, 2004, quoted from www.pacer.org)

Among school age youth (ages 6–21), specific learning disabilities were the most prevalent disability and had the largest increase in service receipt from 1976–2001. It increased threefold—from 2% to 6%. (U.S. Department of Education, National Center for Education Statistics, 2006)

The U.S. Centers for Disease Control and Prevention estimates that the number of children who received special education for autism and related disorders increased from 22,664 in 1994 to 141,022 in 2003. (Unger, 2006)

Autism is the fastest growing disability in the U.S., more prevalent than childhood cancer and juvenile diabetes. More boys than girls are affected with a ratio of 4:1. (Rivera, 2007)

In April 2007, researchers from the Federal Centers for Disease Control and Prevention and the Interdisciplinary Council on Developmental and Learning Disorders presented a report that said about 17% of U.S. children have a developmental disability such as autism, mental retardation and attention deficit-hyperactivity disorders, but that fewer than half are diagnosed before starting school. (Tanner, 2007)

Black students with disabilities were more likely than students of any other race or ethnicity to spend less than 40% of their day in a regular classroom and were the most likely to be placed outside of a regular school. (National Center for Education Statistics, 2005)

Lynda Price, an associate professor of special education at Temple University, estimates that as many as one in 10 adults may have a learning disability and that the vast majority conceal it from workplace supervisors. (Zimmerman, 2006)

After evaluating data submitted from states, the U.S. Department of Education released evaluations in June 2007 of each state's efforts to teach children with disabilities from infants to secondary school students. Most states received grades of *needs assistance* or *needs intervention*, with only nine making the highest grade, *meets the requirements,* for students aged 3 to 21. For services for infants through 2-year-olds, 15 states met requirements while the others ranked as needing assistance or needs intervention. None of the states received the lowest category since 2007 was the baseline year for the data. In addition, states now need to submit state performance plans (SPP) which tell of their intended improvement plans for the next six years. (Samuels, 2007)

The accountability bar is now raised, with states paying attention to the data. Each state also must submit an APR, which is its Annual Performance Report of progress toward the SPP. So it seems that IEPs under IDEA and LEAs have led to SPPs with APRs! (Translation: Individualized Education Programs under the Individuals with Disabilities Education Act and Local Education Agencies have led to State Performance Plans and Annual Performance Reports!) The following table outlines some statistics about the approximately 54 million people in the United States with disabilities compared to those without disabilities.

Table 1.6   Disability Comparisons Across Genders, Ages, Populations, and Locations

Gender	8% of boys	4% of girls	**Aged 5–15**
Gender	12% of men	11% of women	**Aged 16–64**
Gender	38% of men	42% of women	**Aged 65 or older**
Employed	42% of men (4 million)	34% of women (3.5 million)	**Aged 21–64**
Sensory disability involving sight or hearing	4.1% of noninstitutionalized civilian population	10.8 million people	**Aged 5 or older**
Conditions that limit basic physical activities such as walking, climbing stairs, reaching, lifting, or carrying	9% of noninstitutionalized civilian population	23.6 million people	**Aged 5 or older**
Physical, mental, or emotional condition causing difficulties in learning. Can include remembering and concentrating	5.1% of noninstitutionalized civilian population	13.5 million people	**Aged 5 or older**
Physical, mental, or emotional condition causing difficulties in home settings. Can include difficulty in dressing, bathing, or moving inside the home	2.7% of noninstitutionalized civilian population	7 million people	**Aged 5 or older**
Difficulty going outside the home such as visiting a doctor or shopping	4.9% of noninstitutionalized civilian population	10.7 million people	**Aged 16 or older**
Condition that affects ability to work at a job or business	11.8 million people		**Aged 16–64**

Source: http://usinfo.state.gov/scv/Archive/2005/Aug/17-688397.html

Difference Is Not a Deficiency!

Teachers today have increased education and awareness about disabilities. Increased visibility has also led to more acceptance. Today's changing attitudes try to dissolve stereotypes to treat all students with dignity. However, at times the labels or names themselves can be the obstacles. Racism, ageism, sexism, and *disabilitism* still exist, even though much legislation has attempted to prevent these negative prejudicial practices and mindsets. Civil rights and educational laws prohibit discrimination based on different abilities, yet the laws do not always translate into positive everyday practices in schools and beyond.

Working collectively, some members of society still need to realize that a difference does not translate to a deficiency. There is no social ladder of competencies, with disabilities placed on lower rungs. It would be naive to say that all individuals are as capable and intelligent, because all individuals are not the same. Some students with more severe disabilities will consistently require help with daily activities such as mobility, toileting, feeding, and more. Even if students with more severe developmental needs are given the same opportunities, the results will differ. However, it is not naive to say that all students can achieve their highest potentials with *different types of ladders*. This begins in a school setting with peer education and self-advocacy for all. When challenges are presented to students, it means that teachers possess high expectations for all, wanting students to maximize their assets. Challenges are not intended to frustrate students, but to recognize that each student is capable of achieving individualized cognitive advances. This should never be translated into a classroom setting with teachers assuming negative results and automatically diluting objectives from a lesson's content. If students are not introduced to the curriculum content because the assumption is that they *won't get it,* then students are set up for future failures. Since the curriculum spirals, the *knowledge foundation* will then weaken. Increased placements in general education classrooms are affording students with disabilities more opportunities and matching strategies to help them understand curriculum concepts. In addition, improved attitudes toward students with disabilities through positive peer interactions eventually become societal gains with experiences stored, translated, and applied to adult environments.

Complications occur when moral, medical, social, political, and cultural issues interfere with the learning. Students should not be expected to conform to and match standards set by outsiders, without ascertaining whether or not the learners have the prerequisite skills, knowledge, and experiences. Many families with differing cultural values from those of the school system often do not understand these standards. Also true is that some families have expectations that differ from those set at school levels. Some families have higher expectations and some families have lower ones. Other families have realistic viewpoints and expectations for daily and future achievements that are sometimes not recognized by the school. Compromise, communication, and cooperation correct mismatched and misguided expectations and replace them with realistic goals.

It is a challenge for all if stereotypical attitudes are shown by peers, teachers, administrators, legislators, and other adults in the community toward those with differences. Fortunately today, fair treatments overrule those archaic prejudicial attitudes. Politicians are lobbied to change laws and acknowledge inequities. Attempts to end discrimination with educational laws try to diminish the disparity among scores across disability categories, socioeconomic levels, and races. The next section outlines some of these legislative issues in schools and communities.

LEGISLATION SAYS... AND THE CLASSROOM DOES

Like tortoises who have hard shells to protect themselves from predators in their environments, people with disabilities must be protected from predators with *disabilitiphobia* and their sometimes unfriendly, unwelcoming, unproductive environments. It's unfortunate that society needs courts to mandate fair treatments to people with disabilities. Why can't everyone just be on automatic pilot to *do the right thing?* How fortunate that many people of all abilities and ages do not need legislation to spell out the right way to act toward those with disabilities.

Even with legislation, however, disability discrimination still occurs, with people testing the laws' limits and limiting a student's potential. Ultimately, this results in further disabling the potential of a person with a disability. However, when schools foster accepting attitudes, then the peers who will become the future neighbors, coworkers, employers, or employees of a student with a disability will not need a law to tell them just what constitutes appropriate behavior and fairness!

ADA—Americans with Disabilities Act

(Hopefully, one day to be *A Dream Actualized.*)

The Americans with Disabilities Act was passed in 1990 in the United States, but it has been continually interpreted, translated, expanded, and somewhat modified through individual court cases since that date. It's a civil rights law that guarantees equal opportunity for individuals with disabilities in employment, public accommodation, transportation, state and local government services, and telecommunications. Even though the law itself remains intact, it has been amended and tested in the courts. This is partly because of its wording and what ADA states and sometimes what it does not specify.

ADA says that an individual with a disability

1. has a physical or mental disability that limits one or more major life activities,

2. has a record of such impairment, or

3. is regarded as having such an impairment.

The following table outlines and compares what is and what is not considered to be a disability under ADA. Sometimes there is a fine line that specifies what is and what is not protected. For example, sometimes being careless, disorganized, irresponsible, or stubborn may be considered as negative personality traits, yet can be part of a disability, as well. Students with oppositional defiant disorder or AD/HD may display such traits. ADA affects school settings in various circumstances. An example would be that when students with disabilities are gainfully employed in the community, they cannot be discriminated against or denied opportunities if they are competent for the job, based upon their disability. If a student with a disability was denied physical access to his or her classrooms or extracurricular activities due to structural barriers, that would be an ADA concern. If a student had a dog companion and was denied school or community access, that would also be an ADA matter. If a Board of Education meeting was held on the second floor of a building without an elevator and a student or parent in a wheelchair could not attend, that would also be an ADA concern. Not providing a sign language interpreter during a parent–teacher conference or an IEP meeting, if interpretive needs were known in advance, would also be an ADA concern in a school setting. It addresses the following areas with deliverable results that are at times placed on a courtroom's agenda.

Table 1.7   ADA Domains: To ADA or Not to ADA

ADA Domains	Specifics such as
Public accommodations	Bringing a wheelchair on a beach or to a sports event Going to a restroom Enjoying a park
Commercial facilities	Shopping at malls Dining at restaurants Obtaining hotel accommodations Riding a rollercoaster
Employment	Securing a job (if qualified) without a disability interfering with being hired and keeping that job Being treated fairly at that job or employment
Transportation	Having access to a bus, train station, taxi cab, plane, and beyond
State and Local Governments	Attending and participating in a local Board of Education meeting Running for public office Voting
Telecommunications	Talking on a telephone Having computer access

REMOVING BARRIERS

Barriers have been erased by removing inaccessible facilities and replacing them with appropriate environments and conditions. Students using wheelchairs for mobility now have appropriately designed ramps, elevators, and physical spaces. The student using a wheelchair is not to be discriminated against in the school and the work environment when compared to a student or coworker

Table 1.8   Table of Considered Disabilities

Considered a Disability	Not Considered a Disability
Physiological disorder or condition, including effects to neurological, musculoskeletal, special sense organs, respiratory, cardiovascular, reproductive, digestive, endocrine, hemic, lymphatic, and genitourinary systems Mental impairments can include mental retardation—known in some states as intellectual disability or organic brain syndrome—and also emotional or mental illness, and specific learning disabilities	Disadvantages stemming from • Environmental • Cultural • Economic factors
Permanent disabilities that people are born with and ones that will not change or significantly improve over time	Some temporary disabilities that vary in symptoms are sketchy issues, such as ascertaining just what length of time a person has to hold a disability in order for it to be considered as interfering with a major life activity
Emotional impairments, e.g., bipolar disorder, passive-aggressive personality disorder	Personality traits such as being careless, disorganized, or irresponsible
Person who cannot read because he or she has dyslexia or perceptual disorders	A person who cannot read because he or she dropped out of school
Person with a psychiatric diagnosis of stress disorder	Someone under *situational* stress
Person who is blind or has considerable visual impairments	Someone with 20/60 vision
A person who cannot walk or has limited mobility	A person who cannot run fast in a marathon
Someone with a disabling permanent back injury	Someone who complains of back pain, and then plays a game of football or works in another job that requires physical labor
Someone who had cancer or had a mental illness at one time (having a record of the disability)	Someone with a broken leg or who is going through a mentally upsetting time, such as a loss, death, or divorce

Source: National Institute on Disability and Rehabilitation Research: Core Curriculum (Adaptive Environments), http://www.ed.gov/about/offices/list/osers/nidrr/index.html, and Bureau of International Information Programs, U.S. Department of State (2005).

who is able to walk. A child who is blind can no longer be denied access to job opportunities if he or she is qualified. A girl who is deaf can show her ability to complete the same job as someone with better hearing. A student who initially had difficulties learning now has increased opportunities to become a productive adult. He or she is now allowed access to the same opportunities as everyone else in public accommodations, commercial facilities, employment, transportation, and telecommunications. The *idea* was for ADA to be translated to *A Dream Actualized!*

Even though ADA has allowed people with disabilities to participate in many more aspects of society, the law is still not perfect. Some establishments that initially waited to be challenged before complying with the law discovered that ADA was here to stay, and other establishments and employers are still challenging the law. At the time of publication, ADA is being discussed on the hearing floor of the Senate. The ADA Restoration Act of 2007 is designed to amend ADA by not allowing employers to say a person is too disabled to do the job, but not disabled enough to be protected under ADA. Specific disabilities caught in this grey area of the law include, but are not limited to, individuals with epilepsy, physical impairments, hearing loss, and mental illness who are able to regulate their disabilities with medication, prosthetics, or hearing aids. The ADA Restoration Act of 2007 is a bill that proposes to amend ADA to require courts to focus on whether a person has experienced discrimination *on the basis of disability*, rather than first requiring individuals with disabilities to demonstrate that they are substantially limited in some major life activity as the language now states. This way, more protection would be restored to the individual with the disability, rather than protecting the employer, which was not ADA's original intent. This restoration act is trying to alter the definition of a disability to allow a high quality of opportunity and participation for people with disabilities and thereby end all types of discrimination. However, the best part about ADA and other legislative laws is that they are not stagnant, but rather are consistently revisited and improved to remove barriers presented by unfair societal practices in schools and communities.

Universal Design

The following quotes and principles about *universal design* emphasize the need for appropriate pre-service and in-service teacher education about how to *universally* reach students in prepared classrooms.

> Universal design focuses attention on the one standard that matters most, providing the education that each student needs. Just as electronic devices and public buildings can be designed to be used equally well by all individuals, schools can be redesigned to allow equal and easy access to appropriate learning for all students. (Rycik, 2005)

> The idea of teachers considering all students and their individual needs before designing instruction and assessment practices has been a long time coming. What a difference this approach makes to teachers who no longer have to adjust and adapt their lessons and assessments to accommodate the students because the needed flexibility is already built in. (McNary, Glasgow, & Hicks, 2005)

> The Individuals with Disabilities Education Act mandates that schools provide accessible materials to students with exceptionalities at the same time as their peers without disabilities. This, combined with advances in universally designed instructional materials, will give students with disabilities better access to the general education curriculum and promote their educational achievement. (Hopkins, 2006)

Universal design was originally an architectural term geared toward making buildings accessible, yet it's now an even more *universal* term. The main focus is to have products and services available without having to redesign structures for each person's needs. Examples include having Braille numbers written in hotels on room doors and in elevators to indicate floors without a person who is blind first having to request it. Someone who is blind can *see* that the supports are all in place. Curb cuts for people who use wheelchairs have also helped those with wheeled suitcases or shopping carts, those on bicycles or roller skates, or even someone pushing a baby stroller. Universal design branches out to people beyond its originally intended audience. Another example is how closed captioning, originally intended to help those who have hearing differences, now helps people with cultural and language differences understand and associate oral conversation with the written word. Captions also accommodate students who have auditory processing difficulties or dyslexia by encouraging them to read along with the spoken words.

Teachers can incorporate this philosophy into their classrooms, making educational designs and basic principles of instruction accessible. This can go above and beyond *universally friendly* environmental designs, to include *universal strategies* that benefit learners with and without disabilities. Universal design increases all students' access to the general education curriculum and sets up students with and without disabilities for *inclusionary classroom successes.* UDI (universally designed instruction) tries to include all learners' possible needs by having available supports and frameworks already built into lessons, taking a proactive, rather than a reactive, *What do I do now?* approach. Later on, this is translated into creating universal lifelong learners.

Universal design does not mean that students are all simultaneously learning or mastering identical concepts at the same level of understanding. It translates to a classroom with tools and strategies already in place for children to achieve greater school successes. Now when students and teachers travel down that classroom road, they are equipped with materials and strategies already anticipated to implement and receive instruction. The following table gives specific classroom applications that apply the principles of universal design to help students work toward the achievement of higher learning, behavioral, and social outcomes.

IDEA—Individuals with Disabilities Education Act

(My definition: **It D**elivers **E**ducational **A**ccess!)

First it was P.L. 94-142, the Education for All Handicapped Children Act (EHA), back in 1975, guaranteeing a FAPE (free, appropriate public education) to children with disabilities in the United States. This law changed and improved the way students with disabilities were identified, educated, and evaluated with trios of initials such as *IEPs, LREs,* and *LEAs* (spelled out as individualized education programs, least restrictive environments, and local education agencies). P.L. 94-142 also provided due process protections for children and their families. Children with disabilities no longer faced educational exclusion, but were given equal access to learning opportunities, and consequently a better future.

In 1983, the law expanded to include preschool special education programs, early intervention, and transition programs. Then amendments to EHA (P.L. 99-457), in 1986, mandated services to children starting at birth. Infants, toddlers, and preschoolers were all included through early intervention

Table 1.9   Classroom Application of Universal Design Principles With Access for All

Descriptions	Objectives
Content-related visual dictionaries	To help students better understand vocabulary by offering semiabstract connections to written texts
Thematic clip art	To increase conceptual understandings, helping students to visualize the learning
Textbooks and literature on tape	Easier to follow comprehension of stories and information
Cut up tennis balls on the bottoms of chairs	To lower extra noises and distractions and assist students with attention issues
Increased technology, e.g., Smartboards, word prediction programs	Help with note taking and focusing, especially beneficial for students with fine motor issues, such as dysgraphia and students with attention issues
Lesson plans that consider individual students' needs, likes, and dislikes, e.g., more strategies built into lessons to help students with learning, such as outlines, graphic organizers, color coding, or using interest inventories	Motivate and connect students to learning on their instructional level rather than their frustrational levels Allows not only students with perceptual issues to understand concepts, but also gives better organizational skills to all students
Treating all students with dignity	Higher student self-esteem, which translates to taking ownership of learning and attempting even more difficult tasks
Computer technology	Help all students gain access to information, allowing for individual sensory, physical, and cognitive levels, e.g., talking Web sites, math and reading software, worksheets and graphic organizers, curriculum-connected visuals, animated graphics, along with PowerPoint slide presentations
Portable handheld speaking electronic dictionaries	To allow all learners to hear the information to reinforce the written word, aside from helping those students who are blind and dyslexic to increase understandings of vocabulary, literature, and concepts
Modeling lessons with increased praise	To reinforce academic, social, emotional, and behavioral needs and levels of students

programs that insured future successes, laying down the groundwork to build a solid foundation for a child with a disability to achieve a successful future. Crucial early beginnings were addressed! More changes came in 1990 with P.L. 101-476, when the EHA became IDEA, the Individuals with Disabilities Education Act. This was a major change, since it was the beginning of people-first language, meaning it was not the disability that came first, but the individual! Services were made available to students with autism, traumatic brain injury, students in educational transition, those needing social services, and more. The 1997 amendments (P.L. 105-17) then specified that students would receive transition planning, beginning at age 14. Concern shifted to a child receiving his or her education in the LRE and having that linked to the home environment, with schools and families as partners.

Like ADA, the best part about IDEA is the lack of stagnation. IDEA keeps improving in name and meritorious content. IDEA was again reauthorized and improved in 2004 (P.L. 108-446) to IDEIA 2004 (the Individuals with Disabilities Education Improvement Act). A statement of academic achievement and functional performance or nonacademic goals is now included, with emphasis on students knowing how to get along in the real world. Other highlights include more home input and participation in the IEP, periodic or quarterly progress reports of goals, and not just using a discrepancy model for identifying students with learning disabilities. In addition, teachers need to be highly qualified with more preparation, knowledge, and skills. However, it still remains that schools are not required to provide the best or optimal conditions, but *appropriate ones* that are commensurate with the education and opportunities provided to students without disabilities. More specific details follow.

Districts are now allowed to use other identification processes besides the IQ-discrepancy model to identify students with learning disabilities in tiered models. This involves students' responses to scientifically based instructional practices or research-based interventions (or response to intervention [RTI]). It allows educators to develop criteria for learning disability determination by gathering a variety of data, rather than relying on just one criterion to determine eligibility. Responsiveness to intervention is concerned with monitoring students' levels to prevent academic failures. Research on RTI is still in its infancy, but it holds many promises for students with learning needs in classrooms and schools. Screening, interventions, and monitoring on three different tiers involve implementing comprehensive programs with increased accountability. The ultimate objective is to ensure higher outcomes for students with disabilities. In addition, IDEIA calls for early intervening services (EIS) to be available to students who may not be identified under the special education umbrella, but who may be in general education settings and may also need academic interventions. This includes students in all grades, with a greater emphasis on providing services for students in younger grades before they experience repeated academic and related behavioral frustrations and failures. This IDEA 2004 commitment includes providing professional development to try to circumvent the overidentification of students needing special education services.

Individualized education programs (IEPs) do not have to include benchmarks, unless there are severe cognitive impairments. Measurable academic and functional goal statements still state the student's present level of academic achievement, his or her functional classroom performance, and how the disability impacts upon the programs. Another significant change involves the transition age, which is now set at age 16 or younger if necessary, while the prior IDEA mandated transition services at age 14. Measurable postsecondary goals must take into account a student's age-appropriate interests, even if the student chooses not to attend the IEP meeting. These goals include appropriate training, education, employment, and independent living skills.

IDEA 2004, from NCLB (No Child Left Behind) influences, now requires SE teachers to be highly qualified in the core subjects that they teach. Each state may have its own HOUSSE (High, Objective Uniform State Standard of

Evaluation) for the determination of special education teacher subject competency. The purpose is to allow students the same access to information, regardless of their disability. That includes receiving information in a timely fashion from competent personnel.

IDEA 2004 discipline rules apply to a case-by-case determination of a disability, placement issues, and manifestation determination. The law provides for an *interim alternative education setting* (IAES), which includes allowing the IEP team to consider services when the placement change will last for more than 10 consecutive days and if drugs, weapons, or serious bodily injury are involved. Parents or guardians must be notified of a placement change. The manifestation determination must state whether the conduct was related to the disability or whether it was the result of a district's failure to implement the IEP. Other considerations include the school's knowledge of a disability even if the student is not classified. This gives children certain IDEA protections in circumstances such as prior concern expressed by families and school personnel. It would exclude evaluations that determined no disability or in cases where the parents or guardians refused services or an evaluation.

Overall, students with special needs now are within the realm of achieving a high-quality education in literacy, numeracy, language, communication, and social and behavioral skills in natural settings with their peers. This includes timely interventions with families' involvement enhanced to maximize students' potential. These continual reauthorizations of the law show that complacency concerning students with disabilities is not an option, and now the law is offering increased protections!

Services and supports also spill over to nonacademic settings to allow students with disabilities more participation beyond the classrooms. Examples of potential extracurricular activities include allowing a student with dyslexia to perform in a school play with extra help to read his or her lines, or providing a student in a wheelchair with access and accommodations to play on a volleyball or basketball court with his or her peers who do not have disabilities. Increased interactions with peers outside the confines of the classroom walls will be a win–win for all!

Current laws and inclusion policies also result in more students with disabilities attending college. It is not a requirement, but students now have more options! This not only includes those with learning disabilities or attendance at *special* colleges, but it also includes students with autism, Down syndrome, and other emotional, intellectual and developmental disabilities attending the same campuses as their age-appropriate peers. The Education Life section of the *New York Times* (Kaufman, 2006) stated that although many of these students will not be taking Shakespeare or physics courses, they are now being prepared to enter the workforce beyond just having entry-level jobs. Social skills gains are attainable due to modeling, peer mentoring, adult guidance, and family assistance. Legislation has positively impacted postsecondary school opportunities for young adults. This translates into both personal and societal gains.

How is this all possible? It goes back to everyone's positive and encouraging attitudes. This includes school personnel, families, communities, peers, and the students themselves. Differentiation applies not only to instruction, but also to encouraging positive attitudes that spurred and continue to spur legislative protection for students with disabilities! The ultimate goal, for students with disabilities to lead independent and productive adult lives, is now a priority in school settings from the early ages onward!

An Analogous IEP: Learning Road Map

 Writing measurable IEP goals with reasonable accommodations that align to academic standards does not have to be an arduous task. Aside from being required by the law, an IEP (*It's Educationally Prudent*) is a practical tool that says, "Let's figure out a *learning road map* for this student."

Table 1.10   Table of School Mapping

Mapping Your Destination	*School Map*	
What's your starting point?	State the child's present level of academic achievement and functional performance.	
Measure the distance traveled over a certain time.	How will child's progress toward meeting the goals outlined be measured? (Progress can be reported concurrently with report cards or sent home at set time intervals.)	
Research the best route.	To the greatest extent possible, base IEP recommendations on peer-reviewed research. Gather input from all personnel.	
When should the journey begin?	Age 3 and Child Find, which is Part C of IDEA, providing for early interventions and services for students with disabilities, from birth to age 21. This early location and identification appropriately targets and addresses developmental, physical, cognitive, and emotional needs of students with disabilities with appropriate services.	
Will your trip be timed?	Benchmarks and short-term objectives are only needed for children with disabilities who take alternate assessments aligned to alternate achievement standards (those with more severe cognitive impairments). IEPs still have annual goals, accommodations, and modifications listed. Some states also require benchmarks for students in replacement programs.	
Who is going on the journey?	Depends upon LEA (local education agency) and parental agreement in writing. A staff member can be excused from a meeting if that member's area of expertise is not being modified or discussed. Even if a member is excused from attending, written input may be required. Most important, if age, maturity, and cognitive level are appropriate, the student should be a meaningful participant and attend IEP meeting, prepared to give input with perceptions, personal concerns, needs, and goals.	
What if I travel to a different state?	Aha, here's where the plot thickens: Some states have different rules, regulations, interpretations, and alignments with federal laws. However, IDEA is a federally mandated law and must be implemented in all 50 states.	
What driving regulations are expected or enforced?	High expectations that are *driven by results*, not driven by process, litigation, and regulation	
What additional forms do I need for my journey?	More focus on learning outcomes and teaching, rather than meetings and excessive paperwork	

Source: *In Case*, The Newsletter for the Council of Administrators of Special Education (2005, September/October), Vol. 47, No. 2, Section 504, http://Thomas.loc.gov.

Beyond the Foot in the Door and Into the Strategies

Inclusion is not merely about students with intellectual, physical, or sensory differences physically attending the same "regular" classes as those students with higher cognitive abilities or those born with *perfect* scores on the Apgar scale. Without the proper preparation, scaffolding, and mindsets, the *foot in the door* can become an embarrassing and frustrating experience for students with disabilities. Teachers, students, families, and peers must be sensitized in effective ways that mirror the real world, with learning kept at an optimum level in natural settings.

The following are some classroom issues that go *beyond the door:*

Table 1.11   Table of "Beyond the Door" Situations

Environmental	• Set up classroom to offer maximum mobility and access for students with physical and visual impairments. • Seat students with attention issues and visual impairments away from windows (e.g., glare and other distractions). Minimize chair noises by placing cut-up tennis balls on the bottom of chair legs to eliminate extra sounds. • Allow students to use headphones to listen to soothing music, work on computer Web sites, or follow specific tailored directions. • Circulate about the classroom, talking at the front, back, and sides of the room, with necessary proximity to focus students' attentions.
Academic	• Allow individual and differentiated objectives, grading, and/or assessments that consider students' efforts, with realistic and constructive feedback. • Pace lessons, with step-by-step explanations. • Allow for appropriate amount of practice, application, and acceleration. • Consistently and frequently, formally and informally, reevaluate and monitor student progress to determine effectiveness of instructional interventions.
Social	• Have other students in the class act as peer coaches. • Encourage more student reflection and self-advocacy. • Vary cooperative grouping and assignments that allow students to demonstrate their strengths and interests. • Give students opportunities to *play with the academics*, enjoying the facts! • Establish an atmosphere that treats students as contributing, valued, and productive members, e.g., give students realistic classroom responsibilities.
Behavioral	• Post student/teacher-created rules. • Assure students that you dislike their behavior displayed, not them! • Watch for signs of behavioral effects on other students. • Notice and record the antecedents for inappropriate behavior. • *Catch* students being good, and increase the praise. • Talk to families for their input, and offer ideas on how to implement feasible home behavioral charts to establish consistency with school strategies.
Cultural	• Honor students' cultures by including activities and literature from a variety of cultures, global locations, ages, and genres. • Provide supplemental materials in student's primary language to increase background knowledge and familiarity with vocabulary words and concepts. • Watch out for signs of cultural anomie (feelings of not belonging). • Include the student's level of proficiency. • Encourage students to share their differing thoughts and perceptions.

(Continued)

Table 1.11 (Continued)

	• Set up and model a classroom environment that says, *Being different is okay!* • Use resources from educational organizations such as www.teachingtolerance.org www.adl.org
Perceptual	• Ask students to paraphrase what they heard to check auditory processing. • Be certain that worksheets are uncluttered and contain graphic organizers that outline the main ideas, concepts, and connecting or supporting details (see www.inspiration.com, www.kidspiration.com). • Use fun art activities to improve visual discrimination, e.g., puzzles, sketching, cut-up jigsaw-like curriculum photographs (Google-images, www.pics4learning.com, www. puzzlemaker.com). • Incorporate more informal listening activities that test the students' focusing, e.g., stating the sequence, main idea, or relevant details of what they heard. • Use highlighting tape (www.crystalspringsbooks.com) or colored transparencies.
Sensory	• Face students who may be lip reading, but do not exaggerate words. • Be aware of the social isolation students with hearing and visual issues face. • Have appropriate manipulatives, e.g., talking calculators, magnification pages, books on tape, more visuals, clutter-free worksheets, visual dictionaries, or selections of thematic clip art, Braille library, or sign language books, if needed. • Address over- and undersensory stimulation, e.g., announcements, tactile triggers, and gradually sensitize or introduce sounds to students. • Increase dis*ability* awareness for peers. • Be sensitive to individual needs, not the label!
Physical	• Have differing implements for students to manipulate, e.g., pencil grips; larger sized crayons; turkey baster instead of eyedropper in science experiments; larger-sized scissors for cutting, scissors with springs to leave them in an open position; letter, number, and picture stencils; computer access, e.g., different mouse, larger magnification screen, word prediction programs, use of individualized macros. • Speak eye level to students in wheelchairs to avoid neck strain for them. • Lessen physical requirements and replace assignment with appropriate content-related task, e.g., if students are playing volleyball, one student who could not physically participate can check the heart rate by measuring pulses, keep score, or monitor correct rotation.

The following picture passage, *A Rebus of the Many Hats Teachers Wear,* delivers a message about disability attitudes through the combination of words and visuals. Very often, students do not comprehend what they are reading and can be confused by vocabulary words that may be too difficult to pronounce. Even if students can pronounce the words, the words may not be within their bank of prior knowledge or understood within the context of the sentence or passage. For example, while reading *The Wish Giver,* by Bill Brittain, some students had difficulty answering a written comprehension question on whether one of the characters, Adam, should have been content, now that the water was plentiful. They knew the gist of the story but were not sure what the words *content* or *plentiful* meant. There are reading and software programs that circumvent this issue through picture-assisted literacy and content-related graphics to help struggling readers improve their fluency, decoding, comprehension, vocabulary, and organizational skills. Stories and topics can range from Jackie Robinson to penguins to outlining concepts such as "the triumphs and tragedies of the Roman Empire." The following rebus story delineates the possibilities available for educators to honor the learner with more visual-spatial skills to improve his or her literacy levels. On-target strategies sometimes involve changing the appearance of the reading landscape!

A Rebus of the Many Hats Teachers Wear

 It's most important for educators to keep their strategies

on target,  even when dealing with some

students, colleagues,  parents, and the administration

 may be like walking on eggshells. At all costs, tug-of-war

situations  should be avoided! The lines between

 general education and special education are no longer clearly

drawn. Services overlap, with the classroom viewed as the first place to

deliver interventions. There are sometimes no warning 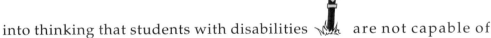 signs or

clear-cut paths to follow. However, do not 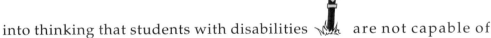 let anyone fool you

into thinking that students with disabilities 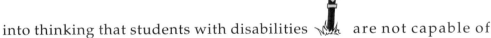 are not capable of

achieving great successes. As an educator, you just need to pitch your

best strategy and catch the results, being the coach along the way,

 helping students to fend off negative attitudes.

Review and compare two items in Appendix B. Both are entitled, *Valuable and Applicable Things to Do in All Classrooms on a Daily Basis,* with 18 delineated points. One is written with pictures while the other has the words only. Which one's message is more strongly received or will be better remembered? The point is to honor learners who often appreciate accompanying visuals to reinforce abstract concepts. Teachers and students can construct their own *visual learning*

books to accompany or preteach more difficult reading passages and unfamiliar or abstract content and vocabulary. This chart depicts visuals with messages that better explain difficult vocabulary and concepts across the curriculum and grades.

Table 1.12   Content-Related Visuals for Grades K–12

Visuals Across Grades and Subjects	Science/ Health	Social Studies/ History/Economics	Math	Reading/ Vocabulary
K–2	magnetism	Kwanzaa	9:00	flour vs. flower
3–5	eclipse	fossil	equations	happy ecstatic
6–8	DON'T DO DRUGS	peasant vs. nobility	pentagonal prism	multitasking
9–12	neuron	balancing the budget	perpendicular	capitalize on strengths

Online Sites and Other Sources to Investigate for Visual Learners

Eyewitness Books: http://us.dk.com

Mayer-Johnson: http://www.mayer-johnson.com. Has Boardmaker software programs, cards, and many other products for symbol-based communication and learning for students.

Online videos and teaching resources with district subscription: http://www.unitedstreaming.com

Pics4Learning: http://www.pics4learning.com. A copyright-friendly image library for teachers and students with a wide range of content-related pictures.

Picture-Assisted Reading and Writing Slater Software: www.slatersoftware.com

Usborne Books: http://www.usborneonline.com

Webs and outlines with related pictures: www.kidspiration.com, www.inspiration.com

How Others Interact With and Acknowledge Disabilities and Differences

Chapter Highlights: This second chapter highlights how differences and disabilities are viewed across nations, cultures, age groups, classrooms, literature, and movies.

Classroom Connections: Sometimes it is unfamiliarity and lack of exposure that creates schisms and prejudicial views. Specific books and lists of movies with paired questions and *dislabeling activities* are included for students in Grades K–12 to become more familiar with differences.

Ways to Differentiate Attitudes: Discussion of simulations and reflective activities for understandings about disabilities and attitudes toward differences.

The following quotes and views on disabilities highlight the complexities involved:

It is teachers' attitudes that will determine the success of students with disabilities. . . . Teachers with positive attitudes due to their knowledge of disabilities and experiences with students who are disabled will help to make inclusion feasible. (Burke, 2004)

The future of disabilities, indeed the future of human diversity, may lie in the resolution of the conflicting visions of human perfection and of a world that values and embraces human variation. (Smith, 2003)

It's not the label that's the problem, but the baggage associated with it. (A software developer who was diagnosed with Asperger syndrome in his 30s, quoted by Szalavitz, 2007)

It is hoped that his step-by-step rise in confidence and self-worth will lead to a greater tolerance and respect for others, regardless of ability or disability. (Peek, 1996)

Having a name for something in some cases can help you do something about it, but parents and teachers need to focus on children's strengths and reward accomplishments, rather than on what labels imply about ability and potential. (Szalavitz, 2007)

Progress is often influenced by how students act and feel about themselves. At times, students with disabilities may seem passive and defenseless because of existing limitations in areas of

- Communication
- Physical development
- Cognitive levels
- Social or emotional needs
- Adaptive development

Adults then try to compensate for these limitations by doing more, which in reality is teaching the child less. For example, if a student could not tie his or her own shoes, and the adult always did it instead, then how will the student improve his or her ability to tie shoes? In this scenario, a student is overcompensated with help if a parent or adult enables the child, thereby negating the opportunity for a student to learn and experience the necessary skills involved. Teachers can model procedures and give direct instruction of skills or concepts in a step-by-step manner, and then require students to perform some of the subskills on their own, allowing them to develop more competencies. This type of guidance can be given in lessons ranging from phonics to calculus.

Other classroom students, teachers, neighbors, and family members may exhibit a condescending attitude, show pity, or even distance themselves from a child with a disability because of their own uneasiness or lack of knowledge. That scenario can be seen when students with autism are placed in schools where the general education teachers and students shy away from students with disabilities, exhibiting no recognition or contact with them as peers. The answer here remains to formally and gradually educate others. Misconceptions are not developed at a given moment in time, but evolve through the years of either positive or negative environmental, situational, and chosen experiences. Everyone needs to realize that people with disabilities

1. Possess and are entitled to future goals and dreams

2. Can appropriately participate and succeed in academic and social arenas

3. Benefit from consistent encouragement and support

Review the rubrics in the appendix that assess disability attitudes for students, peers, teachers, staff, family, and community members. Some of the other appendix tables also encourage *challenging versus enabling* students, and developing appropriate attitudes along with academic and behavioral strategies and documentation. The following table lists some perceptions and comments students aged 9–12 gave before, during, and after an assembly presentation from a person with cerebral palsy who uses a wheelchair. He candidly shared his life with them in a question/answer format to confront and dispel any myths or preconceived ideas they had. Although it doesn't express all views of students in this age group about every person who uses a wheelchair, the table offers snapshots of students' minds, telling what the students previously thought, what they learned, and what they still wonder about a person with a physical impairment. Many thanks to Stanley who graciously shares his life with students in my town one day each year! His visits over the past decade are memorable ones with lifelong lessons that will certainly be applied by many of these students the next time they meet someone who has a physical disability. He teaches a lesson on what to do, just by being who he is, and always with a smile!

SPORTSMANLIKE BEHAVIOR

When teachers instruct students with special needs, *sportsmanlike behavior* is the rule! Analogously speaking, teachers are sometimes *educational coaches* who can encourage students to put forth their best performance. If you've ever been involved in a sports game or competition that lost sight of the fun of the game and became an ill-conceived competitive contest, then you know that the consequences and results are far from fruitful or enjoyable. This chart details the proper behavior that a well-disciplined teacher with a *sporting attitude* would exhibit. This applies to his or her interactions with students, colleagues, families, and the administration. *Good sports* put the *right plays* into action with all of their students. These educators help children with disabilities succeed in school settings and certainly deserve many trophies for their arduous efforts on and off the *educational field*. Teachers can definitely level the *playing field*, otherwise known as their classroom!

WORLDWIDE ATTITUDES ABOUT DISABILITIES IN SCHOOL SETTINGS

The World Institute on Disability (www.wid.org) has an international program that is currently working globally on education issues, to ensure that children with disabilities in many countries around the world are going to school with more inclusion and integration with their peers. They are also seeking to expand special development training for teachers. Social integration and inclusive education, along with changing legislative policies, more worldwide community independence for individuals with disabilities, and the exchange of research are some focuses of this organization.

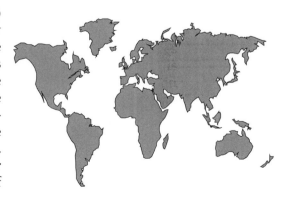

In addition, many countries around the world have modeled their laws and disability services after some of the legislative and educational practices that

Table 2.1   Student Responses From a *Disability* Awareness Assembly

Some things I know about disabilities	Some things I learned	Some things I still wonder
People can still enjoy life even though they have a disability.	I learned that he likes his disability. He doesn't sleep in his chair.	How do they feel about their disability?
Treat them the same.	It takes people with disabilities longer to do things.	Are disabled people embarrassed to go out in public?
They don't have a lot of abilities but they are still determined.	He has children who don't care if he has a disability.	Do people with disabilities feel separated from other people?
Disability is not a bad thing all of the time.	Don't be afraid about people who have disabilities.	I completely understand and learned a lot today.
People with disabilities are the same as regular people.	To be nice to people with a disability; they have feelings too.	Do they play video games?
It's hard growing up!	It's not so bad having disabilities.	Do his brothers and sisters have disabilities too?
You cannot be fully smart.	Some people have confidence.	Why didn't he get a driver's license?
Some people have trouble remembering.	People with disabilities can go to college.	Nothing.
You are likely to be made fun of.	Many difficulties, but can sometimes do more than people without disabilities.	Could we find a cure for disabilities?
Disabilities aren't a disease.	They are not so different from us. People can be the same.	How do people get their disabilities?
They need some help.	There are service dogs that aren't Seeing Eye dogs.	Do people with disabilities have a normal life?
People with disabilities can play sports.	People can go to the movies.	Should we treat them the same as regular people?
Not all of their body parts work.	They can have lower sinks and people that wake them up.	Has he ever tried to walk?
They get around in different ways.	Animals could help people with disabilities.	Do you feel left out?

Some things I know about disabilities	Some things I learned	Some things I still wonder
People with disabilities have the same personalities.	It's hard to travel and dress. It sometimes takes 5x longer to do something.	Is it hard getting out of the wheelchair?
They may be mean and may be nice like the real world.	People with disabilities can marry people without disabilities.	What would it be like if someone doesn't help them?
They still eat and shower like us.	People with disabilities don't mind it.	Do children with disabilities ever feel excluded from other kids?
Their lives are sometimes action-packed.	They can be just like a regular person and still have fun.	What are all the types of disabilities?
They are different and alike in some ways.	When you get to know a person with a disability, you sometimes forget.	Do people enjoy their disabilities?
	Someone with a disability doesn't necessarily have to be a bad person.	Are you mad that you have a disability?
	He can ride a motorcycle.	How do people acquire a disability if they're not born with it?
	They live just like us.	What disabilities do his friends have?
	You can still be a normal person.	Why do people make fun of people with disabilities?
	People don't know how to act around them.	
	Not everyone is born with a disability.	
	People with disabilities can live good lives.	
	It is hard getting ready for work.	
	Disabilities don't stop you from doing things.	
	You don't have fewer rights than anyone.	
	Disabled people can do more than I thought.	

Table 2.2   Sportsmanlike Behavior of Teachers and Related Staff Who Exhibit the Right Plays

Teachers and other staff members are like referees who collaborate and communicate with each other while recognizing and honoring families' needs. Just like *refs* make the right calls, these educators administer and deliver the best practices for students while exhibiting respect for all of the players on the *classroom field*.
Teachers are the ones *keeping score* and not just the final scores or summative test grades, but these teachers manage to recognize and reward students for not only mastery, but their efforts and progress toward accomplishments. Formative scores are used to gauge the educator's instruction.
Teachers and related staff are like athletes who are *well disciplined* and show up for games and practices on time. These educators meet deadlines with evaluations, consultations, and conferences for each marking period. They even share quarterly progress, home strategies, and levels with families and effectively coplan lessons and interdisciplinary units with colleagues.
These educational staff members are *never out of bounds* since they are on target with strategies and universal designs that match and even anticipate students' unique needs.
Realizing that traveling with the ball is not a sportsmanlike way to behave, these staff members *bounce ideas off each other* and don't point fingers of blame.
These educational players don't charge ahead without a game plan in mind. There are pre-, inter-, and postplanning of lessons and *constant reflections* and adjustments in pace and content to improve that next game plan or lesson!
Running in the wrong direction with the ball would not happen with these staff members because they plan *focused* lessons that merit students' strengths, including what the child already knows and future goals.
Hogging the ball would be unheard of since these staff members plan and share thoughts and lessons. There's *collaboration* among multidisciplinary education teams, administration, support staff, families, and the students themselves.
Elbowing now has a new definition with *fine motor/hands-on activities* that use manipulatives and appropriate kinesthetic-tactile modalities to accompany and concretize lessons.
These staff members do not argue calls, but *accept constructive criticism* from administration, support staff, colleagues, students, and families. When disputes arise, honesty and respect prevail.
Goal tending is replaced with *fair practices* that adhere to legislative rules as documented in individualized education programs (IEPs). Students without IEPs also benefit from appropriate interventions when best strategies are applied in inclusive classrooms.
Penalties are replaced with *praise, rewards, and positive recognition* for students, educators, and all related staff. Students experience feelings of *self-worth* when academic and social strides are achieved under the school staff's auspices who are otherwise known as the *facilitative educational coaches*.

exist today in the United States. For example, in Canada the IEP is call an IPP, Individualized Program Plan, while in Cyprus and many other countries it's also called an IEP. Just like the United States, many countries have increased opportunities in recent decades for individuals with disabilities in school settings and beyond. Yet, further strides are needed in the United States and abroad.

In 2003, a study commissioned by the Special Olympics, with collaboration from the Center for Social Development and Education, the Gallup Organization, Research and Evaluation Services of Northern Ireland, and the Center for Survey Research, released the findings from a study, *The Multinational Study of Attitudes Toward Individuals with Intellectual Disabilities*. The following statistics are some of the results from the random sampling of 8,000 persons in 10 countries across the world who responded. Many of the respondents said that their answers do not necessarily reflect their attitudes, but how they view *others'* attitudes toward the societal inclusion of individuals with intellectual disabilities. The 10 countries sampled included Brazil, China, Egypt, Germany, Japan, Nigeria, the Republic of Ireland, Russia, the UK (Northern Ireland), and the United States. The margin of error was plus or minus 3%. Some of the findings revealed the following:

- 53% of the people believed that the major obstacle for the inclusion of individuals with intellectual disabilities is society's negative attitudes.
- 78% believed that the lack of school resources and teacher preparedness are obstacles in education.
- 53% thought that the inclusion of students with intellectual disabilities would impede the learning of other classmates, create discipline problems, and cause safety risks to others in the classroom.
- 54% believed that negative media portrayal posed an obstacle to the inclusion of those with intellectual disabilities. (http://www.special olympics.org)

Timothy Shriver, the director of Special Olympics, summed it up by saying,

The results of this survey show that while there has been some progress in changing the public's perception of the abilities of persons with intellectual disabilities, there is still much work to be done. (Halperin & Merrick, 2006)

The following quotes reveal additional global practices, needs, and attitudes toward maximizing the potentials of persons with disabilities.

The rights of students with disabilities to be educated in their local mainstream school [are] becoming more and more accepted in most countries, and many reforms are being put into place to achieve this goal. [There is] no reason to segregate students with disabilities in public education systems. (Rustemier, n.d.)

Pressure from groups of people who are disabled in the UK has resulted in legislative changes such as the Disability Discrimination Act (1995), stating equitable participation for people with disabilities. It is reported that even with the legislation, people with disabilities in the UK are less likely to hold a degree qualification, be gainfully employed, or own a home. (DEMOS, 2002)

The issues of naming children and youth with disabilities as a specified target group has once again been the topic of heated discussion among world leaders. . . . World Forum on Education for All by 2015 in Dakar, Senegal questions: How will the progress of children and youth with disabilities . . . be monitored when they are not specified as a key target group in the national plans and education programs of their countries? (Price, 2000)

The next statistic taken alone is astounding, but within the context of Vietnam's history with Agent Orange, the toxic herbicide and defoliant used for warfare by the U.S. Armed Forces during the Vietnam War, it makes you realize how environmental factors come into play.

With 6 million disabled people, Vietnam has one of the world's highest rates of disability per capita. . . . The Vietnamese National Assembly passed the National Ordinance on Disabled persons in 1998 . . . to create favourable conditions for people with disabilities to exercise their political, economic, cultural, and social rights. [This] raised awareness . . . but it's still short in implementation. (Bullock, 2005)

Another factor that can influence statistics is population density, growth, and migration. Many families migrated to Ontario, Canada, to take advantage of its reputation for having a good educational system for students with special needs. The following two quotes elaborate further.

From 1998 to 2004, the proportion of special needs children in Ontario's schools more than doubled from 1.3 percent to 2.8 percent. There are now more than 50,000 identified. . . . [Special education] programs cost $1.9 billion annually—or 800 million more than the province spends on the entire community college system. . . . The special education debate is far from over. It may have just begun in earnest. (Urquhart, 2005)

The province pledged an extra $10 million . . . in another step in [a] long-term plan to improve and expand services for families of special needs children. ("Province Digs Deeper for Disabled," 2005)

The next two quotes speak about Ireland's schools and teachers needing more financial resources and reduced class size, common desires of many school systems.

I'd like to see a fair increase in money and resources for *special needs* education . . . [I'm] concerned with what seems to be a slow movement in reducing the pupil–teacher ratio below the current levels of 20–1. (Special ed teacher in Ireland, cited in O'Brien, 2004)

It's time that we exposed the myth that inclusion and integration are possible without class-size reductions. . . . The government's [Ireland's] failure to reduce class size was having a negative effect on pupils. (Flynn, 2005)

Some additional worldviews on inclusion and special education follow.

An angry mother of a child with autism confronted Tony Blair about the closures of special schools. . . . A Tory leader, Michael Howard, promised to end the presumption that *special needs children* should go to mainstream schools. ("Tories Put Blair's Challenger in Special Needs in Spotlight," 2005)

Mexican teachers have voiced that they need and want better methods for dealing with student behaviour in their classrooms. (Aranda, Sanchez-Escobedo, & Williams, 2002)

As in many areas of the former Soviet Union, professional services for Georgian citizens with disabilities are limited both in scope and nature. Persons with disabilities are seriously marginalized.... [S]ome are institutionalized in conditions that have been described as violating basic civil rights. (Hobbs, Szydlowski, West, & Germava, 2002)

Most Eastern European countries with economies in transition had significant problems in supporting families with persons with disabilities. (Alexei Tulbure, Moldova's Permanent Representative to the UN, chair of the 2008 session of the Commission on Social Development, quoted in UN News Centre, 2007)

The European experience of inclusive education is gathering momentum and more and more pupils from special schools are being educated with their able-bodied peers. (Humphreys, Tyne, & Gallagher, 2003)

Limited English proficiency is the most stressful factor for Korean immigrants and a main barrier for successful communication with educators.... [They have a] difficult time building genuine trust and interactive relationships with American teachers because of the language limitations. (Lee & Vail, 2003)

The Hans Knudsen Institute in Denmark is associated with companies that offer education, vocational skill training, rehabilitation, and sheltered employment for individuals with disabilities. It was the result of the work of a man, Hans Knudsen, back in the 19th century, who wanted to assist people with disabilities to become more independent. (Bjerring Nielson, Director of the Hans Knudsen Institute, http://cec-live.2rad.net/intl/progpract.html#hans)

The European Agency for Development in Special Needs Education investigates the current and future uses of communication and information technology for students with disabilities. (http://www.european-agency.org)

A report on effective factors for inclusion of students with special educational needs from 20 European nations identifies these as the top two challenges:

1. Handling of differences/diversities in European classrooms

2. Behavioral, social, and emotional problems (http://www.european-agency.org/iecp/iecp_intro.htm)

The Portuguese Ministry of Education released a resource guide that is designed to help teachers who work with students with multiple disabilities. Inclusive strategies are in the areas of communication, sensory issues, orientation, and mobility. (EuroNews on Special Needs Education, 2002)

The Philippines set up a special care developmental unit (SCDC) in 1990 that offers interventions for special learners to improve social skills, fine/gross motor skills, speech/communication, cognitive and self-help skills, and many areas for community integration. (Division of Special Education International Services—Programs and Practices, http://www.cec.sped.org/intl/progpract.html#inclusive)

In Singapore, special education is conceived of as distinct from general education. Empirical information regarding the inclusion of students with special needs in general education classrooms in Singapore is scarce. (Heng & Tam, 2006)

In 1979 Peru set up a Center (CASP Centro Ann Sullivan del Peru) that offers services to people with autism and severe and profound retardation. Included are community, home, and school services for families, businesses and students. (Division of Special Education International Services—Programs and Practices, http://www.cec.sped.org/intl/progpract.html#inclusive)

The Autism Genome Project has 120 scientists and 50 institutions in 19 countries working to identify specific genes and variants and their interactions with environmental factors. (http://www.sciencedaily.com/releases/2007/02/070218183245.htm)

UNESCO (an international agency within the United Nations) has as one of its priorities to help parents, organizations of people with disabilities, and professional communities move towards more inclusive societies, using education as their groundwork. (http://www.european-agency.org)

The *Australian* reports that schools could be failing students with AD/HD by treating them as backward. . . . Neglect of students' academic and social needs during primary school years often resulted in problems in the middle school years. The article adds that medication for students with AD/HD is not the solution and states, *Pills don't give you skills.* (Sproul, 2006)

Senior doctors from Britain's Royal College of Obstetricians and Gynaecology are urging health professionals to consider permitting the euthanasia of *seriously disabled* newborn babies. (Christian, 2006)

The National Union of Teachers is reversing its inclusion support, claiming that some children's educational needs were not met when they were placed in "totally inappropriate" schools where they inevitably failed. (Halpin, 2006)

The Ghana Education Service must continue to encourage and create the appropriate infrastructure, incentives and financial support to help teachers and school professionals implement effective inclusive practices. (Obi, Mamah, & Avoke, 2007)

Worldwide, there is a push for general educators to learn from special educators and vice versa so as to achieve greater understanding of what might be accomplished together that cannot otherwise be accomplished. (Heng & Tam, 2006)

The Division of International Special Education and Services (DISES), a division of the Council of Exceptional Children, is on the Web at www .cec.sped.org/intl/ and offers additional worldwide insights, research, and resources.

CULTURAL INFLUENCES

Defining the word *culture* is difficult. This becomes even more compounded when students with disabilities have their own cultures that supersede or tightly coexist with the *mainstream culture,* as defined by the students who are more able-bodied. Students from different cultures are often misdiagnosed as needing special education services since language barriers can interfere with the evaluation process. There is a difference between students' cognitive academic language proficiency (CALP) and their basic interpersonal communication skills (BICS).

BICS and CALP were terms developed by Jim Cummins (1984). Using basic conversation or gestures to communicate socially (BICS) is different from how a student performs in the classroom during lectures or on standardized tests using CALP. Some students with special needs are able to communicate well with their peers, but then due to language differences coupled with learning or reading disabilities are unable to succeed in school or have their unique needs correctly diagnosed to allow for appropriate remediation. Academic achievements become even more challenging when the textbook reading assignments would be too difficult even if they were translated to the student's primary language. And that doesn't even address the difficulties that students from another culture with a disability would experience on formalized testing. BICS is much more easily and quickly acquired than CALP but is not sufficient to meet the cognitive and linguistic demands of an academic classroom (Cummins, 1984; Baker & Jones, 1998).

Understanding a child's family background and language development is crucial, yet this information may be difficult to obtain from some parents of students with special needs who are from a different cultural background from the person trying to collect the student information, due to language differences and other issues. In addition, lack of family involvement with school personnel is not always indicative of a lack of concern, but sometimes is a sign of trust and respect for the school system and their decisions. The following quote outlines some of these complexities when families of students with disabilities are contacted by school personnel.

In some countries, teachers are viewed as figures of great authority and a letter requesting parental assistance can be baffling. . . . [It] may be interpreted as an admission on the part of the school that it does not know what it is doing....[Therefore] it's important to include clear explanations to parents. (National Association for Bilingual Educators [NABE], 2002)

There could be many reasons why some families whose cultures differ from the school's majority culture do not attend conferences or become actively involved in school functions. Transportation, child care issues, and language barriers are just a few. Letters sent home should be bilingually translated to ensure productive communication. The idea is for school–home support of academics to be consistently reinforced and validated. Some educators and the families of students both with and without disabilities need more guidance on how this could be achieved.

The same holds true for evaluations of students, including both formal and informal assessments. It is difficult to ascertain the sometimes fine line between whether a child from another culture who is experiencing difficulties has cognitive or cultural issues. At times, with improper testing that is insensitive to language barriers, what looks like a disability may surface. Was the disability created by the inappropriate directions, wording, or lack of background knowledge, or does the student truly not understand the assignments or assessments, even if they were given in his or her own primary language?

What about social relationships? They, too, may become complicated and interfere with a student's school progress. Peers may shy away from or isolate someone who does not conform to the group. Just eating different foods or wearing different clothing styles may target some students for ridicule or avoidance by other students. Here the teacher needs to play a lead role in educating the rest of the class that no one society has a monopoly on culture. An "okay to be different" attitude here is crucial, starting from the younger grades and continuing through adolescence. If appropriate, families or the students themselves can educate others in the class who may have limited exposure to that particular culture. School need not be a lonely place for a child from another culture. Peers can help, not discriminate!

Cultural issues are indeed tangled ones. At times, expectations at home can conflict with the *school culture*. A student from another culture may become confused and feel displaced about the differing rules, trying to do *the right thing* in both places to please adults and peers in each surrounding. Being a *chameleon* here is not the answer! Feelings of anomie, not belonging in either culture, may lead to behavioral issues that interfere with school performance. Children from another culture may very well develop frustrations, which can then lead to learning, emotional, behavioral, and social problems. Lower self esteem will then negatively impact motivation. Understanding teachers, counselors, families, and peers as advocates are essential promoters of positive changes to transform attitudes for students from other cultures, both those individuals with and without disabilities.

Both the culture of the teaching population and that of the student population have undergone changes in the past few decades and will see even more in the future. According to the U.S. Census Bureau, by 2030, students who speak a language other than English at home will constitute 40% of the school-age population. Teachers not only need more knowledge about specific disabilities, but about a child's cultural background, too. In addition, a student's cultural background should not further disable a student with a disability.

We have a growing number of teachers who have English Language Learners (ELL) in their classroom but who have little or no preparation. (Shreve, 2005)

How can educators address these issues?

- Sit ELL students next to a willing peer who can translate.
- Have classroom activities that promote self-esteem and character building.
- Encourage students to share facts about their own culture, e.g., give Powerpoint presentations, or invite community speakers, families, or organizations.
- Label objects in the room in both primary and secondary languages.
- Use more visual prompts such as those at www.enchantedlearning.com, clip art, or diagrams.
- Dramatize concepts with body language.
- Teach students how to respect themselves and others.
- Wither away the belief of students who say, "I'm better than anyone else," and replace it with an attitude that says, "We can all learn from each other!"
- Initiate and consistently *cultivate* home communication.
- Establish prior knowledge.
- Provide bilingual text and talking dictionaries and translators (see, for example, www.franklin.com).
- Supply students with background knowledge in their primary language.
- Address hate-filled remarks or actions directly, since apathy by the teacher will be interpreted as acceptance.

Here are some additional *cultivating* resources to explore:

Division for Culturally and Linguistically Diverse Exceptional Learners (DDEL): www.cec.sped.org/Content/NavigationMenu/AboutCEC/ Diversity/DiversityInitiatives/DDEL1/default.htm. DDEL advocates for students with diverse needs through collaboration, professional development, and more. Publications include *Multiple Voices for Ethnically Diverse Exceptional Learners.*

Southern Poverty Law Center Teaching Tolerance: www.tolerance.org. Teaching Tolerance offers educational kits and free subscriptions to its magazine for classroom teachers, school librarians, school counselors, school administrators, professors of education, leaders of homeschool networks, youth directors at houses of worship, and employees of youth-serving nonprofit organizations. This organization promotes diversity and equity across the nation and world through stories, lessons, and more.

CultureGrams: www.culturegrams.com. Country reports on 190 cultures of the world. Great way to obtain up-to-date information on a variety of countries and cultures to increase students' exposure and at the same time validate the cultures of students represented in your school.

Dave's ESL Café: www.daveseslcafe.com. Ideas, activities, and resources for students and teachers, with links to ESL Web sites.

Multiple Intelligences: www.igs.net/~cmorris/inventories_on_mi.html and www.surfaquarium.com/MI/inventory.htm (includes nine intelligences).

Multiple intelligences are a way to allow students with diversities to show what they know in different ways. Schools often value primarily verbal-linguistic and logical-mathematical intelligences, instead of also honoring other intelligences in the instructional design of classroom lessons and assessments. Students with diversities need to be given opportunities to capitalize upon their strengths. Teachers can investigate their own preferred intelligences so that they are sensitive to reaching diverse students.

Effective Reading Programs for English Language Learners and Other Language-Minority Students: www.bestevidence.org/_images/word_docs/ELL_9_06.doc. Listing and evaluation of reading programs for English language learners and other language-minority students in the elementary grades. (Entire report is available online at www.successforall.org/_images/pdfs/ell_20060907091650.pdf.)

Boggle's World: www.bogglesworldesl.com. This Web site has teaching resources for TESOL, TEFL, and ESL K–12 students with English skills along with printable worksheets and lessons.

Activities for ESL Students: http://a4esl.org. This project of *The Internet TESL Journal* (iteslj.org) has quizzes, tests, puzzles, podcasts, and lessons submitted by teachers.

TESOL—Teachers of English to Speakers of Other Languages: www.tesol.org. 700 South Washington Street, Suite 200, Alexandria, VA 22314. Phone: (888) 547–3369.

Anti-Defamation League: www.adl.org. 823 United Nations Plaza, New York, NY 10017. Phone: (800) 343–5540. Provides resources, research, and advocacy to teach about differences in school settings and communities.

AGEISM

 Although this book focuses on students in K–12 classrooms, it is also important to address the adults who are the products of our school systems. Some older people with disabilities who were schooled in the pre–P.L. 94-142 era were not given the same inclusive opportunities as students are today. Many agencies are now trying to meet this population's growing needs.

Rights for people with disabilities certainly extend beyond the school years. Individuals with disabilities deserve the same opportunities as their peers, regardless if they are seated in high chairs, classroom chairs, wheelchairs, or rocking chairs! As an Easter Seals poster once proclaimed, "You don't have to stand up to be counted!" Age is sometimes also misunderstood. Older people can sometimes be victims of discrimination. If that older person has a disability, he or she may sometimes receive even less respect from society.

Age is used as criteria to determine when children begin receiving educational services, when transitional plans should be created, and at what age these services are terminated (e.g., IDEA covers students up to age 21). Age determines when teenagers can vote, drive a car, serve in the military, or be considered as an adult in the eyes of the law. No matter what age a person is, he or she still deserves the same rights, respect, and opportunities to show his or her abilities. When given the best interventions, children in schools today will hopefully become productive adults, and later become senior citizens who fondly remember inclusive school experiences. School settings will influence the lives of students as they age, too!

INDIVIDUAL CHOICES ABOUT INCLUSION

Even though today's buzz word is inclusion, opinions about inclusion differ. Not everyone with a disability has a carte blanche philosophy that inclusion is the best or only option for school success. People with disabilities or families of students with disabilities will have had either positive or negative prior school or societal experiences, or both. Some faced acceptance and some faced rejection, which consequently led to feelings of higher or lower self-esteem, accordingly. As a result of their individual experiences, some people with similar types of disability concerns bond together to form a group identity and a collective voice. Together as a group or *culture,* people can share collective hopes, aspirations, and resilience to combat the oppression, discrimination, and sometimes just misunderstanding of others. As a group, their voices are heard, helping them to forge ahead and prosper despite the existence of negativity or lack of knowledge about their differences.

People are of course entitled to have differing opinions about disabilities and *best practices.* For example, I remember the disagreement expressed by a graduate student whom I instructed in Pennsylvania over the LRE (least restrictive environment) continuum. Her thinking was that the general education classroom in a neighborhood school is the least restrictive environment. She taught in a separate school for students who are deaf or hearing impaired. She resented the fact that her teaching environment was labeled as being more restrictive than a general education classroom. This educator believed that for her students' needs, a *regular* school would be more restrictive, since the staff of a general education classroom did not have the same extensive training on how to accommodate specific auditory needs of students who are deaf and those who have specific hearing impairments.

To further illustrate this point, a group of people decided that, rather than face conformity, they wanted to create their own environment, where a disability is not viewed by others as a deficit, but just a way of life. For example, to erase the worries about understandings, tolerance, acceptance, and comfort levels of others, they wanted to create a planned *signing community* in South Dakota, intended for people who use sign language, including those who are deaf and their relatives and friends who also sign. They wanted the primary way to communicate to be through sign language. Even though American Sign Language is the fourth most widely used language in the United States (http://clerccenter.gallaudet.edu/infotogo/) it is the only one not heard. Their intention was to create a town, Laurent (named after Laurent Clerc who formed the first school for the deaf in the United States), that is utterly sensitive to those with hearing impairments. They planned on including elements such as

- Fire and police cars with more lights and fewer sirens
- Businesses and homes with reduced glare
- More open spaces with easy visibility for signing

- An ASL (American Sign Language) public school system
- All businesses and services accessible in sign language, e.g., post office, restaurants, movies, theaters, and more.

The town founders' intentions were not to discriminate against or exclude those with hearing abilities, but to include them, too. Individual choices were intended for homebuyers, by acknowledging that Laurent was both a sign language and agricultural community. These choices were intended to allow people with and without hearing needs to live in this type of rural community as productive economic workers and contributors. Due to a lack of funding, their original plans did not come to complete fruition, but their wheels are still turning as they are looking at other site options.

Individual choices exist for those with and without disabilities. Societal factors such as lack of dignity, exploitation, prejudicial attitudes, insensitive words, abuse, degrading viewpoints, and judgmental eyes only serve to isolate students with disabilities and the adults they become. When the obverse is evident, dignity, respect, equality, positive remarks, comfort, upgrading viewpoints, and nonjudgmental eyes open doors for more opportunities. People who speak with sign language understand smiles, too. Students with disabilities respond to applauding audiences; they deserve more curtain calls in all theaters!

MANNEQUINS THAT SPEAK LOUDLY

How delightful that I walked into Kohl's department store a few years ago, and saw two mannequins, side by side. One was in a wheelchair, while the other one was standing erect. It even seemed like the two mannequins were friends. The best part was that it wasn't even *Disability Awareness Week* or anything like that.

This is a great message being sent out to the public. How do we expect attitudes to change, if people do not take these kinds of steps? The person in the wheelchair *gained many steps* by Kohl's message. These mannequins were communicating that *it's okay to be different,* and still have a fashion sense. Having a disability does not mean that a person can't hold the same societal desires.

Now how is this related to a school setting? Well, first off there are *no dummies!* Second, students shopping in a store like Kohl's are subliminally receiving a message that friendship is not defined by one's abilities. Whether one sits or stands does not influence his or her worth. We need more of this type of community integration. And third, educators need reminders of just how many lessons can be taught outside the school, as well!

DISLABELING ACTIVITIES

Both younger and older students must increase their dis*ability* awareness. Accepting others should come naturally to all of us. However, in some cases, people with "exceptionalities" or "differences" are the recipients of negative and unfounded perceptions and prejudices. There are many curriculum guides for physical education, language arts, mathematics, science, art, social studies, health, and music curriculums. There are also social curriculum guides for teaching children acceptance and sensitivity, but even so, this type of training needs to be continually valued and modeled by both teachers and administrators for the peers of students with disabilities.

In today's inclusive classrooms, the curriculum should also teach students how to view people beyond what they see or think they know, especially emphasizing that there is no *typical student*. Students need help realizing that there are differences among all of us. These are the very things that make us special and unique! Through early training, students can learn to accept people as they really are and maximize the potential of just who people with disabilities can be. Families also need more awareness of the *bigger picture* of inclusion and how it relates to their children and other students with and without disabilities. A positive classroom climate with community and family support creates an atmosphere of acceptance where *all* individuals are valued! The following story, entitled *Two Horses*, by Alison Cotter delineates the impact we have upon each other in school settings and *all fields*, as well!

Two Horses

 Just up the road from my home is a field with two horses in it. From a distance, each looks like every other horse. But if you stop your car, or are walking by, you will notice something quite amazing. Looking into the eyes of one horse will disclose that he is blind. His owner has chosen not to have him put down, but has made a good home for him. This alone is amazing. If nearby and listening, you will hear the sound of a bell. Looking around for the source of the sound, you will see that it comes from the smaller horse in the field. Attached to her halter is a small bell. It lets her friend who is blind know where she is, so he can follow her. As you stand and watch these two friends, you'll see how she is always checking on him, and that he will listen for her bell and then slowly walk to where she is, trusting that she will not lead him astray. When she returns to the shelter of the barn each evening, she stops occasionally and looks back, making sure her friend isn't too far behind to hear the bell. Like the owners of these two horses, people are not thrown away just because of imperfections or because we have problems or challenges. Other people are brought into our lives to help us when we are in need. Sometimes we are like the horse who is blind, being guided by the little ringing bell of those who step forward with a place in our lives. Other times we are the guide horse, helping others see. Good friends are like this. You don't always see them, but you know they are always there. Listen for each others' bells.

Source: Adapted from *Two Horses* by Alison Cotter, a true story about two neighboring horses. Used with permission.

The following K–12 grade level reflective activities and books ring bells that steer students in a direction that fosters acceptances of students of all abilities. Teaching students how to behave with and include others is classroom time well spent, since this skill will later transfer into a lifelong practice, well beyond the school years!

GUIDED LESSONS AND READINGS TO LEARN MORE ABOUT ABILITIES

- Grades K–4: Flowers in Your Classroom Garden
- Grades 3–5: What Makes Me Cook?
- Grades 3–8: Shake It Up!
- Grades 4–8: What's Important to You?
- Grades 7–12: Interpretive Signs

Name _____ Date _____

Grades K–4: Flowers in Your Classroom Garden

Create your own special flower that tells a few special things about you! Remember, if you or someone you know has a disability, it is only one "petal" on that "flower." With the right watering, we all can bloom to make up an amazing classroom garden!

For example your petals can say: *loves pets, writer, dancer, happy, funny, scared of spiders*, and more!

My Flower

Teacher note: These flowers can be planted/posted in a classroom garden!

Source: Karten, T. (2005). *Inclusion Strategies That Work!* Thousand Oaks, CA: Corwin Press.

Grades 3–5: What Makes Me Cook?

Just like the way chefs need to measure ingredients with the right kitchen cooking tools, students in the classroom need different recipes for success. Answer the following questions about yourself and then interview a peer.

Table 2.3

Questions: What Makes Us Cook or Learn?	Myself— My Mixture/ Responses	Responses from someone else in the class I interviewed
How much time do you need to study for tests if you want a good grade?		
What's a hot or sticky classroom situation that you would want to avoid?		
What added special help do you need to do your best? Is it extra help from teachers, your peers, or someone else?		
What can you or others do to prevent *getting burned* and ensure that the classroom is always a *cool place*?		
What other materials, books, tools, or strategies would help you to learn?		

Grades 3–8: Shake It Up!

Younger and older students need to consistently escalate their dis*ability* awareness. Accepting others is something that should come naturally to all, but without proper training in this area, students who are different may be the recipients of other students' negative and unfounded perceptions. This activity teaches students of all ages how to view people beyond what they see or think they know about them. It attempts to hit the core, to help students understand people as they really are, and to maximize the potentials of who they can be. If we as a society want the contributions of all citizens, this training is needed at all ages through a variety of thought-provoking activities. Positive classroom climates create atmospheres of acceptance where individuals of all abilities are valued.

In the first activity, the teacher places the following items in three separate, identical empty coffee cans: the #1 can has a dollar bill, the #2 can has 20 pennies, and the #3 can has 1 quarter. The teacher then shakes each can and asks the class, which one do they think is worth more? The moral here is that sometimes the more valuable things are not always the easiest to identify and also may be the quietest. What you hear or see on the outside does not tell the whole story!

In the second activity, the teacher again places items in three separate, identical empty coffee cans. Now, the #1 can has a dollar bill, the #2 can has 100 pennies, and the #3 can has 4 quarters. The teacher then shakes each can and asks the class, which one do they think is worth more? The moral here is that you don't always know what's on the inside by what you see or hear on the outside. In this case, the cans are all equal, but in different ways. People are equal in different ways, too!

In the third activity, the teacher places equal amounts of rice grains in a coffee can, opaque orange juice container, and paper bag; use your best judgment here with quantity—no need to count the grains! The teacher then asks the students, "What do you think is on the inside of these containers?" Elicit student responses and then have a class discussion. The moral here is that even though things appear different on the outside, the contents or insides of each are basically the same. Every person on this planet has the same worth, regardless of what we all look like on the outside.

In the fourth activity, ask the students which they think is worth more, rice or money. Discuss how if a person were stranded on a desert island, the rice would be worth more than the money! The moral here is that each person has different needs!

Shake it up! teaches about the value of money and of people, too! We're the same in some ways, and different as well. Some people may be a little shaky about their thoughts, but others are willing to shake up their thinking, with or without the use of cans!

Reproducible 2.1

Shake It Up

Activity #1: Circle the can that you think is the most valuable:

#1 Can   #2 Can   #3 Can

Activity #2: Circle the can that you think is the most valuable:

#1 Can   #2 Can   #3 Can

Activity #3: "What do you think is on the inside of these containers?"

Coffee can _____

Juice container _____

Paper bag _____

Activity #4: Circle which is worth more.

Rice   Money

Something to think about: What do you think it means when someone says, "You can't judge a book by its cover"?

I think it means

_____

_____

_____

_____

Grades 4–8: What's Important to You?

What do you wish that the classroom had to make the learning more interesting and fun? Include ideas that match your strengths and needs.

Name _____ Date _____

Grades 7–12: Interpretive Signs

Can you describe analogous school situations that some of these road signs might represent for a student with a disability, performing academics or interacting with peers? Cooperatively brainstorm your thoughts with your peers.

PEER EDUCATION ON DIFFERENCES

Without direct instruction about disabilities, it is difficult for peers to understand the personal experiences, characteristics, and needs of someone who sees, feels, and looks at the world differently. It's the same world, yet the opportunities are not always the same for everyone. Miseducation and the lack of knowledge or experience of teachers and other students will limit students' abilities. Certainly, pity is not an option! Students with disabilities very often want no special treatment, and prefer to be treated like anyone else.

A multivariate cross-sectional analysis in Canada given across socioeconomic levels revealed some results concerning attitudes toward students with disabilities. The study used everyday language and different drawings across genders and disabilities to elicit responses. Most important, it revealed that negative biases need addressing at early ages to circumvent future negative social isolation for students with disabilities. The study purports that some of the confusion in the literature regarding the roles of age, gender, and disability type in children's attitudes has been the result of the tendency to examine these issues in isolation from one another. This study advocates that more exploration is needed to determine the impact of quantitative and qualitative time spent with students with disabilities (Nowicki, 2006).

Opportunities for friendships were at one time greatly limited for students with disabilities. Peers without disabilities, in the not-so-distant past, were not only uneducated about disabilities, but also segregated from a student with a disability. Students with disabilities were friends with other students with disabilities, while the *general education students* mingled with each other in their segregated classes. There was far less education about disabilities, and it was sometimes even nonexistent or thought to be unwarranted.

In recent times, children have learned from an early age through inclusive classrooms that not only can they be friends with someone with a disability, but they can support each other in different ways. Through familiarity, students' varied experiences replace the need to *gawk* or the misunderstandings of what is no longer the unfamiliar. As a result, children's acceptance and expectation levels have meritoriously risen.

Now that such progress has happened, more peer education about different types of disabilities is warranted. Students need to understand things about their peers. Not all students in a classroom need to be doing the exact same work since students may very well be performing on different levels, entering the classroom at alternate starting points, with various experiences, competencies, and background knowledge. The fact that students have a spectrum of abilities needs to be an accepted norm. Speaking in a conversational tone to a student who is deaf, or being on eye level with a student in a wheelchair to avoid that student experiencing constant neck pain are also examples of disability knowledge that must be known by teachers and shared with students. Teachers can create opportunities for appropriate, sensitive, and cooperative interactions among peers. Students need to be taught that it's okay to ask a student with a disability what his or her preferences are or if you can offer assistance with things like carrying books, turning the page, making a copy of your notes, helping with social calls, or maybe even encouraging peers to assist each other with problem solving and cooperative projects.

Most important, peers need exact instructions and coaching on the best ways to help out fellow students. If a child has a disability and displays cognitive, behavioral, or physical characteristics that need explaining, then it is the responsibility of the teacher to prepare students in the classroom for possible scenarios and describe acceptable responsive behavior. If appropriate, families and the students themselves can advocate for particular needs. In addition, students can answer questions about each other's behavior, e.g., *Tell how Miguel helped you in the cooperative group*. It is equally important for students with and without disabilities to reflect on their own behaviors, as well. Even if a student exhibits inappropriate classroom behavior, there is a lesson to be learned from that, too. Not every situation can be outlined or predicted, and consequently there will be teach*able* moments!

Peering Into Teachable Moments

The U.S. Department of Labor's Office of Disability Employment Policy (ODEP) has funded pilot projects to promote mentoring programs for youth with disabilities. Research has shown that mentoring is especially effective in helping youth with disabilities transition into the workplace and adulthood (www.dol.gov/odep/pubs/fact/cultivate.htm).

Mentoring can involve students with or without disabilities helping other students with or without disabilities. Research substantiates that students learning transitional skills, modeling, and ways to jump from high school to the years beyond, whether it is postsecondary education or the workforce, benefit from peer mentoring programs (Moccia, Schumaker, Hazel, Vernon, & Deshler, 1989; Rhodes, Grossman, & Resch, 2000). An e-mentoring model for youth with disabilities is being conducted through a program, *Connecting to Success*, that was developed at the University of Minnesota (ici1.umn.edu/ementoring/default.html). This electronic communication allows students with different schedules and in different locations to interact through e-mails. Mentoring programs offer excellent opportunities for students; however, this cannot occur without the right training and proactive preparation. The next table reflects some considerations for educators, peers/mentors, and mentees to review. Teachers, guidance counselors, administrators, and others can use this table to monitor and document the peer program.

When there is proper implementation and ongoing evaluation of peer mentoring/tutoring programs, then everyone in school benefits from the development of higher social and academic skills:

> Peer tutoring is one of the most effective tactics available to assist students with learning disabilities in the differentiated classroom and can increase the quality and amount of instruction that students with learning disabilities receive. (Bender, 2002)

A colleague of mine shared one of the best quotes I have ever heard. While this educator was teaching a middle school math lesson, he was trying to explain a concept to a student, but the student just wasn't getting it. Another student overheard the teacher's efforts and offered to help this student with some peer tutoring. In less than a minute, the student with the misunderstandings understood the procedure and concepts. The peer tutor apologetically looked at the teacher and said, *"Kids understand kids!"*

Table 2.4 Implementation of Peer Mentoring Programs for Students With Disabilities

Questions/Concerns	Possible Considerations & Examples	Mentor & Mentee Focus/Additional Comments/Other Considerations/ Plans/Notes/Strategies/Collaborations
1. Name the specifics, e.g., the type and duration of the peer mentoring program.	Frequency, location, e-mails, face-to-face, phone conversations, letters, project-based, ongoing, time-limited, student-ratio, school, home, work, community, daily/ weekly/monthly schedules	
2. What knowledge does the peer mentor need to have about the peer or student's disability?	Social, behavioral, emotional, cognitive, physical, academic, medical considerations, and family dynamics	
3. What skills and resources are required and who will train the mentor and/or educator?	Specific concepts, more reading instruction, learning how to use task analysis, ways to model and help but not enable, computer-assisted programs, software, knowing how to teach study skills, knowledge of VA/KT strategies, and multiple intelligences as a means of instruction and assessment	
4. What types of accommodations or modifications will be needed, and will there be administrative support, e.g., funding, scheduled planning time?	Lower reading, but higher-interest level content-related fiction and nonfiction books, math manipulatives, books on tape, Braille, translator, sign interpreter, scribe, additional technology, seating, ways to focus and maximize attention	
5. Who will oversee the mentor to determine effectiveness?	Progress reports, informal or formal assessments, reflective sheets for mentors and mentees, adult observation	
6. How will confidentiality issues be addressed?	About disability itself, medical concerns, personal, physical, academic, personality needs and levels, home/family situations, and any other information shared between peers and staff	

Many educators will attest to the fact that students will spend more time on task learning from each other than when learning from the teacher. Now, when you have students with learning, physical, or emotional and behavioral difficulties in a classroom with peers who don't have the same needs, it is up to the teacher to establish an atmosphere that models appropriate ways to be the best student and to lead others on that path as well. It's a *win–win* lesson in character education that goes well beyond a workbook page.

Peers who display a helping, yet not condescending attitude toward students with disabilities are truly recognizing and maximizing their own abilities as well. Acceptance eventually leads to growth and friendships. Basically, there is no race but the human one, and that includes people with and without a disability!

Simulations and Glimpses

Disability simulations do nothing but reinforce negative stereotypes about persons with disabilities. *Awareness Days* can be beneficial if they are done properly; it is important for the public to meet with persons with disabilities and to interact with us. (Valerie Brew-Parrish, polio survivor and longtime disability activist, www.raggededgemagazine .com/archive/aware.htm)

Simulations are miniscule glimpses into the lives of individuals with disabilities. Tying a blindfold on your eyes, placing cotton in your ears, sitting in a wheelchair, or cutting paper while wearing mittens may imitate some physical and sensory frustrations individuals with disabilities experience, but the scope of these activities is limited. I've personally guided elementary through graduate-level students to try some imitative activities. My objective was to demonstrate the point that until you walk a mile in someone else's moccasins, you have no idea how the person is feeling. After hearing more perspectives, I now realize that these types of simulations do not erase, but at times can actually perpetuate misconceptions about disabilities if the activities are not delivered appropriately.

Understandings about the everyday lives of individuals with disabilities cannot be accomplished solely through simulations. What about the social and psychological dynamics involved? Simulations are brief snapshots that may evoke feelings of pity and general hopelessness in both participants and observers. The realness is missing, so the perceptions and observations are somewhat skewed. A 12-year-old may pretend to be a baby or a 25-year-old, yet the premise here would be shaky: a 12-year-old is still living in a 12-year-old's body. Would a person of color paint him- or herself white to understand more about being Caucasian, or would someone from the Caucasian race paint him- or herself another color to gain different insights and perspectives? How could a person with a *5-minute difference or disability* understand the significance and total impact of that difference on a person's daily life? Simulations are imitations, not replications!

A better way to understand more about disabilities and differences is to hang out, listen to, and have direct personal experiences with individuals with disabilities in social and academic settings. Positive and more realistic examples of individuals with disabilities can also be obtained by reading books, viewing movies, and talking to someone with a disability. These are some ways to gain more accurate understandings than can be accomplished by trying to be *temporarily disabled*. Students in schools should not walk away thinking that the terrifying feelings they may have had when they simulated a disability are what a person with a disability continually experiences. Simulations can have such unintended negative outcomes, if not handled properly. That includes introducing the purpose of the simulation, reflecting upon the experience in a debriefing, and conveying the point that the simulation is a fractional part of what some think they perceive or understand about disabilities, yet can't even imagine.

If simulations are conducted, a reflective sheet such as the following one is recommended. The discussions are equally, if not more crucial than the activities themselves. Debriefing erases the often unsound disability simulation conclusions.

Reproducible 2.2

Reflective Debriefing Questions for Ability Simulations

1. How did you feel when you couldn't _____?

2. What were you thinking as you watched or heard others?

3. Would you like to try the activity again?

4. What strategies helped you cope?

5. What have you learned from this activity?

6. Would you recommend this exercise to a friend?

7. What's the difference between this simulated activity and the experience of someone who has an actual disability?

8. What effect does labeling have on individuals?

9. What could you do to gain more knowledge about different abilities?

10. List a Web site that has accurate information to learn more about people with differing abilities.

Source: Adapted from Karten, T. (2005). *Inclusion Strategies That Work! Research-Based Methods for the Classroom.* Thousand Oaks, CA: Corwin Press.

It's All About How You Interpret What You See

Ti si darh rof osem lihcdner ot rednutsnad eaebcus they ese nights fidfernetly nath oyu od.

Translation: It is hard for some children to understand because they see things differently than you do.

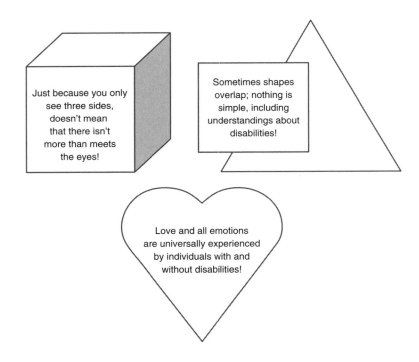

Just because you only see three sides, doesn't mean that there isn't more than meets the eyes!

Sometimes shapes overlap; nothing is simple, including understandings about disabilities!

Love and all emotions are universally experienced by individuals with and without disabilities!

Books That Embrace Differences: Literature Ties With Guided Questions for Disability Awareness in Grades K–12

The following books and movies are not just about disabilities and differences, but also about children dealing with life. Even though some of these are picture books, written for an elementary reading level, the concepts are mature adult ones. Many of the books and movies have themes that do not solely focus on a disability, but also deal with pluralistic issues, such as family dynamics, sibling relationships, peer pressure, goal setting, and school dilemmas. This chapter includes sets of questions that go with some of the books and movies listed, offering opportunities for self-reflections to develop reading and listening comprehension and writing skills, along with better attitudes about disabilities.

The assessments offer a chance for students to demonstrate higher-level thinking skills through a variety of activities honoring the multiple differences of diverse readers. There are no answer keys, since many of the questions are open-ended ones. The absence of an answer key encourages creativity and the merits of different, but justified responses. No answer keys also allows for teacher differences in expectations of their students, and encourages professionals to read the literature and view the movies as well!

Overall, both fiction and nonfiction literature and movies are ways for students to learn more about a variety of subjects. In this case, it's an opportunity for students to differentiate and develop sensitive dis*ability* attitudes. Harried teachers need not be concerned as to when they can fit this into their busy curriculum, since many reading, writing, and research skills are included in these questions and the lessons they generate. In addition, multiple intelligences are honored since the types of questions, including open-ended ones, are differentiated to match classroom diversity.

Books That Embrace Differences for Grades K–2

The following books can be *read-alouds* that help students increase their background and exposure to people with different abilities. Students can discuss the content of the books with a partner or collectively as a class. Teachers may also need to scaffold and provide additional support or explanations to some students. Students can draw pictures and talk about the characters, plot, setting, and story endings, just like they would discuss any other book. Depending upon ages and abilities, students can scribe their answers to another peer or adult, or if their writing skills are more advanced, write a short paragraph on their own without dictation about the stories, or answer all or some of the basic or higher-level comprehension questions.

Silent Lotus, by Jean M. Lee (deafness)

Rolling Along With Goldilocks and the Three Bears, by Cindy Meyers

I'm Like You, You're Like Me, by Cindy Gainer

Ian's Walk, by Laurie Lears (autism)

Leo the Late Bloomer, by Robert Kraus (abilities that bloom)

Be Good to Eddie Lee, by Virginia Fleming (Down syndrome)

I Have a Sister—My Sister Is Deaf, by Jeanne Whitehouse Peterson

Our Brother Has Down's Syndrome, by Shelley Cairo

Luna and the Big Blur, by Shirley Day (visual needs)

The Don't-Give-Up Kid, by Jeanne Gehret (learning differences)

Where's Chimpy? by Berniece Rabe (Down syndrome)

Knots on a Counting Rope, by Bill Martin Jr. and John Archambault (blindness)

When Sophie Gets Angry—Really, Really Angry, by Molly Bang

My Friend With Autism, by Beverly Bishop

Apartment 3, by Ezra Keats (blindness)

Joey and Sam, by Ilana Katz (autism)

Sneetches, by Dr. Seuss (differences)

My Friend Isabelle, by Eliza Woloson (Down syndrome)

What's Wrong With Timmy? by Maria Shriver (cognitive/developmental disabilities)

Eagle Eyes, by Jeanne Gehret (AD/HD)

Talk to Me, by Sue Brearley (language disabilities)

Don't Call Me Special: A First Look at Disability, by Pat Thomas (interactions)

Reproducible 2.3

Silent Lotus

By Jeanne M. Lee

1. Do you think this is a good title for the book?

2. What is a lotus?

3. How did Lotus express herself?

4. Do you think Lotus was happy?

5. If you were Lotus, what would you wish for?

6. Ask an adult to help you find where *Kampuchea* is today on a world map.

7. If you met someone like Lotus, what would you tell her?

8. Choreograph (design) a dance for Lotus.

9. Why was Lotus fascinated by the cranes, herons, and white egrets?

10. Draw your favorite scene from the book.

Reproducible 2.4

Rolling Along With Goldilocks and the Three Bears

By Cindy Meyers
Illustrated by Carol Morgan

1. Describe the Bears' house.

2. Do you know anyone who has a physical disability?

3. Why does Baby Bear go to physical therapy?

4. What was different about Baby Bear's bed?

5. What did Goldilocks think about the wheelchair?

6. Do you think that *spunky* was a good adjective to describe Baby Bear?

7. How did the Bear family treat each other?

8. How does this story compare to another one you may have read?

9. Create a toy for Baby Bear.

10. Could you be friends with someone who uses a wheelchair?

Reproducible 2.5

I'm Like You, You're Like Me

By Cindy Gainer

1. Name some fun things that you and your friends do together.

2. Tell how you are different from some of your friends.

3. Why is it fun to look at your baby pictures?

4. How does your family celebrate their favorite holiday?

5. Describe a time when you were not accepted or included by others.

6. Does everyone learn in the same way?

7. Name some different emotions (feelings).

8. Draw or find pictures of your favorite and least favorite foods.

9. Write a word by each letter that describes the concepts (what you read about) in this book:

   A
   C
   C
   E
   P
   T
   A
   N
   C
   E

10. With an adult's help, find out how children in another country have fun, like the kind of games they play, songs they sing, toys they play with, and more.

Reproducible 2.6

Ian's Walk:
A Story About Autism

By Laurie Lears

Illustrations by Karen Ritz

1. What do you like about Ian?

2. How does Ian react to the fan in the diner?

3. What does Ian do when the fire truck rushes by?

4. Why do you think Ian wrinkles his nose at the flowers, but likes sniffing the wall instead?

5. If you were Tara or Julie, how would feel about having a brother like Ian?

6. Do you know anyone who acts like Ian?

7. Why does Julie's stomach do a flip-flop when Ian disappears?

8. Why do you think Ian likes the bell?

9. How is their walk home from the park different from the one the children took to the park?

10. Do you know anyone who has autism?

Reproducible 2.7

Leo the Late Bloomer

By Robert Kraus

Pictures by Jose Aruego

1. Have you ever felt like Leo did?

2. Why is Leo described as a *late bloomer?*

3. What are some of Leo's difficulties?

4. What do Leo's parents think about him?

5. Draw your favorite scene from the book.

6. Why do you think Leo's mom believes *patience* is important?

7. How does the book describe the changing seasons?

8. How could you help a flower bloom?

9. Why do you think the author compares Leo to a flower?

10. Can you think of a time when your hard work paid off?

Reproducible 2.8

Be Good to Eddie Lee

By Virginia Fleming
Illustrated by Floyd Cooper

1. Why does Christy describe Eddie Lee as a mistake?

2. Why does Christy's mom want her to be nice to Eddie Lee?

3. How do you think Eddie feels when JimBud and Christy tell him to go home?

4. Have you ever gone exploring by a lake?

5. What is described as BEE-U-TI-FUL?

6. Why does Christy say Eddie is a genius?

7. Could you be friends with Eddie Lee?
   Where would you go exploring?

8. What lesson do the children learn when they look at their reflections in the lake?

9. With a teacher or another grown-up, research the actor Chris Burke on the computer. How is he similar to or different from Eddie Lee?

10. What's the most important thing about being a friend?

Reproducible 2.9

I Have a Sister—My Sister Is Deaf

By Jeanne Whitehouse Peterson
Pictures by Deborah Kogan Ray

1. How do you think the narrator feels about her sister?

2. Do you know anyone who has difficulty hearing?

3. How could her sister tell that the radio was playing?

4. Have you ever been scared by the sound of thunder?

5. Would you be friends with someone who is deaf?

6. Why do you think her sister who is deaf yells so loudly?

7. What does the narrator mean when she says that her sister talks with her fingers?

8. How does the narrator get her sister's attention?

9. Can listening to a lot of loud music on headphones be harmful to your hearing?

10. Can children who are deaf learn the same things as someone with perfect hearing?

Reproducible 2.10

Our Brother Has Down's Syndrome

By Shelley Cairo

1. Draw pictures of a cell and chromosomes. Look up the definitions of these words in a dictionary or on the computer.

2. Can Down syndrome go away?

3. Does Jai cry or smile just like other children?

4. Tell about some fun things Jai likes to do.

5. Could someone with Down syndrome get a job when he or she is older?

6. How do Jai's siblings help him?

7. Do you have a brother or sister who sometimes needs help? If you don't have a brother or sister, do you think if you did you would help him or her if needed?

8. Would you invite someone with Down syndrome to your birthday party?

9. Why would someone make fun of a person with Down syndrome?

10. Is it a good thing that people have differences?

Reproducible 2.11

Luna and the Big Blur

By Shirley Day
Illustrated by Don Morris

1. Why does Luna dislike her glasses?

2. Describe Luna's family.

3. Did you ever have a strange dream like Luna did?

4. What happened to Luna the day she didn't wear her glasses?

5. Was her *happy* dream true?

6. What does *nearsighted* mean?

7. Do you have things that make you different from others?

8. What is special about Luna's name?

9. Have things ever looked blurry to you?

10. Design your own pair of glasses.

Reproducible 2.12

The Don't-Give-Up Kid and Learning Differences

By Jeanne Gehret

1. Why does Alex's mom call him the "don't-give-up kid"?

2. Why do you think Alex reads the word "top" 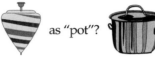 as "pot"?

3. Explain why Alex doesn't have many friends at school.

4. Describe the difference between Mrs. Potter and Mrs. Baxter.

5. Research the inventor, Thomas Edison, telling about his school experiences.

6. How do kids get learning differences?

7. Did you ever have trouble reading?

8. What's your favorite subject in school?

9. Which school subject do you think is the toughest?

10. Describe a time you wanted to give up on something, but then figured out a way to do it.

Reproducible 2.13

Where's Chimpy?

By Berniece Rabe

1. Did your parents ever read bedtime stories to you?

2. What was your favorite story?

3. Why is Misty upset when she can't find Chimpy?

4. Write a list of the places where Dad and Misty look for Chimpy.

5. Tell what things Misty finds while looking for Chimpy.

6. Did you ever have a favorite stuffed animal when you were younger?

7. Do you know anyone who has Down syndrome like Misty?

8. What is Down syndrome?

9. Write a poem about Misty and Chimpy.

10. Why is it *ironic* or somewhat strange that Dad can't find his glasses?

Reproducible 2.14

Knots on a Counting Rope

By Bill Martin Jr. and John Archambault
Illustrated by Ted Rand

1. Describe the relationship between the grandfather and his grandson.

2. How did the grandson get the name, *Boy-Strength-of-Blue-Horses*?

3. Why did the grandfather say he was born with a dark curtain in front of his eyes?

4. Draw a picture of how *blue* is defined in this story.

5. How did Rainbow help the boy to see?

6. Have you ever gone horseback riding?

7. Even though Rainbow and the boy did not win the race, what was accomplished?

8. Do you agree with the statement, *"His dreams are more beautiful than rainbows and sunsets."*

9. Did this story remind you of anything you learned in social studies about Native Americans?

10. What did the knots on the counting rope symbolize?

Books That Embrace Differences for Grades 3–5

The following books help students increase their exposure and sensitivity to differing abilities. After reading a book, invite students to discuss it with a partner or in small groups. Students can draw pictures and talk about the characters, plot, setting, and story endings. Invite them to share what they have learned about differences.

Putting on the Brakes: Young People's Guide to Understanding Attention Deficit Hyperactivity Disorder, by Patricia O. Quinn, MD, and Judith M. Stern, MA

Hank Zipzer, the World's Greatest Underachiever: I Got a "D" in Salami, by Henry Winkler and Lin Oliver (learning differences)

Dyslexia, by Dr. Alvin Silverstein, Virginia Silverstein, and Laura Silverstein Nunn

How to Behave and Why, by Munro Leaf (character building, behavioral issues)

Oh Brother! Growing Up with a Special Needs Sibling, by Natalie Hale

Blue Bottle Mystery: An Asperger Adventure and *All Cats Have Asperger Syndrome,* by Kathy Hoopmann

Different Like Me: My Book of Autism Heroes, by Marc Thomas and Jennifer Elder

In Their Own Words: Helen Keller, by George Sullivan (blindness-deafness and courage)

Learning to Slow Down and Pay Attention: A Book for Kids About AD/HD, by Kathleen Nadeau, PhD, and Ellen B. Dixon, PhD

Loser, by Jerry Spinelli (learning differences)

Small Steps: The Year I Got Polio, by Peg Kehret (physical differences)

Special Brothers and Sisters: Stories and Tips for Siblings of Children With a Disability or Serious Illness, edited by Annette Hames and Monica McCaffrey

Thank you, Mr. Falker, by Patricia Polacco (dyslexia)

The Summer of the Swans, by Betsy Byars (sibling with a cognitive disability)

The Year of Miss Agnes, by Kirkpatrick Hill (different type of classroom in AK)

There's a Boy in the Girls' Bathroom, by Louis Sachar (behavioral issues)

Up and Down the Worry Hill: A Children's Book About Obsessive-Compulsive Disorder and Its Treatment, by Aureen Pinto Wagner, PhD

Matt the Moody Hermit Crab, by Caroline McGee (bipolar disorder)

My Name Is Brain Brian, by Jeanne Betancourt (ages 9–12, dyslexia)

Reproducible 2.15

Putting on the Brakes:

Young People's Guide to Understanding
Attention Deficit/Hyperactivity Disorder

By Patricia Quinn and Judith M. Stern

1. Describe some difficulties children with AD/HD might have in school.

2. How is *hyperactivity* compared to a racing car?

3. Have you ever been *impulsive*?

4. Draw a diagram of the brain. (see page 26)

5. Tell about a time that you experienced one of the emotions listed on page 29.

6. Have you ever felt *overloaded* in class when the teacher was giving out too much information?

7. Describe a time that you experienced an emotion listed on page 32.

8. Where can children with AD/HD get support?

9. What makes a good friend?

10. Identify some ways that you can be more organized in school.

Reproducible 2.16

Hank Zipzer, the World's Greatest Underachiever: I Got a "D" in Salami

By Henry Winkler and Lin Oliver

1. In Chapter 1, Henry says that at first he knows his spelling words, and then they "seem to orbit off into space somewhere." Has that ever happened to you when you study for a test and feel prepared, and then you seem to forget everything the next day?

2. The teacher, Mrs. Adolf, describes spelling as great fun. Do you agree with her? Look over the following list of activities and rank them, placing a 1 by your favorite fun thing to do and a 6 by your least favorite activity.

   ____ Listening to music   ____ Spelling words

   ____ Drawing a picture   ____ Solving math problems

   ____ Doing a puzzle   ____ Taking a walk outside

3. When Hank was upset about his report card grades, Frankie told him to just *give it more gas* while Ashley said he needed *more pedal to the metal*. What did his friends mean by their comments?

4. Have you ever been in a situation where you told a lie and then got into a lot of trouble, like Hank? Tell what happened.

5. Explain what Hank's dad meant when he said he no longer had a *D in salami*.

Reproducible 2.17

Dyslexia

*By Dr. Alvin Silverstein, Virginia
Silverstein, and Laura Silverstein Nunn*

1. What is dyslexia?

2. Name five famous people who have dyslexia.

3. Did you ever have difficulty reading?

4. Why do people with dyslexia sometimes feel stupid?

5. Describe the different jobs that the right and left part of the brain do. (see page 19)

6. Is there a cure for dyslexia?

7. Can you break up the word *dyslexia* into syllables?

8. Can children with dyslexia make the honor roll?

9. Have you or anyone you know ever been disorganized? If so, how could you or that person get more organized?

10. Look up the word *self-esteem* in the glossary. Now tell how you can improve your own self-esteem.

Reproducible 2.18

How to Behave and Why

By Munro Leaf

1. Why does the author say being honest is important?

2. What's the secret of fairness?

3. Describe something a selfish person would do.

4. Does the author think being strong is about having big muscles? If not, where does strength come from?

5. Name some ways you are wise.

6. Do you think that living with other people is like *sailing together in a boat*? Explain your answer.

7. Do you know anyone who needs more reminders on how to behave?

8. Draw a picture of two imaginary people, one who is well behaved and someone who is not well behaved.

9. Do you think behavior is something people can get better at?

10. Tell what might happen if your classroom had a teacher who was not honest or fair.

Reproducible 2.19

Oh Brother! Growing Up with a Special Needs Sibling

By Natalie Hale

1. How would you describe Rebecca and Jonathan's home life?

2. Why did Rebecca decide to tell her friends about Jonathan before they came to play at her house?

3. Is Becca sad about her brother's disability?

4. If you were Becca and Jonathan's parents, what rules would you think are the most important for both of your children?

5. In the chapter, *Will It Happen to Me?* how does the children's mom explain the word *genetics*? (pp. 24–25)

6. Explain a time in your life when you thought nobody knew or understood what you were feeling.

7. If you were Jonathan, would you like to have a sister like Becca?

Reproducible 2.20

Blue Bottle Mystery: An Asperger Adventure

By Kathy Hoopmann

1. Why do you think Ms. Browning-Lever breaks Ben's ruler?

2. Describe how the blue bottle's *magic* affects Ben and Andy's lives.

3. Ben has a system or way of picking his six Lotto numbers. Identify what six Lotto numbers you would select. How would you choose them?

4. Why does Ben start flapping when Dad talks about moving?

5. Describe a time that you or someone you know felt like Ben did about not wanting to be different anymore.

6. Describe what these terms mean:

   Jump to it! _____

   This is the last straw! _____

7. Ben does not like surprises. Do you like surprises? If so, tell about a surprise that happened to you.

8. Do you think it is ironic (strange or odd) that Ben's teacher, Sue, is Dad's old friend?

9. These three-syllable words were in Chapter 12, *The House Warming Party*. Divide them into syllables and illustrate any two words.

Word	Syllables		
Asperger	As	per	ger
verandah			
trampoline			
enormous			
computer			
basketball			

10. Would you be friends with Ben if he was in your class?

Books That Embrace Differences for Grades 6–8

The following books help students increase their exposure and sensitivity to differing abilities. After reading a book, invite students to discuss the theme and concepts presented with a partner or in small cooperative literature groups. Students can draw pictures in a storyboard or PowerPoint presentation; write essays; and talk about the characters, plots, settings, and story endings with each other. Invite them to share what they have learned about people's abilities in written, oral, visual, and dramatic reports.

Zipper, the Kid With AD/HD, by Caroline Janover

The Man Who Loved Clowns, by June Rae Wood (Down syndrome)

Al Capone Does My Shirts, by Gennifer Choldenko (Autism)

Freak the Mighty, by Rodman Philbrick (physical and learning differences)

Views From Our Shoes: Growing Up With a Brother or Sister With Special Needs, edited by Donald Meyer

The Survival Guide for Kids With LD, by Gary Fisher, PhD, and Rhonda Cummings, EdD

Singing Hands, by Delia Ray (hearing differences)

Joey Pigza Swallowed the Key, by Jack Gantos (behavioral differences)

A Corner of the Universe, by Ann M. Martin (acceptance of familial social differences)

Millicent Min: Girl Genius, by Lisa Yee (more advanced abilities)

16 Extraordinary Americans With Disabilities, by Nancy Lobb

Chuck Close, Up Close, by Jan and Jordan Greenberg (learning and physical differences)

Of Sound Mind, by Jean Ferris (deafness)

One Step at a Time, by Deborah Kent (visual differences)

Riding the Bus With My Sister, by Rachel Simon (developmental differences)

Star Girl, by Jerry Spinelli (nonconformity)

The Acorn People, by Ron Jones (lessons learned from children with disabilities)

The View From Saturday, by E. L. Konigsburg (physical differences)

Stuck in Neutral, by Terry Trueman (severe physical disability)

My Thirteenth Winter: A Memoir, by Samantha Abeel (dyscalculia)

The Sibling Slam Book: What It's Really Like to Have a Brother or Sister With Special Needs, edited by Don Meyer

Reproducible 2.21

Zipper, the Kid With AD/HD

By Caroline Janover

1. Do you know someone who acts like Zipper (Zach) does?

2. Describe Zach's mom and dad.

3. What happens when Zach forgets his lunch?

4. Do you think Zach needed to write an apology note to Mrs. Gambini?

5. How does Josh feel when he messes up the poster and Zipper yells at him?

6. Why does Zach like to visit *Picking Pete*?

7. How does Josh's team react when he forgets about the game?

8. Did you ever go to a homework club? If so, how did it help you? If not, do you think you would ever want or need to go?

9. What explanation does Zach give for taking the magazine from the store? What should he have done instead?

10. Zach plays the drums. Did you ever play a musical instrument? If you have played an instrument, how did you feel about the sounds you produced? Was it easy to learn? How much practice was needed? If you have never played an instrument, would you like to learn one day?

Reproducible 2.22

The Man Who Loved Clowns

By June Rae Wood

1. Do you know someone who is similar to Delrita's Uncle Punky?

2. If you were Delrita, do you think you would be ashamed of Punky or have *ambivalent* feelings?

3. One of this book's themes is about dealing with grief. Describe how the characters handled some of their unfortunate situations.

4. Delrita's hobby is whittling wooden figures. Describe a piece of art or an object that you or a friend created.

5. Defend or argue the viewpoint that Punky was ready to live an independent life.

6. How can we as a society help everyone to realize and maximize their potentials?

7. Research this site, www.ndss.org, and list five facts you have learned about Down syndrome.

8. Describe some ways you can turn *Down* syndrome into an *up* syndrome.

Reproducible 2.23

Al Capone Does My Shirts

By Gennifer Choldenko

1. In the story, the author describes Natalie as "sometimes living in her own world, which is sometimes a good or bad world." Have you ever experienced that sentiment about your world?

2. Alcatraz is located on an island in the San Francisco Bay. Research and identify five cities within a 150-mile radius of Alcatraz.

3. Explain what the cons meant when they said that "it takes twelve minutes to get to Alcatraz, but twenty years to get back."

4. What two questions would you ask Al Capone if you ever met him?

5. Research this site, www.autism-society.org, and list five new facts you discovered about autism.

6. Why did Piper's *laundry scheme* backfire?

7. Moose Flanagan's moving experience was an awkward period of adjustment for him. Describe a difficult time when you experienced a change in your life.

8. Explain the author's analogy on the last page when she compares *life* to *a game*.

Reproducible 2.24

Freak the Mighty

By Rodman Philbrick

1. Explain what Max means when the book opens and he says, "I never had a brain until Freak came along and let me borrow his for a while."

2. Freak has a vivid imagination and often refers to medieval times. Have you ever escaped what was happening by thinking about a different time or place from where you were? If you could choose to live in any setting, where would it be?

3. Explain what Freak means by a *biogenic intervention.*

4. Write a creative paragraph on a topic of choice using five words from Freak's Dictionary in the back of the book.

5. Max and Freak are like a unit. Describe a time in your life when you have felt that way about a friend or family member.

6. How can family influences have positive and negative impacts on children's lives?

7. Describe an unsavory character in this book.

8. Relate the comment, "You can't judge a book by its cover," to the novel, *Freak the Mighty.*

Reproducible 2.25

Views From Our Shoes: Growing Up With a Brother or Sister With Special Needs

Edited by Donald Meyer

1. Compare and contrast the viewpoints from two different siblings in the book.

2. Why do you think this book is entitled *Views From Our Shoes*?

3. How is being a sister or brother of someone with special needs different from being a sister or brother of someone without special needs?

4. What have you learned from this book?

5. Do you or any of your friends have a brother or sister with special needs?

6. Review the glossary of disabilities at the back of the book. Describe one of these terms in your own words.

7. Why is it important for *supported living* to be offered to children with disabilities?

8. How do you think you would feel if you had a brother or sister who did things differently?

9. Visit one of the Web sites listed in the appendix and describe more information you have discovered about a disability.

10. Write a poem for one of the siblings in the book.

Check out *The Sibling Slam Book: What It's Really Like to Have a Brother or Sister With Special Needs*, edited by Donald J. Meyer (for Grades 6–12).

Reproducible 2.26

The School Survival Guide for Kids With LD: Ways to Make Learning Easier and More Fun

By Rhoda Cummings and Gary Fisher

1. Tell some ways color coding can help kids stay organized.

2. Who is Bruce Jenner? (check the index)

3. What are some helpful ways you can stick up for yourself? (pp. 120–122)

4. What are some strategies you can use to help you solve math problems?

5. Name some ways to improve your writing.

6. Who can you ask for help if the work is too difficult? (Chapter 8)

7. Have you ever had difficulty with a school subject? What have you done to deal with that difficulty?

8. How can you improve your test grades?

9. What are some ways you can be a better reader?

10. Look at the charts on pages 148–150. Try to design your own chart or table on the computer, using the Table tool, that can help you or a friend organize information for a school subject or outside activity.

Reproducible 2.27

Singing Hands

By Delia Ray

1. Identify how this book's characters and plot would be different if the time setting were the present, instead of 1948.

2. Gussie's dad used a Smith Corona typewriter. Create a timeline, beginning with this typewriter, that shows the major innovations and discoveries that led to today's computers.

3. Gussie remarked, *"The whole Negro family had to file to the colored section in the very back of the bus."* Research and detail other injustices that existed due to discriminatory segregation policies in the South.

4. Identify synonyms and antonyms for each of these nouns Mrs. Fernley assigned on Gussie's first *Weekly Word List:*

Table 2.6

Word	*Synonym*	*Antonym*
knavery		
imprudence		
impropriety		
mortification		
perfidy		
ignominy		
acrimony		

5. Choose one of the following stories, operas, or poems mentioned in *Singing Hands* and write a brief synopsis that includes details about the characters, setting, and plot.

   a. *Madame Butterfly* (John Luther Long's short story or Puccini's opera)

   b. *Casey at the Bat,* by Ernest Thayer

   c. *The Hunchback of Notre Dame,* by Victor Hugo

   d. *The Tell-Tale Heart,* by Edgar Allan Poe

   e. *Pegasus* (Greek myth)

6. The author, Delia Ray, notes that the 1930s–1970s was a time when society ignored and often shunned people who were then called *the handicapped.* Many people believed it was shameful to sign since you should disguise your disability. Respond to this viewpoint from two perspectives:

   a. a person from the *Ears*   b. someone who is deaf

7. Delia's parents had some innovative and adaptive tools in their home, such as a light bulb connected to a doorbell and a flashing light instead of a beep on an alarm clock that alerted them of the sounds. Investigate and identify how technological advances have improved opportunities for people with hearing impairments and other disabilities.

8. Working with a peer, figure out what is being said when each of you sign a sentence using the alphabetic finger spelling shown in the beginning of the book. As a challenge, try singing and signing "The Star Spangled Banner" with emotions, not sounds!

Books That Embrace Differences for Grades 9–12 and Beyond!

Of Mice and Men, by John Steinbeck (developmental disabilities)

The Curious Incident of the Dog in the Night-Time, by Mark Haddon (autism spectrum disorder)

The Memory Keeper's Daughter, by Kim Edwards (Down syndrome)

Animals in Translation: Using the Mysteries of Autism to Decode Animal Behavior, by Temple Grandin and Catherine Johnson

The Real Rain Man: Kim Peek, by Fran Peek (autism)

A Sense of the World: How a Blind Man Became History's Greatest Traveler, by Jason Roberts

Running With Scissors: A Memoir, by Augusten Burroughs (emotional/ family issues)

The Dive From Clausen's Pier, by Ann Packer (physical disability)

The Glass Castle: A Memoir, by Jeannette Walls (emotional/family issues)

The Heart Is a Lonely Hunter by Carson McCullers (cultural differences and deafness/muteness)

Icy Sparks, by Gwyn Hyman Rubio (Tourette's syndrome)

Extraordinary People With Disabilities, by Deborah Kent

Born on a Blue Day: Inside the Mind of an Autistic Savant, by Daniel Tammet

Care Packages: Letters to Christopher Reeve From Strangers and Other Friends, by Dana Reeve

Connections in the Land of Disability, by Alan Brightman

Awakening to Disabilities: Nothing About Us Without Us, by Karen Stone

No Pity: People With Disabilities Forging a New Civil Rights Movement, by Joseph P. Shapiro

Make Them Go Away: Clint Eastwood, Christopher Reeve and the Case Against Disability Rights, by Mary Johnson

The Man Who Mistook His Wife for a Hat and Other Clinical Tales and *An Anthropologist on Mars: Seven Paradoxical Tales,* by Oliver Sacks (neurological disorders)

In Search of Better Angels: Stories of Disability in the Human Family, by J. David Smith

Flowers for Algernon, by Daniel Keyes (basis for the movie, *Charly,* about a man with a developmental disability)

The Quiet Room: A Journey Out of the Torment of Madness, by Lori Schiller and Amanda Bennett

Raymond's Room, by Dale Dileo (speaks of the segregation of people with disabilities)

Falling Boy, by Alison McGhee (physical disability)

First Person Plural: My Life as a Multiple, by Cameron West, PhD

Different Is Not Bad, Different Is the World: A Book About Disabilities, by Sally L. Smith

Reproducible 2.28

Of Mice and Men

By John Steinbeck

1. Explain whether you believe that the relationship George Milton shared with Lennie Small could likely happen in real life.

2. Detail two instances of how George protected Lennie.

3. After researching the lives of migrant workers, write a brief paragraph that highlights a typical day in their lives.

4. Describe Lennie's reaction when he accidentally kills Curley's wife.

5. Give Curley's wife a name and explain the reason for your name choice.

6. Tell which of the book's characters could be depicted as lonely or alienated. Support your choices with explanations.

7. Research the organization called The Arc, at www.thearc.org, and identify the available employment Lennie would have had if he lived today.

8. If you were in George's place, would you have made the same decision or a different one at the end of the book?

9. Explain the symbolism in the title of the book. How would you change the title?

10. Illustrate an emotional scene from *Of Mice and Men*. Your drawing can be made freehand or using clipart.

Reproducible 2.29

The Curious Incident of the Dog in the Night-Time

By Mark Haddon

1. Christopher compares prime numbers to life, since they are both logical but have rules that are difficult to figure out. Defend or refute his position.

2. Have you ever glanced at something instead of really looking at it, as the author describes? If so, describe that experience.

3. The narrator says that he can describe many comings and goings by pressing fast forward, rewind, and pause buttons in his brain, comparing his thoughts to a DVD player. Describe a recent event by pressing your own buttons.

4. Create a two-columned chart that highlights what you perceive to be Christopher's strengths and weaknesses. Give specific anecdotes from the book to support your statements.

5. Compare and contrast the character traits of Christopher's mom and dad. You can use a Venn diagram to respond.

6. Research and list five other capital cities in Europe within a 300-mile radius of London.

7. How did Wellington help Christopher learn many life lessons?

8. Revise and complete the title below to create your own novel. Design your own creative cover to match the new title.

   The Curious Incident of the _____

Reproducible 2.30

The Memory Keeper's Daughter

By Kim Edwards

1. How was the doctor's reaction to the birth of his daughter with Down syndrome typical of attitudes in 1964?

2. Choose one of the following characters in the book and write a first-person narrative from their perspective that explains what they thought about Dr. Henry's initial decision to institutionalize his daughter.

Table 2.7

Paul	Caroline
Norah	Al
Rosemary	Phoebe herself

3. Investigate Pittsburgh and list five of its contributions as an industrial and cultural city.

4. Draw a portrait of Dr. Henry similar to one he would photograph of himself.

5. Paul found music to be his escape. Tell about the favorite songs you like to listen to or sing, or which instruments you like to play.

6. Compare and contrast Paul's and Phoebe's lives, telling about their personalities, choices, education, and priorities.

7. This book is about a decision made to keep a secret from others. Tell about a time someone kept a secret from you or when you kept a secret from someone else. What were your emotions and reactions when the truth was revealed? If this has not happened to you, then just describe the effect that this secret had on Dr. David Henry, his family, and the other characters in the book.

8. Research this site, www.ndsccenter.org, and tell why self-advocacy is a vital and common practice today for people with Down syndrome and other disabilities.

Reproducible 2.31

Animals in Translation

By Temple Grandin and Catherine Johnson

1. Temple Grandin mentions B. F. Skinner, a famous psychologist. Research Skinner's accomplishments and his influence on our knowledge about behavior.

2. Describe a personal situation when using task analysis, as mentioned in Chapter 1, *My Story* (p. 13), would be helpful.

3. In the section, *What Do Animals See?*, in Chapter 2, *How Animals Perceive the World*, the idea of *seeing detail* is described as when an animal or a person with autism is seeing the real world instead of his or her idea of the world. How did Temple Grandin use this thinking to help her with McDonald's needs?

4. Explain why Ms. Grandin chooses not to watch violent movies. (Chapter 3, *Animal Feelings*, in the section, *No Freud for Dogs*)

5. Describe the contrast between two-legged and four-legged creatures' reactions to pain. (Chapter 5, *Pain and Suffering*, in the section, *Autism and Pain,* pp. 187–189)

6. Define these terms: (Chapter 5, *Pain and Suffering*, pp. 214–225)
   a. conscious memory
   b. unconscious memory
   c. fear learning
   d. hyper-specific fear

7. Tell why Temple Grandin needs to create a computer video of a meat plant in her imagination. (Chapter 6, *How Animals Think*, in the section, *Learning That's Easy for People, Hard for Animals,* pp. 251–254)

8. In Chapter 6, *How Animals Think*, in the section, *Words Get in the Way*, why was a salad bowl visualized at the same time as the Super Bowl?

9. Explain why math savants can do calendar calculators while other people cannot. (Chapter 6, *Animals Genius: Extreme Talents*, in the section, *Autistic Savants*)

10. Give examples of two behaviors from the *Troubleshooting Guide* in the back of the book.

Reproducible 2.32

The Real Rain Man: Kim Peek

By Fran Peek

1. Fran Peek tells how his son Kim spent less than 10 minutes in first grade and was then tutored by retired teachers. Compare and contrast the treatment of students with disabilities in schools throughout the decades:

   a. At the time of Kim's schooling in the 1950s–1970s

   b. After Public Law 94-142 was passed (the precursor of IDEA) to now

2. Kim's biggest nightmare is to be *bookless.* Describe your biggest nightmare.

3. Name at least 10 professions that would benefit from Kim's strength with numbers.

4. Fran Peek says that when Kim was labeled *retarded*, it clouded his abilities and robbed him of his potential for 37 years. Labels and categories exist all around us today, such as those regarding clothing, food, or music. Debate or defend the use of labels with items and/or people.

5. In Part III, in the section, *Beauty Is in the Beholder,* the following quote by Confucius is given: *"Everything has its beauty, but not everyone sees it."* Explain this quote in relation to Kim Peek. Then research and paraphrase three additional quotes from Confucius.

6. Fran and Kim Peek are big advocates of The Arc. Do online research about this organization's philosophies and how people have benefited from their services. (www.thearc.org)

7. According to Kim's dad, along with his beloved books and music, family and friends are still Kim's primary anchor. Describe your primary and secondary anchors.

(Continued)

(Continued)

8. Facts come easily to Kim, but concepts are more difficult. In the table below, choose a topic in history, science, mathematics, music, or art, and list five facts about it and five related concepts.

Topic: _____

Table 2.8

Facts	Concepts

9. Kim loves music. List popular songs and artists from each of these decades of Kim's life.

Table 2.9

Decade	Song Title	Artist/Group
1950s		
1960s		
1970s		
1980s		
1990s		
2000		

10. Read the headlines in the appendix, and then write your own headline about Kim Peek.

Reproducible 2.33

Movies About Abilities

Directions: Choose one of the movies in the box below to view. Then design your own five questions and write a brief review of the movie. Pay particular attention to how the person with a disability was portrayed and how that person was treated by others in society. Sample questions and a sample review of the movie, *House of D*, are shown as follows.

Table 2.10

Charly	*I Am Sam*	*Of Mice and Men*
As Good As It Gets!	*Anger Management*	*What's Eating Gilbert Grape?*
Something About Mary	*Forrest Gump*	*Radio*
To Kill a Mockingbird	*Running With Scissors*	*Patch Adams*
Coming Home	*Edward Scissorhands*	*The Miracle Worker*
My Left Foot	*One Flew Over the Cuckoo's Nest*	*Rain Man*
My Other Sister	*Mr. Holland's Opus*	*Scent of a Woman*
A Beautiful Mind	*Children of a Lesser God*	*Awakenings*
The Ringer	*The Mighty*	*Rear Window* (1998 version)

House of D—Movie Review

The movie's protagonist, Tom, reflects upon his life in New York City and his relationships with Pappas, a janitor and friend with developmental issues who worked at his school; his mom; and a woman he sought advice from. Robin Williams portrays Pappas with candor, yet at times, he seems to show more intuitiveness and inferential skills than a person with intellectual challenges would realistically possess, for example, in the airport scene at the ticket counter. The film gives a credible portrayal of the impact of Pappas's family on his life. Overall, Robin Williams's gestures and behavior were realistic. Pappas had a certain level of independence and productivity, yet he experienced setbacks as well. The movie is about changes, choices, and environmental influences. It is upbeat despite the many twists and turns experienced by several of the characters in their settings.

Review this site to find more movies about disabilities: www.disabilityfilms.co.uk.

House of D—Questions

1. What did Pappas mean at the end of the movie when he said that he was no longer retarded?

2. How did the other boys act toward Pappas?

3. Describe the French classroom lesson in your own words.

4. Compare and contrast Tom's mother's issues with issues Pappas experienced.

5. If Pappas was an adolescent living in the twenty-first century instead of the 1950s, what different educational, social, and political opportunities would be available? Elaborate on how his life might have taken another direction.

PART II

Classroom Implications

3

Entering the Inclusive Classroom

Chapter Highlights: Highlights of this chapter include assessing, modifying, and adapting the curriculum. Specific classroom implications and sensitivities for inclusion and disability awareness are highlighted. Discussion of technology possibilities for students with disabilities is also offered in this chapter.

Classroom Connections: Sample classroom scenarios are given that connect IEP goals with students' strengths and the curriculum. Ideas for ways to accommodate, modify, accelerate, and review lessons are shared.

Ways to Differentiate Attitudes: A listing of disability sensitivities is given that ranges from cognitive to social, physical, perceptual, and sensory considerations to help students respond to instructional interventions.

IDEAS ABOUT DISABILITIES

In the preface to *Inclusion Strategies That Work!* (Corwin Press, 2005), I listed these *inclusionary* mind-sets.

Prior Inclusion Confusion

1. What's inclusion?

2. I won't do inclusion.

3. I don't know how to do inclusion.

4. Who's included?

5. Can I have training for inclusion?

6. I need more planning time.

7. It's not working.

8. More direct skill instruction is needed.

9. What's differentiated instruction?

10. When do I retire?

Now, with NCLB and more emphasis on accountability, the shift has changed from teachers asking, "Why are these students with disabilities included?" to "How can I raise all of my students' achievement levels?"

Translation: Teachers are no longer wondering *if* students with disabilities can learn, but are arduously figuring out ways to advance their school and then *life productivity!*

In addition, the age of the teaching population has also changed. Many younger educators have themselves been educated in classrooms alongside students with special needs. These teachers are products of an *educational tide* that merits peers who are colearning. Many staff members who were educated in this *post-P.L. 94-142 era* subliminally and automatically accept inclusion. They don't require it to be sold to them. Other educators, who went to school in the *pre-P.L. 94-142 era,* are delighted to be part of this educational tide as well. The third group consists of combined younger and older educators who need more convincing and training to accept both the high and low *classroom tides,* to help students who are included to stay afloat. Overall, the following quote sums it up best:

> Inclusion can be promoted in the classroom...implementing cooperative learning, multiple intelligences, technology, balanced approach to literacy, thematic/interdisciplinary curriculum approaches, and teaching practices that make subject matter more relevant and meaningful. (Villa & Thousand, 2003)

What's Inclusion?

The Latin root word of *include* means to embrace, while *exclude* means to shut out. Sometimes students are placed in a classroom under the guise of being included, when in actuality such a placement is really not embracing them, but setting them up for failure, if the appropriate mindsets do not adequately prepare them for classroom success.

What Inclusion Is Not

- Placing students who are reading three grade levels below the rest of the class within a general education classroom without appropriate supports or alternate materials. You are then teaching them a lesson in frustration!
- Having students with disabilities take the same assessments as their peers, and then writing a clause in their IEP that even though they do not meet grade-level proficiency, acceptable progress is a 10% gain. (10% of what?! And who's measuring? This needs to be explained and documented with dates and evidence of baseline knowledge and progress.)
- Diluting the work before preassessing a student's needs or competencies
- Limited to physical inclusion, without academic and social inclusion
- Any setting that limits a student's potential!

Inclusive Education Includes

1. Students who have individualized education programs (IEPs) that give merit to their strengths, competencies, potentials, and the curriculum

2. Teachers with parity of roles collaborating together to best meet the diverse needs of the entire heterogeneous class while they implement effective interventions

3. Administrators supporting their staff with adequate and appropriate resources, time for instructional planning, trust in their judgments, along with constructive criticism

4. Communicating children's needs to families who reinforce learning at home

5. Encouraging and promoting positive classroom and life attitudes

Reproducible 3.1 has the definition on the left side and the vocabulary word on the right side. It's a sensitive way to have students match answers without requiring them to read through longer definitions in all of the choice selections. See how many of the definitions on the left you can match with the correct word from the right-hand column. Keep in mind that some words' definitions may overlap!

This Is How the Kids Feel

While teaching a group of graduate students who were presenting a lesson, another graduate student responded to a question incorrectly. One of the presenters quickly said, "Oh, that's okay, good try!" The student who gave the incorrect answer was still humiliated and quietly said to me, "So this is how the kids feel! We really need to do more activities like this to understand just what it feels like when you don't know!" We as educators sometimes forget what students experience when they are students with special needs in an inclusive classroom. We need to sharpen our sensitivities and reflect on our preparation, knowledge, confidence, and collaborative roles with others. Instruction and realistic praise delivered in nonthreatening classrooms promote feelings of self-confidence that help students gain academic and social strides. There's a huge connection between the intellect and affect!

The tables on pages 106–110 are reflective ones for teachers to look at their own competencies and their classroom plans for specific lessons. Even though there is no template for each lesson, certain common ingredients maximize students' abilities across the curriculum. Proactively thinking, planning, and implementing these elements should not be viewed as arduous or burdensome educational tasks. With the right attitude, it's much easier to accomplish the best results for all students in every school setting; these charts visually represent that concept!

Matching Sample IEP Goals With Classroom Lessons

The following sample lessons are suitable for a first grade, sixth grade, and a high school class. These charts show ways for teachers to feasibly address IEP goals in classroom lessons for students with differing needs and strengths.

Reproducible 3.1

Can You Match These Definitions With the Correct Terms?

Inclusive Vocabulary

strengths teachers need to focus on   process

topic/subject matter   modifications

how teachers implement strategies   abilities

what all parties need   meaningful

what learning needs to be   support

adaptations in learning   content

two or more teachers   preplanning
working/planning together

thinking about learning beforehand   attitude

testing students' knowledge   collaboration

how teachers need to work together   assessment

different ways of being smart   cooperatively

a positive one is needed by all   multiple intelligences

Table 3.1   Reflective Table for Teachers Who Serve Students With Special Needs

How Would You Rate Your Skills? Name: _____				
Use a scale from 1–5, with 5 being the strongest rating, while 1 means you need the most improvement or have concerns about your skills in the areas of inclusion, in class support, pull-out support, and replacement or self-contained programs. Write N/A if you think the descriptor is not applicable.	Inclusion (all-day program)	In-Class Support	Pull-Out Support	Replacement/ Self-Contained Programs
Lesson Preparation				
Curriculum Knowledge				
Collegial Communication				
Strategies				
Coplanning				
Role With Parents/Guardians				
Role With SE Students				
Role With GE Students				
Role During Classroom Lessons				
Level of Confidence				
What I think about me . . .				
Strengths				
Weaknesses				
What I Love!				
What I'm Not Sure About				
What I Would Change/ Improve				
What I Wonder About Other Thoughts/Issues/Comments				

Table 3.2   Table of Modes and Methods

Unit:				Concept/Learning Objective:
Class: Student:				
Motivating Activity/Materials:				

Step-by-Step Procedures/Methods:

Date of Initial Lesson: **Revisitation Plans/Dates to Review Concepts:**

Highlight Anticipated People Involved With Collaboration	*Highlight Goals & Curriculum*	*Highlight Differentiation: Accommodations Modifications Parallel Activity*	*Highlight Assessment Options*	*Communicate Connecting Classroom Concerns, Comments, & Considerations*
GE teachers	social/behavioral	establish prior knowledge	Adult	
SE teachers	academic	centers/stations	Peer	
Student	emotional	acceleration	Self	
Peers	physical	Technology (specify):	frequent formal and informal monitoring	
Family	perceptual		portfolios	
Custodian	critical thinking skills	note taking help outlines, graphic organizers	teacher observation dated anecdotal logs/notes	
Administration	communication	preteach vocabulary	multiple intelligences	
Physical/Occupational Therapist	cognitive auditory—remember, process, discriminate visual—match, recognize, classify	home/family collaboration	alternate test format & grading, varied/simplified/modified expectations	
Educational Support Team	word decoding analysis	research assignments	chapter/unit tests/quizzes	
Instructional Assistants	math computations	journal writing	individual or cooperative research projects	
Grade Level Teachers	word problems	written examples/modeling, templates	class participation	
Former Teachers	language arts	individual guidance/reteaching	more time allowed or dividing the test into sections	
Coteachers	functional skills	VA/KT options, e.g., brain breaks, graphics	additional assignments, e.g., extra credit	
Supervisors	gross/fine motor skills	multiple intelligences	homework grades	
Speech/Language Therapists	interdisciplinary connections	manipulatives, e.g., counters, calculators, magnetic letters	log progress, efforts, achievements over time/KWL journals	
Guidance Counselor	review	tiered activities	read test questions	
School Secretary	study skills	study guide	conferencing	
Others (specify):	organizational support	mnemonics	skits or performances	
	other:	vary instruction delivery, e.g., games	alternate: student/teacher-created choices	

Table 3.3   Matching Sample IEP Goals With Classroom Lessons

Lesson Objectives	To advance social, emotional, academic and perceptual skills by listening to the book, *Sneetches,* by Dr. Seuss. a. Students will use auditory and visual acuities to identify rhyming words. b. Students will answer reading comprehension questions to identify the main idea, details, sequencing, inferences, and the story's theme. c. Students will increase their own self-esteem and improve peer interactions through guided teacher questions and role-playing as Sneetches with and without stars.
Classroom Grade	First-grade class
IEP Goals	Student will improve social, emotional, behavioral skills: a. Increase positive self-references, e.g., *I did a good job!* b. Exhibit social reciprocity with classroom peers during academics. c. Decrease waving and shaking of hands. Student will improve expressive language skills: a. Communicate needs and correctly respond to specific oral questions 80% of the time. b. Increase the frequency of appropriate conversations.
Student Classification	Autism
Student Strengths	Loves animations, responds well to music, beams when verbally praised, likes computer work, strong kinesthetic and visual modalities
Student Weaknesses	Often has inappropriate attachments for objects, focused interests, prefers to be alone, will exhibit repetitive language, lower cognitive level
Accommodations Modifications Parallel Activity	Allow the student to write rhyming words in color-coded lists that have the shape of the endings outlined, e.g., configuration boxes. Ask student to copy the letters of his or her name in a salt tray or with shaving cream. Copy pictures from the story from the beginning, middle, and end, and ask the student to sequence them with the help of a peer or adult, e.g., instructional assistant, or a coteacher. Integrate computer programs, e.g., www.palsprogram.com, http://www.dttrainer.com, http://www.computhera.com. Reward student for verbal responses and appropriate conversations with peers. Have student use verbal manding (requests) with peers and adults. Scan pictures from the book on the computer and place them in an animated PowerPoint presentation to increase understandings. Reward increased eye contact and responsiveness to oral questions and requests. Give the student nontoxic clay, a kneaded eraser, or a soft foam ball to replace the waving and hand flapping. Create a rhyming song about the Sneetches for all students.
Assessments	Reward partial strides toward goals, e.g., decreased hand flapping; use applied behavior analysis to help with academic and behavioral goals; make informal observations; teach the student self-monitoring, e.g., with positive self-references or more computer time.
Other Concerns	Student requires frequent supervision and monitoring to stay on task. More eyes in the classroom need to ensure that this inclusive environment services the student with autism and his or her peers; appropriate support is needed from administration, multidisciplinary teams, colleagues, and classroom helpers.
Bottom Line	Everyone in the classroom benefits from increased social awareness. This lesson about Sneetches can then be related to differences exhibited by some children, such as knowing that a student who has a classification of autism is a contributing and *star student*, too!

Table 3.4   Matching Sample IEP Goals With Classroom Lessons (cont.)

Lesson Objective	Students will demonstrate understandings of the Kush empire during classroom lessons by answering written and oral questions.
Classroom Grade	Grade 6
IEP Goals	Student will improve study skills and classroom behavior: a. Write legible notes during classroom lessons 85% of the time. b. Summarize main points of readings 85% of the time. c. Paraphrase readings 85% of the time. d. Work cooperatively with peers 90% of the time.
Student Classification	Emotionally disturbed
Student Strengths	Understands and follows rules with reminders, responds well in structured environments with frequent monitoring, good decoding skills, wants to fit in
Student Weaknesses	Poor readability of handwriting, weak fine motor skills, low focus, inconsistent motivation, minimal self-esteem, inappropriate interactions with peers, weak reading comprehension and organizational skills
Accommodations Modifications Parallel Activity	Directly teach him or her the textbook's format, showing how the bold headings are the main ideas with subheadings to delineate more Kush details. Offer the student graphic organizers or index cards to sort and sequence ideas and events. Preteach the meanings of more difficult or unfamiliar vocabulary words. Use guided support and monitoring during cooperative lessons. Give the student an assigned role, e.g., connector, researcher. Try to allow student choices in assignments that connect to something he or she is familiar with, e.g., compare Kush's wealthy economy from gold mines to the economy of a local business or your own finances. Use personal behavioral log or incentive chart to monitor and graph daily and weekly peer interactions. Assign a peer mentor/coach. Maximize technology, e.g., Smartboard. Coordinate and consult with OT teacher to find out what services are appropriate to strengthen weak fine motor skills. Allow student to tape record answers or have a peer scribe responses. Allow the student to copy notes from a peer. Give the student an outline of the lesson to follow along.
Assessments	Orally read the questions to the student if comprehension issues interfere with responses. Vary types of assessments, from paper & pencil to portfolios. Give the student more empowerment and ownership of learning with a list of approved Kush projects to choose from. Have student keep a social journal for more behavioral reflections and home communication.
Other Concerns	Family dynamics are complicated since the student is allowed to assume authoritative role within the home environment. Need scheduled time to collaborate with the OT teacher for classroom ideas to address fine motor skills.
Bottom Line	Consistency, structure, and more student metacognition. Praise partial strides. Teach and post acceptable social rules and spelled out consequences for repeated infractions. Increase character education programs. Frequent conferencing and communication with families to offer ideas about how to continue behavioral rules in the home, e.g., signed log, e-mail. Time and support from administration to plan with other teachers and to reinforce behavioral rules, if necessary.

Table 3.5   Matching Sample IEP Goals With Classroom Lessons (cont.)

Lesson Objective	Through cooperative research assignments, students will increase and demonstrate their understandings about global warming/climate changes, the greenhouse effect, and the causative effects of these changes on Earth.
Classroom Grade Level	Grade 11
IEP Goals	a. Student will identify the main idea and concepts in nonfiction reading. b. Student will compose a five-paragraph essay using appropriate grammar, syntax, capitalization, and punctuation.
Student Classification	Specific learning disability in areas of reading comprehension, word decoding, and written language
Student Strengths	Excellent verbal reasoning, strong mathematical skills, excellent peer interactions
Student Weaknesses	Will not ask for help; weak writing skills; difficulties with reading comprehension, vocabulary, spelling, auditory processing; does not hand in assignments by given dates
Accommodations Modifications Parallel Activity	Teach and monitor student's organizational skills to track short- and long-term assignments, reports, quizzes, and tests, e.g., calendar; assignment book, Palm Pilot, computer folders. Ask student to graph weather patterns over time to value his or her math skills. Teach student to think of mnemonics to memorize concepts, e.g., wage = warming atmosphere, greenhouse effect. Increase usage of visuals to explain vocabulary: Usborne Science Encyclopedia, http://www.pics4learning.com. Preteach vocabulary. Have content-related books on the greenhouse effect available at lower reading levels. Allow student to use writing planners and frames to organize and sequence written thoughts. Teach writing revision skills. Use a handheld electronic Franklin speller. Allow student to refer to a list of commonly misspelled words. Directly teach listening skills. Ask student to paraphrase his or her understandings. Set up debates to capitalize upon the student's verbal skills. Include more cooperative learning groups with trained peer mentors who can help ease student's reading issues.
Assessments	Administer clutter-free tests with questions that honor the student's knowledge of the concepts, without requiring him or her to decode more difficult vocabulary. Count classroom participation and cooperative learning assignments as part of the grade. Orally read test questions to the student in a quieter, alternate setting, or have the student listen to a taped version of the test with headphones. Hone in on the student's math strengths and good verbal skills
Other Concerns	This student needs to be at the IEP meeting to voice needs and be an integral part of the planning committee to take more of a share in his or her IEP goals. Address transition skills and goals following high school graduation, e.g., entering the workforce, postsecondary education, writing a resume.
Bottom Line	At this age, it is imperative that the student hones his or her self-advocacy and self-determination skills to improve learning experiences and to maximize strengths for school performances and beyond.

RTI: Response to Intervention—Living the Research

RTI is not just for special education. It's a system of providing education that works for all kids. (Samuels, 2006)

While the RTI model provides a valid means for identifying students, another benefit of RTI is that it merges special education into the overall policies of *No Child Left Behind (NCLB)* such as having clear standards, useful measurement, and sound instructional practices. (Wedl, 2005)

Rather than devoting extensive resources to finding out whether students "have" disabilities, we should devote those resources to assessing students' exact instructional needs using models like Response to Intervention. (Harry & Klingner, 2007)

The response-to-intervention (RTI) process incorporates low-inference and functional assessment procedures that can link directly to group and individual intervention planning. (Fairbanks, Sugai, Guardino, & Lathrop, 2007)

Moving to an RTI approach, especially, if it ends up primarily being a problem-solving approach, may introduce considerably more clinical judgment into the identification process than was present prior to IDEA 2004. (Hallahan et al., 2007)

Unlike prereferral, RTI is not a formal part of the special education referral process. RTI is a general education initiative with the goal being to help general education embrace a method intended to help students early on so special education does not become part of their future. (McCoun, 2006)

Some Facts About RTI

1. It is based on research.
2. There is frequent gathering of student data.
3. It encourages systematic instructional modifications.
4. RTI is not unique to special education.
5. Its focus is to improve educational performance.
6. The ability-achievement IQ-discrepancy model is not the only means of identification of students with learning disabilities.
7. The RTI model allows students in early grades to receive scientifically-based instruction as soon as possible.
8. It monitors data to determine the effectiveness of interventions.
9. Interventions can be multitiered with increased intensity, frequency, and duration.

As an example of number 9 above, the first tier may have interventions with the whole class, then Tier 2 may offer interventions to a group with specific skills, while Tier 3 can involve individual instruction. The problem-solving model approach may be used with the tiers. (National Research Center on Learning Disabilities [NRCLD], http://www.nrcld.org/html/research/rti/concepts.html.)

However, many unknowns exist about RTI. Some of the most prominent are the following:

a. Little research has been conducted on RTI on older students or for subjects other than reading.

b. There is debate over whether general or special education is responsible for RTI.

c. Teachers' fidelity to honor and apply research-based practiced practices is unproven.

d. Specific ways to effectively implement RTI in classrooms and schools have not been developed (Hopkins, 2006).

Ultimately, there are no universal programs since there are no universal students, but through careful planning, students with disabilities will  continue to have brighter futures with better early-school, research-based interventions. Both special and general educators who increase their own disability awareness with appropriate strategies and attitudes are the conduits for the interventions to succeed. Pre-service teachers, families, administrators, all personnel, and the students themselves are the ones who can effectively promote these very interventions by always being ready to *catch* and *pitch* the best preparation, attitudes, and support.

In the past, in order for a student to be classified as having a learning disability, there needed to be a discrepancy between the intelligence quotient and academic achievements. Now, school districts can use other models such as RTI to determine if a student is in need of services. The bonus here is that the label of LD (learning disabled) is not a branding one, but one that focuses upon students achieving higher academic levels when given appropriate interventions delivered by prepared and qualified teachers.

Response to intervention replaces *the wait to fail attitude* with frequent monitoring and the application of guided teacher strategies with the following accountability steps:

1. Establish a student's baseline knowledge, e.g., reading 10 out of 15 words, solving 12 out of 25 grade-level math problems.

2. Implement appropriate strategies and remediation based upon individual/group needs and focuses, e.g., decide how long strategies will be used, along with when, where, and who will implement and monitor the interventions and strategies.

3. Monitor students during the regular intervals, e.g., fall, winter, spring.

4. Gauge effectiveness of instructional models implemented.

5. Decide whether to stay the course, discontinue, redirect, or reassess.

With proper implementation, RTI propagates the idea that if a student is *disabled*, that certainly does not mean that he or she is *unable* to learn! The provided interventions are meant to strengthen and maximize students' abilities and assets. The following table outlines some possible cognitive, physical, cultural, social, emotional, perceptual, and sensory sensitivities that need to be taken into account to better assist students to respond to classroom interventions.

Table 3.6   Disability Sensitivities That Help Students Respond to Interventions

Student with ____ needs	*Disability Sensitivities*
cognitive	Will understand the curriculum with accommodations such as • Having access to the same content, using lower-level reading materials, paraphrasing of vocabulary and concepts, preteaching, extra time and practice, mini lessons, changing scope and sequence • Visuals or concrete experiences to explain abstract concepts (e.g., illustrated worksheets, more graphic organizers, videos, animated online sites, field trips) • Strategies that incorporate personal interests, modeling of difficult problems, repetition, and metacognitive opportunities to increase self-awareness to not only improve content knowledge, but also skill development in effective learning strategies • Seeing a rubric, model, or example of acceptable performance levels and completed products
physical	May require a classroom environment with • Less handwritten assignments, but more templates, graphic organizers, and outlines to ease fine motor issues • Physical access to all points (e.g., lunchroom, clubs, all areas within the school and classroom) • Appropriate technology, e.g., word prediction programs, slant boards
cultural	Will require realizations that • School culture may be different from messages received from student's home cultural environment and family needs • No one has a monopoly on culture • Learning styles of students from different cultures vary • Individuals within the same culture are at times both individualized and group referenced

(Continued)

Table 3.6 (Continued)

Student with ____ needs	Disability Sensitivities
social/ behavioral	Will benefit from • Guided assignments with spelled out cooperative roles and expectations • Modeling of appropriate behavior in real and hypothetical situations • Social stories that delineate upcoming situations and expectations • Trained peer mentors • Increased behavioral metacognition • Behavioral plans with consistent rules, rewards, and consequences • Decreased group sizes
emotional	Will benefit from • Journaling opportunities to express themselves • Educating peers about possible *acting out* behaviors some students in the class may display, along with instruction about appropriate responses • Graphing daily moods • Corrective feedback • More self-advocacy and self-determination • Acceptable channeling outlets, e.g., art, music, dance, exercise, yoga, *quiet room*
perceptual	Will benefit from • Clutterless and simplified worksheets, rewriting information on index cards • Reduction of extraneous visual and auditory distractions • Appropriately sized print in texts and worksheets • Increased cues and prompting • Computer-based software programs (see http://www.plato.com)
sensory	May require • Not being seated by windows or open doors • More visuals if there are auditory issues • More auditory cues, if there are visual needs • That speakers face the student when talking, if student is reading lips • Awareness about hypersensitivity to sounds, e.g., fire drills, announcements • No overstimulation, e.g., too many classroom charts, multiple directions at one time

Tools to Help Build Better Learners: Constructivist Teachers

Constructivist teachers try to build better learners by allowing them to enjoy the learning experiences to better retain learning discoveries. Constructivism itself can be an intervention when teachers offer guidance that allows students to effectively respond to self-interventions through individual and group problem solving. Students with and without disabilities are unique, yet complex. Both academic and social levels can be increased when students are major players in their improvements. Constructivism takes into account a student's background knowledge, prior learning experiences, culture, interests, and multiple intelligences. In social constructivism, the learner is an integral player in his or her advancements. Instead of lecturing or giving play-by-play, step-by-step instructions on what to do, self-discovery provides a lasting intervention!

RTI will be most effective with careful and frequent compilation of data along with error analysis from formal and informal assessments to collect and interpret effectiveness of programs implemented, e.g., establishment of a baseline level; graphing of progress; dated observational records; portfolios; behavioral logs; journals; collaborative student, teacher, and family reflections; anecdotal observations of functional and academic performances; and more!

Constructivist teachers inquire about students' understandings of concepts before sharing their own understandings of those concepts. (Brooks & Brooks, 1993, p. 107)

The next table visually illustrates how response to intervention meshes with instruction given by constructivist educators for students with and without disabilities. Yes, accommodations and modifications may be applied as needed, but the major theory of constructivism emphasizes a well-filled *educational toolbox* for all students and teachers!

Table 3.7   Response to Intervention With Better Classroom Construction

Constructivist teachers...

clamp learning to prior knowledge	fill in learning gaps by engaging students' curiosity	allow students to link and share ideas through discussion of hypotheses, prediction, and general points of view
don't hammer in ideas, but allow students to *learn by doing* to pull out their strengths	go beyond skill and drill	cut out the nonessential memorization and regurgitation of facts
plan fun activities that incorporate the academic nuts and bolts	smooth out emotions by allowing ample wait time	establish an environment that allows for *wrenching discoveries*
help tighten ideas to students' long-term learning	encourage students to bounce ideas off each other	dig deeply to connect to learners
actively staple learning to curriculum standards	measure and then remeasure students' progress, efforts, and achievements	have a toolbox filled with strategies for students to self-regulate and discover learning concepts

Reproducible 3.2

"There Are No Blankets!"

Well, where's the script? Here's the news flash: there are no written inclusion by-laws that can apply to all learners! There is no one size that fits all or even most! Many of us just don't measure up to someone else's expectations, be they intellectual, behavioral, social, or physical ones. Now, what can be done if there is no blanket that covers every situation a teacher will experience in the classroom?

Just like there are king-sized, queen-sized, double, or twin-sized blankets along with a multitude of stores in which to find them, there are different sensitivities and strategies that match individual learners' needs in a variety of classrooms. I guess that's the reason for the number of books published, along with the abundant teacher manuals to deliver the curriculum standards. There is no blanket that covers it all!

Directions: Try to *blank-it* these open-ended sentences:

1. Students with different abilities need curriculum that _____.

2. Teachers with the right attitudes will _____.

3. Even though there may be 30 students in a class, with varying abilities, my lessons can be productive to all when _____.

4. Appropriate materials to have on hand are _____.

5. If I need more support, I could _____.

6. Communication with _____ will help.

7. Planning involves _____.

8. When families _____, then _____.

9. If administrative policies say _____, then _____.

10. I understand that blanket-styled learning _____.

Other Factors That Enter Into the Classroom Equation

Weigh the odds

Cognitive, educational, personality, and perceptual variables become even more complicated by economic, environmental, and cultural factors. When teachers, families, administrators, and students themselves realize that learning is multifaceted, then this realization will translate to improvements. Nothing is clear-cut, yet a logical and sensitive school environment helps educators to solve classroom equations, despite the many variables presented!

Table 3.8   Variables to Consider

Cognitive	Educational	Personality	Perceptual
intelligence	type of instruction	self-esteem	memory
distractibility	preparation of educators	attitude	spatial relationships
background knowledge	environment	persistence at task	size or sequencing
understandings	class size	motivation to succeed	interpreting auditory or visual stimuli
learning, thinking, reasoning	administrative support	showing initiative	distinguishing the part from the whole or an image from its background
	connections and reinforcement in the home environment	asking for help study skills	attention or inattention to details and patterns

In addition, physical variables involving the classroom environment need to be taken into account as well. This includes the actual setup of a classroom with available materials and manipulatives for centers and exploratory learning. Specific examples of such a classroom would have a computer/research center, and an art corner with paper, crayons, markers, templates, sketching books, and bookshelves with both nonfiction and fiction books with high-interest topics across different grade levels. Physical classroom elements need to be sensitive to students who may require quiet or noisy areas at different times of the day and allow for the completion of specific independent or cooperative chosen activities or teacher assignments.

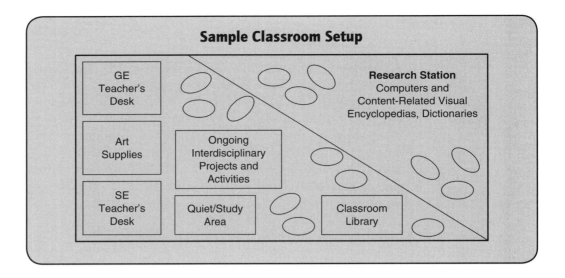

Collaboration and Coteaching Lessons

Collaboration is another factor that when effectively implemented yields improved communications and planning among all teachers, other students, the home, and administration. This school planning includes shared leadership, with an administration that honors students' diverse needs and teachers' knowledge and experiences with both the curriculum and their students. Planning can be school based, grade-level specific, or districtwide with administrations that emotionally and financially support the ongoing collaboration. Together, teachers can plan lessons that include relevant and reflective tasks. Effective coteachers do not debate over classroom control or responsibilities, but share in the planning, teaching, and assessment of all students, without differentiating who is responsible for the learning of students with disabilities. When collaboration is at its best, it's seamless and almost automatic, with teachers often finishing each other's sentences. Some educators are so much on the same page that they frequently even end up wearing the same colored clothing and similar outfits! Collaboration meshes minds, thoughts, and excellent strategies, while honoring the curriculum delivery to help all students achieve their maximum potentials. The next table offers coteaching reflections that teachers can share with each other before, during, or after coteaching.

Some Quotable Coteaching Thoughts

Bridging academic gaps is the shared responsibility of both general educators and special educators. (Heng & Tam, 2006)

Coteaching should be part of a school culture that encourages professionals to work together to achieve a shared goal. (Barth, 2006)

In classrooms filled with students with a variety of learning needs, two teachers can be better than one. (Friend, 2007)

Coteaching is defined as a partnership in which there is a positive impact on both teaching abilities and students' progress. (Cramer & Nevin, 2006)

Table 3.9   Topics to Co-Review

Topics to Co-Review	GE Teacher Comments	SE Teacher Comments
1. Pre-, inter-, postplanning		
2. Instructional/curriculum delivery, content knowledge		
3. Monitoring students during lessons		
4. Assessments: frequency, modifications, accommodations		
5. Teacher roles		
6. Administrative support		
7. Student feedback/reactions		
8. Family contact		
9. Role of instructional assistants		
10. The best part of coteaching		
11. What I would change		
12. Other issues		

When two educators share the roles and responsibilities, the results yield rewarding academic and social benefits to students in inclusive classrooms! (Karten, this volume)

Collaboration involves all parties beyond just two teachers. This collaboration includes families, paraprofessionals, instructional assistants, special subject teachers, occupational therapists, speech/language pathologists, lunchroom assistants, bus drivers, administrators, and classroom teachers. Lines of communication need to be kept open, with face-to-face conferencing, e-mails, written communications, phone calls, and more, without letting time pass with problems in place. It can range from a formal conference to something similar to the message in the following box.

Let's get together to discuss _____.

I'm concerned because _____

_____.

I can meet on these days at these times.

_____   _____   _____

Let me know if this works for you. If not, what are your best days and times to meet? Maybe the principal or instructional support team can arrange classroom coverage so that we can plan and discuss these concerns. Let's figure something out together!

My e-mail is _____.

Thanks, _____

ASSESSING, MODIFYING, AND ADAPTING THE CURRICULUM

Fairytale classrooms do not exist, but educators can definitely figure out ways to connect with students on levels where they can succeed. Both summative and formal assessments must be utilized in productive ways. Most important, the evaluations and assessments are not just about the grades received. Assessments can help teachers figure out where to go next in their instruction, while they deliver vital information to the student, families, and future teachers as well. If there were no errors, then the learning would be superficial! Students sometimes need to know that it's okay to mess up, because those may be the very times when they learn the most! Educators can then also look at the results and say, this is what I need to review to help my students. Another thing to consider is whether the assessment is a fair view of the student's learning, or does it tell the educator that instruction must be enhanced and varied to meet student needs?

In this age of statewide accountability, proficient levels for students are desired by students, families, educators, and administrators. Students want to know that they have performed well, and families want to be proud of their children's achievements. NCLB now has school districts scrutinizing data to see if their districts pass state requirements. These types of summative assessments have taken their place on the classroom stage and have influenced the way educators teach. Suddenly, it's not about what the students know, but more about what the students *should* know because it's on the test!

On the obverse side, formative assessments give teachers information on how to proceed with instruction. Teaching and learning can then be adjusted to meet students' levels. This allows the students to gain additional metacognition

Table 3.10   Fairytales Can Come True!

Suppose some of these *imaginary* characters entered a classroom. How would their diverse needs be met by their educators? What strategies, modifications, adaptations, and assessments could be employed?	
Dilemma Presented	*Recommended Instructional Strategies*
Little Red Riding Hood (LRRH) went through the forest to visit her grandmother, but became lost in the woods and met an unsavory character, the wolf.	• LRRH needs training on how to use a compass as a tool to strengthen her *directionality challenges.* • Preteaching about her *wooded* environment *would* help strengthen her naturalistic intelligence. • Map skills training with graphic organizers for instruction, note taking, and assessments would be beneficial. • More visual clues would help, such as digital pictures of the forest to sequence the steps she should follow. • LRRH could also benefit from direct social skills training to learn how to better handle inappropriate social situations. • The wolf would need to complete an anti-bullying/character education program with pre- and post-observations and assessments of his improvements and a monitored behavioral plan.
Cinderella was going to the ball and lost her shoe. She also had a dysfunctional family environment.	• Cindy requires an intensive self-advocacy program that teaches her to build her self-esteem by helping her to honor and recognize her many strengths. • Cindy could use family counseling with more direct home visits by social workers and agencies to ascertain the quality of Cindy's living conditions. Collaborate with guidance counselor. • Cindy also requires self-help skills to compensate for her family's negative outlook and apathy. • She would benefit from organizational skills training to learn how not to let her pace interfere with her daily routines (e.g., losing a shoe). • Tiered social skill training for the sisters would be helpful. • Cindy could use a PE program with step-by-step training for dance steps. If there are physical issues, Cindy could have PT or perform a parallel activity, e.g., sing.
Jack and Jill went up the hill to fetch a pail of water. Jack fell down and broke his crown.	• Jack may benefit from related services from an occupational therapist who could work with him on his gait and other gross motor issues. • In addition, perhaps more cooperative learning is required. Even though the pair went together, the task of fetching the water was not completed. Additional peers who divide responsibilities could accomplish the task. • They might benefit from more materials (e.g., additional smaller pails) for each of them to hold the same total amount of water, with less in each pail. • It may be helpful to use untimed hill trials and graphing of amount of water retrieved to gauge improvements toward accomplishing the task, rather than reserving judgments and grading based on a completely filled pail.
Mary had a little lamb with fleece as white as snow. Everywhere that Mary went, the lamb was sure to go.	• Although Mary and her lamb are friends, the lamb needs to develop more skills in being independent. • Mary needs instruction and training on how to be a peer tutor who will help, not enable, her friend the lamb. • Differentiation of instruction and assessment for both Mary and the lamb would be beneficial, that is based upon their diverse strengths. • The lamb is to be commended for its good grooming!

along with empowerment and self-direction. It's not about a single test score, but is more of a reflection of the student's overall level. Piaget labeled these processes *accommodation* and *assimilation,* when individuals construct new knowledge from their experiences. Either the learning fits in with their prior knowledge, or the students readjust or accommodate their thought process. This is critical information to have to prevent a downward spiral from occurring if too much time has elapsed. Formative assessments basically tell educators and students what is needed to brush up on before the *learning picture* is matted and framed!

Portfolios are also an excellent alternative. Research on portfolios has proven their value as an assessment tool (Gitomer & Duschl, 1997). Portfolios contain evidence of learning that indicates reflective growth. In addition, communication among students, educators, and families is increased by viewing the tangible documentation that shows progress over time. This type of feedback yields more validity than a single report card grade does, since the contents of the portfolio explain levels of understandings. Portfolios can also enhance student pride as completed works and projects are reviewed independently and cooperatively with peers and adults through conferencing. Portfolio pieces may range from poetry to a science lab review or a content-related visual dictionary that the student drew or filled with applicable computer images. It's not a summative, but an ongoing formative assessment. Portfolios are more about authentic learning strides than a single numerical or letter grade.

Some additional assessment conundrums include the fact that assessments are often influenced by socioeconomic aptitude, what students have learned in prior years, and the aptitude some students were born with. The following quote sums it up well:

> Variations in students' backgrounds fog over the effects of the instructional interventions under study. (Popham, 2006)

To address these variations and circumvent nonacademic related factors such as frustrations, different motivation, and less-than-quality work habits, modifications and adaptations need to be matched with students' levels, backgrounds, and interests. Interventions implemented during instruction and assessment need to be real ones that challenge students, yet recognize differences. Educators who allow their students necessary classroom scaffolding appreciate and honor their students' levels and strengths, without frustrating students with and without disabilities who, like all human beings, have weaker and stronger areas.

> When we teach and assess in ways that respect different strengths, students learn and perform better. (Sternberg, 2006)

The dilemmas arise, since there is a fine line between helping and enabling students. The key is getting the students to realize that they need help before the assessment is given. Students *need to know that they don't know!*
Anatole France, a French novelist living from 1844–1924, poignantly stated,

> An education isn't how much you have committed to memory, or even how much you know. It's being able to differentiate between what you do know and what you don't. (http://www.quotationspage.com/quote/31753.html)

The preceding quotation can be applied to today's learners as well. Unfortunately, many students in diverse classrooms hope to *get by* and not be noticed as being different or unable to learn at the same pace as their peers. That's when differentiated classrooms can honor the different levels with centers, tiered assignments, cooperative learning, multiple intelligences, and more. Differentiation of instruction sometimes involves differentiation of assessments, too. Standardized test achievements are not the only criteria that must be measured and used to gauge students' competencies. In addition, students' efforts and progress deserve accolades by educators, families, and the students themselves as steps toward the mastery of standards. Schools need to determine if the students are responding to the interventions, noting where they were, where they are, and where they are going. Mastery certainly has multiple meanings. How wonderful it would be if students could focus more on what they learned, rather than their grade! So, how do you measure growth and improvements? And just what kind of curricular and student-specific adaptations, accommodations, and modifications are appropriate? The issue of assessments for students with special needs has many complexities yet simplicities as well, as shown with these two quotes:

> The demand for proficiency for all cannot be met because of the inevitable distribution of ability in any human populations. (Rothstein Jacobsen, & Wilder, 2006)

> Formative assessments promote learning when they help students answer three questions: *Where am I going? Where am I now?* and *How can I close the gap?* (Chappuis, 2005)

Overall, valid assessments that are embedded in learning activities can both direct and inform teaching and learning. Many students with disabilities succeed in the classroom if they are given certain accommodations and assessments based upon their individual strengths and areas of need. Accommodations and modifications may be present both during classroom instruction and during assessments. They can include extra time to complete an assignment or test, being able to do test corrections for extra points, allowing a scribe to write answers if fine motor difficulties or illegible handwriting is evidenced, or even having a test orally read. At times, there is consistency and correlation between state and classroom assessments, e.g., both may allow extended time for completion. It's not just about getting the high test scores, but about learning! That includes ways to stretch the learning through appropriate accommodations and modifications. These quotes and the tables in this chapter and the appendix give some additional insights about realistic and reasonable classroom accommodations and modifications. Most important, motivating instruction usually results in more fruitful assessments!

Formal and Informal Assessments With Accountability That Counts!

For the record to serve as more than merely a justification for a final report card grade, the information that we collect on student performance must be instructionally meaningful. (Clymer & Wiliam, 2006)

Schools over-emphasize test results—teachers gauge their own efficacy by them, parents fixate on them, and students come to fear them. Ultimately, test results obscure opportunities to honor and value individual differences and instead translate differences into classifications that place, even trap, students in a range of settings such as remedial and gifted programs. (Brooks & Brooks, 1993, p. 122)

Educators are concerned with the standards that are too stifling and unrealistic or meaningless lessons that cause students to increase their misbehavior, frustration, and anxiety. (Kenning, 2007)

An educator from India summed it up well: "Here when we want the elephant to grow, we feed the elephant, we don't weigh the elephant." (Chen, 2007)

We need to focus on the following:

- Believing ability is incremental and evolutionary
- Giving alternate assessments, varied formats, or retests on the same material, e.g., open-ended questions vs. multiple choice formats, word boxes, project-based assessments within constructivist classrooms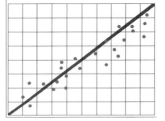
- Teaching while introducing tidbits of what's next
- Finding out what students know before the lesson begins
- Understanding which part or parts students don't understand
- Helping students understand the part or parts they don't understand
- Recognizing students' growths in addition to full mastery
- Encouraging students to monitor their test grades, e.g., graphing their results
- Gauging pacing and instructional interventions by students' achievements
- Meriting oral responses in class participation, cooperative projects, written passages, and reports
- Concentrating on functional skills as well, e.g., knowing your phone number before you are required to solve quadratic equations

Appendix C gives specific ways to document students' progress to see if they are responding to teachers' interventions even before formal assessments are given. The graphs, checklists, and tables presented offer educators ways to monitor literacy, as well as mathematical, social, and functional skills. The next table outlines examples of interventions and related services school providers give to help students achieve mastery of the curriculum with specific guided support.

Just who delivers these services varies from school to school within the same district, from district to district within the same state, and across different states and countries. The following quotes regarding accommodations and modifications

Table 3.11   Types of Services

Types of Services, Interventions, and Student Needs	Possible Providers
Family training, student counseling, and scheduled school or home visits	School psychologist Guidance counselor Social worker
Speech/language and audiology services, signed language, cued language	Speech pathologist Audiologist Teacher of the hearing impaired
Depression, acting-out behavior, social and behavioral issues	School psychologist Outside sources Family/individual counseling
Training for fine or gross motor coordination	Occupational therapist Physical therapist
Additional academic support Specialized instruction Study-skill strategies and interventions	Home communication and collaboration with supportive families Peer tutors Resource center teachers Basic skills intervention teachers Classroom teachers = GE & SE Educational support teams
Vision services	Orientation and mobility trainer
Assistive technology	Computer labs with practice and training for students Staff development opportunities that offer personnel direct instruction, e.g., software, Smartboards, portable keyboards
Psycho-educational assessments that may result in a specific diagnosis (e.g., learning or developmental disability)	Psychologist Learning disabilities teacher consultant
More communication, support, and collaboration with staff, students, and families	School principal Curriculum specialists Staff developers District supervisors Grade-level staff development Instructional support teams

elaborate some of the complexities, concerns, individual outlooks, and classroom possibilities involved in maximizing students' assets.

> Educators should implement adaptations that not only provide students with physical access to general education classrooms but also promote academic and social participation. (Cushing, Clark, Carter, & Kennedy, 2005)

One district in Idaho notes the fallacy in the long-held belief that the brightest students can progress or thrive on their own and emphasizes how these students need to be challenged just like the low- and average-performing peers, giving growth to *all* students. (Clark, 2005)

Whether students are educated in inclusive environments and/or special educational classrooms, curriculum and instruction must be differentiated and adaptation must occur. (Hoover & Patton, 2005)

Accommodations allow students with disabilities the opportunities to achieve maximum and optimum results alongside their peers without disabilities, while modifications allow students with disabilities to achieve somewhat different or modified outcomes. The next table contrasts some specific curriculum examples that indicate the difference between accommodations and modifications.

Technological Access That Accommodates Students' Needs

We live in an incredible age. Maybe future generations will look back at this time as an archaic and primitive one, but the technological breakthroughs that are currently out there for people with disabilities are amazing ones! Today, technology has allowed students to have accommodations that maximize their participation in the general education curriculum, without the students being singled out as being *special* or different! As this section delineates, technology is a desirable and productive accommodation with numerous classroom possibilities. Disabilities are being transformed into possibilities beyond those ever thought conceivable.

People with blindness are faced with a promise of cameras acting as their eyes, with their tongues sending impulses to their brains. BrainPort is a device that retrains the brain nerves in the tongue to send signals to the brain to interpret touch as sight! Sensory substitution by electrotactile stimulation is an amazing thought! Imagine being able to *feel* an image and see it with impulses. It's like rewiring the brain. How incredible that a person who is blind can see a smile and can perform on levels that match his or her peers in more activities than would have been imaginable in prior years.

Students who are deaf are using iPods to do their homework, with teachers recording themselves on VHS tapes signing assignments and vocabulary words. Families at home can see the words at the bottom of the lessons, so they can also help their children with their assignments, even if they themselves cannot sign. Cochlear implants offer some people with hearing issues access to sounds they had never heard before. Lessons can also be uploaded onto iTunes, which students can view from anywhere. The IDEA 2004 regulations outline that the National Instructional Materials Accessibility Standards must be adopted, e.g., publishers providing digital books at the same time peers without disabilities have access to instructional materials. Universally designed technology requires digital font for XML books, which can be manipulated on a computer, cell phone, or PDA (personal digital assistant). The font can then be enlarged and made into speech or Braille. Robotic limbs offer students with physical impairments a new way to improve fine and gross motor skills. The world is now a more inviting one to all students! The next few quotes and table elaborate further.

Table 3.12   Accommodations and Modifications

Accommodation	Modification
Orally reading multistep grade-level math word problems to a student with word decoding difficulties	Letting that student solve one-step math problems on an easier math and reading grade level
Allowing a student to complete a test in another setting with extra time, using the same test and scoring standards as the rest of the class	Allowing a student to complete a test in the same setting without extra time, but deleting parts of the test to allow student to achieve a higher score
Letting a student read a book with a ruled marker or lined transparency that allows him or her to highlight each line, to help the student keep his or her place	Giving the student a lower-level, high-interest book in place of the assigned book
Showing the student a model of an acceptable book report	Accepting a book report that did not follow given parameters
Cutting out pictures of items with different letter sounds for students to sort	Giving the students an alternate assignment to match colors
Allowing students to do odd numbers only on a math practice book page with fractions	Changing the fraction assignment to a math workbook page of adding single-digit numbers
Giving a more concrete learner or one who needs help with organization three index cards with each law of motion defined, rather than pages of notes or text	Deleting requirement that student understand the laws of motion and replacing it with an assignment about dinosaurs
Creating a student study guide that encourages thinking skills rather than rote memorization	Giving a student a study guide that has the exact questions and answers expected
Allowing a student to take class notes with a laptop or digital recorder	Not requiring a student to take class notes or be responsible for class lectures
Assigning specific classroom roles to students during cooperative learning activities	Assigning independent projects to students in lieu of cooperative learning activities

Just because I couldn't speak, they thought I had nothing to say. (A person operating a computer with a headwand, www.scope.org .uk/home/mission.shtml)

Technology offers teachers and students rich, challenging, varied, and motivating opportunities for learning about disabilities. (Salend, 2005)

In Scotland, instead of students who are dyslexic just having a scribe who reads questions and writes dictated answers during exams as an accommodation, they can now use laptops. It was discovered that the students responded better with digital exams on a computer that they could independently scroll and also spell check their answers. ("Dyslexic Pupils to Use Laptops," 2007)

Through functional magnetic resonance imaging and monitoring of the brains of boys with AD/HD who were not on medication, it was discovered that certain parts of the brain are not as developed. This will lead to better medical, social, and psychological treatments. (Switzer, 2007)

Information about disabilities and curriculum topics are readily and quickly available through computer searches, as shown with the following sites and perspectives.

Table 3.13   Web Sites

Web Sites to Learn More About Disabilities	Description
National Dissemination Center for Children with Disabilities (NICHCY) http://nichcy.org	Disabilities fact sheets Parent resources
National Center for Learning Disabilities www.ld.org/	LD Basics with possible characteristics, interventions, and resources
Disability Social History Project www.disabilityhistory.org	Has disability awareness activities appropriate for Grades 6–12 classroom instruction
Boston Children's Museum www.bostonkids.org/educators/disability_awareness.html	Activities, books, and videos that promote an acceptance of differences and similarities
Federal Resources for Educational Excellence http://free.ed.gov	Topical information for curriculum areas and more, e.g., math, history, language arts, science
National Institute of Mental Health www.nimh.nih.gov/	Emotional/behavioral concerns addressed with resources, research, and interventions presented
National Center for Disabilities Services— Abilities! http://www.ncds.org/	Works to promote independence and dignity for people with disabilities, e.g., training programs, access to teleconferencing for communications
www.disabilityisnatural.com, www.pacer.org, www.easter-seals.org	People-first language, "count me in" disability awareness, posters, lessons, friends who care
Web 2.0 tools http://www.atechnews.com/	Using Web tools for social, environmental, and political purposes, e.g., Wikkis and blogs. Students and professionals can share information. Assistive Technology News
What Works Clearinghouse http://ies.ed.gov/ncee/wwc/	Studies and critiques educational interventions
Digital recorders PowerPoint presentations Talking calculators	Help students with communication needs, e.g., voice recognition programs. Helps concrete learners or those with visual or low-memory issues, e.g., giving sound effects. Assists students with learning/sensory/physical issues, e.g., dictating notes, adding more visuals or auditory cues

Fun, yet educational Web sites for students to access to brush up on thinking skills across subject areas:

www.funbrain.com
www.funschool.com
www.playkidsgames.com
www.thekidzpage.com
www.mathcats.com
www.aplusmath.com
www.coolmath4kids.com
www.brainpop.com
www.puzzlemaker.com
www.timeforkids.com
www.wsjclassroomedition.com/teen/index.html

Computers and increased technology offer students with disabilities excellent access to information and increased forms of communication, but there are some important factors to consider in terms of accessibility.

Ask yourself how a student with a learning disability might perceive the tasks and information, how a person who is deaf would understand the content of your Web site without relying on sound, how a person who is blind would access a Web page using a screen reader, and how a student with physical impairments might participate in a chat session. Chances are you'll find yourself saying, "I hadn't thought of it in that context," and you'll make *design* changes that will have a *universal* impact. (Weir, 2005, emphasis original)

Things to consider when students access information online:

Students with disabilities should be taught to use technology to maximize their independence, productivity, and participation in all academic and employment activities. (Burgstahler, 2003)

Table 3.14

1. Organization	Easy to follow flow, without a lot of different folders.
2. Graphics	Choose those that complement the lesson and do not distract from the learning.
3. PowerPoint presentations	Offer them in HTML—accessible to screen readers with learning disabilities, people who are blind, or those who have low vision, using programs such as Kurzweil 3000 to read aloud or JAWS for Windows from Freedom Scientific.
4. Color	Use the same color to organize related points and ideas; avoid excessive color.
5. Introduction	Give overall purpose and synopsis.
6. Directions	Use clear and terse wording.
7. Physical difficulties (operating a mouse)	Encourage speech-to-text software program such as Dragon Naturally Speaking from Scan Soft that is trained to recognize personal speech patterns. Use macros to perform repetitive tasks. Reduce amount of scrolling. Use Headpointer instead of a mouse.
8. Vocabulary level	Students with dyslexia or word decoding issues can be given links to other sites that offer the same content at a lower reading level.
http://www.cast.org/ offers more technology accessibility with many more resources and strategies. http://atechnews.com/ has information on assistive technology.	

Access to information and communication technologies creates opportunities [for] everyone in society, but perhaps no more so than for persons with disabilities. . . . When available to everyone, information technologies foster individuals to reach their full potential, and for persons with disabilities it allows them to play their part in society's development. (UN Enable, 2005)

Available Technological Services, Accommodations, and Programs

- Training of students and staff (sometimes teachers can't keep pace with the advancing and sometimes higher *techno* knowledge of their savvy students)
- Modified utensils for easier physical grasp
- Art software programs for students with perceptual and physical issues
- Powered scooter or wheelchair for mobility
- Software programs and videos for daily living to recreation activities
- Magnifier or copier to enlarge math, reading, and other content area worksheets
- Braille systems for students who are visually impaired
- FM or loop system for students with hearing concerns
- Writing help, from a modified pen and paper to a portable word processor
- Voice recognition software that translates keystrokes into spoken words
- Touch screen communication boards
- Word prediction programs for students with learning or physical issues
- Communication boards for students with expressive language weaknesses
- Electronic dictionaries/books for students with blindness or dyslexia and for ELL learners
- Talking calculators for those with visual and reading issues
- Epistemic games (such as those that simulate jobs, e.g., journalists, urban planners, engineers, graphic artists) for more career development and transitional services
- Slant boards for writing, to ease physical strains
- Computer templates to decrease fine motor and expressive language issues
- Virtual museum trips to concretely reinforce abstract concepts
- STEM skills developed through robotics programs that teach science, technology, engineering, and math skills
- Robots used as mediators for social interactions for students with autism
- Digital textbooks with features that include video clips, animation, and virtual reality
- Curriculum-based video games
- Optical character recognition (OCR) technology that converts scanned images to text and then TTS text to speech (www.readsmart.com) for students with blindness, visual impairment, and dyslexia

The next Web search on autism shows how narrowing down specific questions can help learners gain knowledge on any curriculum topic. Just telling students to do *online research* is not enough since many sites are

Table 3.15   Autism Web Sites

Autism Web Search	
Why is autism sometimes looked at as a spectrum disorder?	www.autism-society.org http://www.njcosac.org http://www.nimh.nih.gov/publicat/autism.cfm http://www.autism-pdd.net/what-is-autism.html http://www.autismspeaks.org
Where can I find *eye-catching* pictures to incorporate into lessons?	www.pics4learning.com www.kidspiration.com, www.inspiration.com www.slatersoftware.com http://us.dk.com http://www.usborneonline.com http://www.unitedstreaming.com
Name some organizations that can offer help to students with autism and their families.	www.nichcy.org http://www.aspennj.org http://www.njcosac.org http://www.autism-fs.org.uk www.autism-society.org http://www.aspenautism.com
Describe some current research studies being conducted with autism.	http://www.autismresearchnetwork.org/AN http://www.autism.fm
What are the differences and similarities between autism and Asperger syndrome?	http://www.asperger.org http://www.njcosac.org www.autism-society.org
Who is Temple Grandin?	http://www.health-reports.com/autism.html http://www.iidc.indiana.edu/irca/fTemple.html http://www.templegrandin.com
How can general education students be peer buddies or allies to students with autism?	http://nationalserviceresources.org/epicenter/practices/index.php?ep_action=view&ep_id=462
Define these terms in reference to verbal behavior: mand, tact, echoic, mimetic, and intraverbal.	http://www.autismusaba.de/lovaasvsvb.html http://www.christinaburkaba.com/AVB.htm
Investigate these computer software programs that are designed to help students with autism.	PALS: Progressive Academic Learning System www.palsprogram.com/ Accelerations: Discrete Trial Trainer http://www.dttrainer.com/jos/index.php CompuThera: http://www.computhera.com

inappropriate ones due to their language, readability, or age level. In addition, offering questions to answer focuses students on specific teacher-selected facts and concepts. The questions on autism in Table 3.15 will probably yield different answers when completed in different years, as the amount of research on this developmental disability is compiling faster with each day that passes! Focus on answering these questions as you explore the specific sites on autism. After completing this one, think how you can then apply this type of computer-constructed Web search to your own grade levels and curriculum topics.

"He Didn't Do His Homework, Either!"

The following vignette explains one of the huge benefits of inclusive classrooms, which is that all students in the class can benefit.

While I was walking around or surfing the classroom, I discovered that one of my students did not do her science homework. While she was filling out the mandatory teacher-assigned punitive homework slip, which then needed to be signed by her parent, I asked to see her assignment pad. Sure enough, the page from the day before was empty, and the homework assignment was never written down. I then directed her to write the missed science homework down, along with other class work that needed to be completed. She promptly obliged, but then looked at me and said, "He didn't do his homework, either!"

Now the student she pointed to was her peer, sitting right next to her. He was not a student with an IEP, but one who also did not complete the science homework. I promptly asked to see his homework assignment pad as well, and instructed him to write the assignment in his pad under the correct date. The first student nodded her head in agreement. She was satisfied that if she was being scrutinized, her peer should receive the same treatment.

How could I or why would I argue? Inclusion is also about fairness and accountability. That doesn't just apply to students with special needs, but to all students. Another time, while listening to students read aloud, I heard one student who had severe decoding issues. I then shared this observation with the "regular" teacher, and together we conducted informal reading assessments geared to assessing this child's needs. We then communicated this information to the child's parents, and the reading ball got rolling for this unclassified student, too.

No More Excuses!

Before educators decide which curriculum to deliver, what books will be the best choice for the subject matter and grade, or which instructional strategies to implement, they need to involve the students as the major players, from the early grades and onward! No matter how persistent, diligent, or prepared a teacher is, all is a waste if students are not the ones who are responsible for their learning. That means no more excuses! I actually compiled a list of "I don't have the homework" excuses with a class one day to emphasize this point. You can share this list with your students, or together with your own students compile a list to help them realize that as educators, we've heard it all! The point of *no more excuses* is that there is no excuse for not having your homework.

In the age of communication, with e-mail, text messaging, e-boards, phones, instant messaging, and more, students have the ability to complete their homework, even if they left the book at school. Encourage students and families to exchange phone numbers with classmates and to develop a network with peers, or *study group allies,* to circumvent these excuses! Sometimes there are socioeconomic factors to consider; even in this age of high technology; some families do not have working phone numbers and some children do not know their phone numbers because they change so frequently. Some households cannot afford a computer and do not have home access to the Internet. Alternative solutions can include having students access the Internet from a public library or a friend or relative's house. Many teachers have Web pages and e-boards with daily and weekly assignments and syllabuses posted. Families need to be privy to this information, too.

Here are some of the *excuses* for which there are no excuses!

"I don't have the homework because . . ."

I was too busy watching TV.

I can't find it!

I did it, but I left it home!

It was too hard!

I didn't know what to do!

I didn't have the time!

I left the book in school!

The dog ate it! (some validity with this one, as evidenced by my own Labrador retriever)

I left it at my grandma's house.

I didn't know what page.

I was too busy at karate.

I don't know why!

Inclusion and ability sensitivities reach those students with IEPs as well as those students who fall between the cracks. Students of all abilities benefit from a lower teacher–student class ratio with two teachers working together in a classroom. Extra eyes can catch the quieter student who needs reassurance, or even the louder student who will then proactively *get the attention* before feeling the need to display *attention-getting* behavior. Students with higher abilities can be directed to more challenging tasks, and those who don't understand the objectives won't object to someone reexplaining the lesson.

Sensitive teachers and assisting classroom adults can match the ability levels of all of their students and at the same time realize how a student's disability may have an impact on his or her progress in the general education classroom. The first step is to have a baseline that lists academic achievement and functional classroom performance for both academic and social avenues. The next step is for educators to figure out how students' strengths can be acknowledged and capitalized upon. Most important is to include the student and his or her family in this planning process so the same skills and rules can be reinforced in all environments. Metacognitive skills for all educators, students, and families promote future strides through learning the curriculum and social, behavioral, and self-help skills. The ultimate goal is proactive communication for further advancements and eventual mastery levels, not frustration from stumbling blocks encountered.

Appendix B gives specific information about matching appropriate accommodations with students' needs while honoring their multiple intelligences. Additional instructional strategies and resources are given for educators, families, and all support staff to reference while helping students with differing physical, cognitive, social, behavioral, and perceptual levels succeed in school settings and beyond, no matter what the *classroom weather* is like.

Classroom Weather

Both WINTER accommodations and SUMMER modifications fall under *the classroom help umbrella.*

However, the classroom AUTUMN weather is sometimes just a bit stormy for students who are caught without the proper attire. SPRING

The following table further clarifies these points.

Table 3.16

Seasonal Classroom Climates	*Weather or Whether or Not It's Working*
Clouds	Fogginess by teachers, students, and parents
Precipitation	When curriculum is becoming too complex and is drenching students
Hail	Student is totally lost in the storm
Snow	Accumulation of misunderstandings throughout the year(s)
Summer	Happiest and *warmest* time for students and teachers
Fall	Panic permeates when summer vacation *leaves*
Winter	Chilling temperature in classroom becomes dangerously low
Spring	Learning growth begins as planted learning seeds flourish
Sunshine	Classroom academic and social warmth with rays of hope
Forecast	With the correct programs and instructional strategies that are designed to maximize assets, students can and will succeed in all kinds of weather!

A Literal Way to Focus on Strengths

We must help all our students discover their strengths and allow them to learn through these strengths. (Nunley, 2006)

Table 3.17

A	Advancements achieved
B	Believing best
C	Consistent communication
D	Dreams delivered
E	Exceeding expectations
F	Following flows
G	Giving grades, gaining goals
H	Honoring hearts
I	Involving individuals
J	Joyous jumps
K	Knowledge kindled
L	Learning leaps
M	Matching minds
N	Nurturing needs
O	Open ownership
P	Positive praise
Q	Quality questions
R	Reaching results
S	Strategies shared
T	Teaching techniques
U	Understanding unknown
V	Valuing values
W	Warranting wishes
X	*Ex*traordinary *ex*tras
Y	Yearly yardsticks
Z	Zealous zooms!

CAPITALIZE ON STRENGTHS:
WHAT TO MINIMIZE AND MAXIMIZE

The bowling ball rolls down the lane, and the anticipation begins. Will it be a gutter ball, a split, or maybe a strike? Just how many pins are knocked down and how many points are scored, depends upon a variety of factors. My father taught me how to bowl. If I stood in the right spot, had a good approach, and held my arm out straight, without curving it off target, then I would be a great bowler. Just because he taught me the rules and showed me some strategies did not mean that I would become a great bowler overnight. I needed to practice and refine my techniques.

Today's classrooms are a bit like a bowling game. Educators, administrators, students, and families are rooting for high scores, implementing a variety of interventions. Students with disabilities will respond to these interventions, but it won't happen overnight. Some bowlers require heavier balls, some need to stand closer to the pins instead of having a running approach, and some may need bumpers at the beginning; while some will make spares and strikes, others will not. High scores and improvements both in bowling lanes and in classrooms are feasible and certainly attainable if everyone continues to practice and refine their skills. That approach will result in *high scores* for both students and educators!

Mastering the Curriculum

Chapter Highlights: This fourth chapter offers specific classroom designs that teachers can use as models to present the curriculum, e.g., layered curriculum, whole-part-whole designs, differentiated objectives, and right angles.

Classroom Connections: Specific classroom suggestions and parallel assignments are given for students with lower cognitive levels and more advanced designs for accelerated lesson objectives are offered for students operating with above-average skills. GAME plans outline how to differentiate objectives for K–12 curriculum connections, letting some students gather facts, others analyze the learning, some manipulate the concepts, while others can further evaluate the learning presented.

Ways to Differentiate Attitudes: Differentiation of learning objectives and collaborative teacher attitudes. Emphasizes how specific lesson designs allow students to demonstrate their prior knowledge and increase their understandings as opposed to rote memorizations.

PRESENTING CURRICULUM

Presenting curriculum objectives to students in a way that they can experience success is not an easy task for educators. Layered curriculum, differentiation of instruction, and right angles are approaches that try to identify and apply diverse instructional goals for classroom learners. Learners with disabilities need to have their skills developed and sharpened in different ways that will allow them to apply, generalize, and retain the learning. The following quotes and lessons acknowledge the complexities and match feasible ways for learning to be maximized.

To differentiate instruction is to recognize students' varying background knowledge, readiness, language, preferences in learning, and to react responsively. (Hall, 2002)

Early Elementary Learners:

By enlivening your classroom with drama games, your students will develop important life skills, enhance oral and communication skills, gain confidence, and have fun while learning. (Sotto, 2006)

Adolescent Learners:

In addition to the obvious physical signs in adolescence, teens and 'tweens are undergoing a major neurological overhaul, which is why that perennial teen mumble "I don't know" may be closer to the truth than we'd realized....It's the most important developmental time for the brain....[We need to] reach them in innovative ways. (Standen, 2006)

So what works for all students, both the younger ones and the older ones, and the ones in between? It's not easy to include fun activities while being cognizant of students' developing brains! Let's go back to the fairy tales, trying the *Goldilocks approach.* Not too much, or too little, but just the right amount of instruction will create productive, lifelong learners, capable of branching out on their own.

It all begins with a game plan, knowing what you want to teach, your objective, and then thinking about what your students already know, which is what their baseline knowledge is. This Goldilocks approach becomes even more complicated because you have to remember that there are also more advanced students in the class. Their needs should not be minimized or sacrificed because you are instructing students with disabilities. They need behavioral, cognitive, and social goals and objectives, too. And then there are the students who won't finish first or last, but may have average skills. Should their needs be addressed, too? Of course! The following planner asks you to think about a content area or skill you would like to teach and then match it to your learners by thinking about their specific learning characteristics, styles, and abilities.

Reproducible 4.1

**Think of your own curriculum and write objectives
you want your students to achieve.**

Table 4.1   Designing Objectives

Grades	Skills/Content Areas
K–2	
3	
4	
5	
6	
7	
8	
9–12	

Designing Objectives

Baseline Knowledge:

Advancing Level:

More Challenging Assignments:

Possible accommodations a child with _____ might need:

Possible accommodations a child with _____ might need:

Possible accommodations a child with _____ might need:

Source: Karten, T. (2007d). *More Inclusion Strategies That Work: Aligning Student Strengths With the Standards.* Thousand Oaks, CA: Corwin Press.

Differentiation of Curriculum Objectives and Instruction in Blended Classrooms

Curricular goals are the springboard from which differentiation ought to begin. In an effectively differentiated classroom, the same powerful understanding-based goals will nearly always "belong" to everyone. (Tomlinson & McTighe, 2006)

As teachers become more aware of students' unique learning styles and intelligences, they become more able to design learning experiences that appeal to their students' different needs and interests. (Gregory & Chapman, 2002)

Several components of differentiated instruction include

    a. Alignment of tasks and objectives to specific learning goals

    b. Concept-focused instruction without emphasizing minute details or obscure facts

    c. Ongoing assessment for readiness and growth

    d. Varying response expectations

    e. Engaging and encouraging all learners to succeed. (Hall, 2002)

[A]lthough essential curricula goals may be similar for all students, methodologies employed in a classroom must be varied to suit the individual needs of all children: i.e., learning must be differentiated to be effective. (Theroux, 2004)

Differentiation means we offer a variety of instructional strategies for the same specific objective....It doesn't necessarily take more time, but it usually takes a different allocation of time. (Nunley, 2006)

It's not the quantity of the work, but the quality that counts. While making accommodations or modifications for varying classroom student levels, some educators think that if they just give the brighter kids more assignments, and make the students with learning disabilities, for example, only do the odd-numbered questions on a math worksheet, then that's a differentiated classroom. What does this type of differentiation accomplish? Not much! In this scenario, although the end product is changed, the instruction is not differentiated. Couldn't both groups achieve understandings of the same learning objective, but be instructed or assessed in different ways? Allowing students to succeed means that you are not overloading them with information, nor will you delete knowledge from their programs. As an educator, you basically think of different ways to simultaneously reach them and teach the same topic, at different levels of proficiency that acknowledge their different classroom starting levels. Another factor to consider here is the pacing of the assignments to instruct students, not to frustrate them, and then to challenge others as well. When accurate records of students' achievements are kept, then the teachers know when to move on and what concepts to review again. Content/topic, process/activities, product/mastery, or environment may be differentiated to address varying classroom student levels. Of course, the differentiation and propagation of positive attitudes is the prerequisite for all.

Some specific differentiation of instruction concepts and instructional strategies include

a. Compacting

If a student demonstrates correct prior knowledge, competencies, and skills, then the student is given higher-level activities. Examples include assignments requiring manipulation of the curriculum using skills of analysis, synthesis, and evaluation.

b. Solo, Cooperative, and Collaborative *Sponging & Anchoring*

Students who finish ahead of time can join other students or independently complete available classroom assignments that have already been introduced to the entire class. These are ways for learners to *soak up* the knowledge while teachers are certain that the concepts don't *set sail!*

c. Cubing

With cubing, students explore a topic, object, person, issue, book, and so forth by describing, comparing, associating, analyzing, applying, and arguing pros and cons, giving different views of agreement or disagreement.

d. Learning Centers

These structured learning center activities will vary according to individual students' levels, interests, learning styles, and the curriculum topics. Teachers can circulate about the classroom to supervise and monitor social and academic skills and needs, inconspicuously giving guided and corrective individual feedback.

e. Problem-Based Learning (PBL)

Students try to independently or cooperatively formulate solutions to real-life issues and situations. It not only challenges students to be self-directed, but it also encourages them to learn how to be a team player. PBL values application of prior knowledge and research skills to solve specific problems and issues presented.

f. Tiering

Educators look at individual student levels and assign matching tasks based upon student competencies. The idea is not to frustrate students, but to challenge and encourage them to explore topics on a level at which they can succeed. Interests and learning profiles are considered before assignments are given. Tiered lessons take into account the readiness levels of students. The standards are divided into lessons that acknowledge students' baseline or prior knowledge and advancing levels.

g. Graphic Organizers

These can help learners understand curriculum concepts from textbook pages by linking facts and details in a *student friendly* way. By rereading the factual information and then referring to the graphic organizers to make sense of it all, students can better process the learning if visual presentations are their

Figure 4.1   Laws of Motion

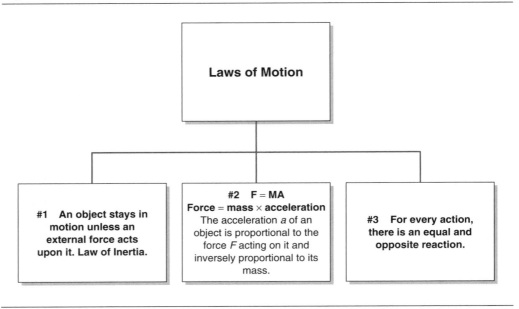

strength. The graphic organizers can also serve as their study guides. They can be just the thing to help students interpret the concepts better (see www.graphic organizers.com/index.htm, www.inspiration.com, www.kidspiration.com).

h. Differentiated Pacing

Curriculum must be presented at a pace that invigorates students, while at the same time acknowledges their individual needs. Students with learning needs do not always benefit from a slower instructional pace, since their attention may wane. Allow students to ask questions, guide them to self-correction and -reflection, and value their feedback. Introduce, guide, review, reinforce, move on, and review again!

i. Cooperative Learning

There are many shapes and forms of cooperative learning, but its basic merits include the development of positive peer relationships with alternate, yet effective instructional approaches. Types include but are not limited to TTYP (talking to your peers), inside-outside circles, and four corners. If cooperative learning activities are set up correctly, there are positive interactions with individual accountability that includes equal and simultaneous participation.

More details about layered curriculum and the right angles of learning with further elaboration and specific curriculum connections follow.

Layered Curriculum

Curriculum was implemented that differentiated assignments in a tiered format to meet the needs of a diverse classroom. Teachers helped each other create units of study and accessed a Web site where teachers from across the nation posted teacher-designed lesson plans. As a result of this initiative, teaching skills improved, and so did the collaborative ethics between regular and special education teachers. (Nunley, 2003)

Layered curriculum applies Bloom's Taxonomy to classroom content and thinking processes:

Layer C = Gather information, facts, basic knowledge (core facts)
Layer B = Manipulate and apply that knowledge (with mastery, can use multiple intelligences, different learning styles)
Layer A = Critical evaluation of real-life issues (with supported research)

Then students receive grades according to their mastery level of layers. This approach asks teachers to critically evaluate their content areas and then design hierarchical instruction. It promotes success, while allowing for individuality. (Nunley, 2006)

Right Angles of Learning

The right angle approach reaches and teaches all learners on their appropriate instructional levels, with a plan for successful outcomes. Some students achieve all objectives, while others obtain partial mastery, working on their individual instructional levels....Not everyone is working on the same level, yet learning improvements in increments are gains and building blocks for more learning. (Karten, 2005)

Students with special needs often do not benefit from curricular materials presented in the same format as their peers without special needs. (Beattie, Jordan, & Algozzine, 2006)

Approaches such as the layered curriculum, differentiated instruction, and right angles recognize differences while at the same time give merit to other *learning spices* and challenges! The intention of all three of these approaches is to separate the curriculum, rather than the students. Students within the classroom may have strengths in one content or skill area and weaknesses in another. If allowed multiple ways to demonstrate their knowledge on a level that values their strengths, the ability rather than the *dis*ability is highlighted. This means lessons with objectives, rather than objections, for all! Classrooms can then be set up accordingly as depicted by the following whole-part-whole example.

Whole-Part-Whole Classroom Design

- Teacher introduces the concept to the whole class.
- Then students are given varying assignments and divided into cooperative groups, while teacher circulates about the room, offering help as needed (Karten, 2005).

Figure 4.2   Right Angle of Reading

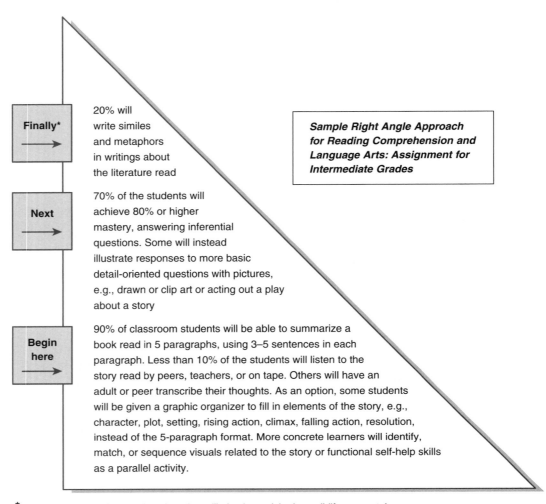

Finally*

20% will
write similes
and metaphors
in writings about
the literature read

*Sample Right Angle Approach
for Reading Comprehension and
Language Arts: Assignment for
Intermediate Grades*

Next

70% of the students will
achieve 80% or higher
mastery, answering inferential
questions. Some will instead
illustrate responses to more basic
detail-oriented questions with pictures,
e.g., drawn or clip art or acting out a play
about a story

**Begin
here**

90% of classroom students will be able to summarize a
book read in 5 paragraphs, using 3–5 sentences in each
paragraph. Less than 10% of the students will listen to the
story read by peers, teachers, or on tape. Others will have an
adult or peer transcribe their thoughts. As an option, some students
will be given a graphic organizer to fill in elements of the story, e.g.,
character, plot, setting, rising action, climax, falling action, resolution,
instead of the 5-paragraph format. More concrete learners will identify,
match, or sequence visuals related to the story or functional self-help skills
as a parallel activity.

*There really is no "finally," since learning will also be revisited to solidify concepts!

Source: Adapted from Karten, T. (2005), *Inclusion Strategies That Work! Research-Based Methods for the Classroom.*
Thousand Oaks, CA: Corwin Press.

Right Angle GAME Plans for Grades K–12

Accordingly, each student needs a GAME plan to follow. There
are no better melodic students' words than, "Aha, now, I get it!"
Bingo! Insights achieved!

Designing effective lessons is more than just rolling the dice
and taking a chance. Curriculum management requires a great
deal more than luck!

Students with disabilities do not always get to choose the
cards they are dealt, but educators in school systems can increase
their knowledge of students' needs and levels by designing
appropriate lessons that are on their instructional, not frustration, level.

For example in a specific classroom lesson,

Some students would

G = Gather the materials

Others could

A = Apply the facts

Some could

M = Manipulate the facts

And another group might

E = Evaluate the information.

If the goal or objective is to teach the class how to play chess, then here's a *game plan:*

G = Some students would learn how to set up the board by following and matching a diagram or model of a properly set up chessboard. These students could also observe ongoing classroom chess games or watch instructional videos or DVDs.

A = Other students would learn the rules about how the different chess pieces move by practicing and playing against a computer software program with step-by-step instructions.

M = Some students could play chess games with each other, to actually manipulate their pieces during classroom game play or even join a school or neighborhood chess club.

E = This group of students could evaluate their moves and think about how different choices would have yielded alternate results. This group could also figure out how thinking through their choices or strategies in other life situations or activities is similar to the moves or decisions they make on a chessboard.

The following examples of curricular lessons are designed for establishing appropriate *instructional GAME plays* throughout the grades and allow students to gather, apply, manipulate, and evaluate their knowledge and skills. This values higher-level thinking skills, which then leads to learning that will not just be remembered for the test, but hopefully for a lifetime! Curriculum topics explored are listed in the table below.

Table 4.2   K–12 Right Angle GAME Plans

K–2	3–5	6–8	9–12
Community	Story Elements	Imperialism	Discrete Mathematics
Patterns	Estimation	Geometry	Economics
Money	Map Skills	Body Systems	Nutrition and Exercise
Earth	Forces	Research Reports	Writing a Thesis

Grades K–2 GAME Plans

Topic: Community

G = These students gather and describe pictures of different communities from magazines and computer graphics, e.g., park, school, forest, lake.

A = Given a collection of pictures of living and nonliving items, these students match which objects belong in each community, e.g., books, fish, swings, bears.

M = These students manipulate the learning by telling what would happen if a living or nonliving item was misplaced, e.g., What would happen to a fish in a forest? Students will think of their own scenarios as well.

E = This group of students tells how different environments are negatively and positively affected by human beings, e.g., pollution, new houses being built.

Topic: Cooking with Patterns

G = Students repeat displayed patterns with models of different pasta shapes or letters from alphabet cereal.

A = Using the same manipulatives, students create their own patterns, following oral and pictorial teacher directions.

M = This group changes patterns according to multiples and skip counting, and gathers letters that form sight words from the alphabet cereal.

E = These students identify patterns with representative symbols, such as letters and numbers, e.g., 1, 2, 3, 3, 2, 1, and AABBBCCCC.

Topic: Money skills

G = These students recognize, name, and/or sort coins and bills.

A = This group of students matches coins and bills with items worth that amount, demonstrating an understanding of the approximate value of the coins and bills.

M = Students in this group manipulate coins by adding and subtracting coins and bills to demonstrate a beginning understanding of decimals, e.g., *mock classroom store.*

E = Students are shown similar items and must decide which is the better value, e.g., two differently sized bags of potato chips.

Topic: About the Earth in the Solar System

G = Students identify the eight planets in order from the sun, making clay models and gathering factual information. Students realize that the Earth's movements affect our daily lives. They physically role-play how the Earth spins, or rotates, on its axis.

A = This group understands the specific effects of the Earth's movements, e.g., a year is the amount of time it takes the Earth to revolve around the sun (365 days); the Earth spinning on its axis translates to days and nights around the world.

M = Students explore the reasons why it is believed that plants, animals, and people live on Earth, and not on other planets.

E = These students learn how space exploration has affected life here on Earth, e.g., medical advances, environmental concerns, everyday products.

Grades 3–5 GAME Plans

Topic: Elements of a Story

G = Students listen to and/or read a story to identify the main characters, setting (where and when it took place), main events, and the story's ending.

A = Students answer oral and written inferential, prediction, and sequencing questions, e.g., *What do you think would happen if...? What was this character's motive for...? Put these events in order.*

M = Students pretend to be the characters and act out the story they heard or read, including important details with appropriate dialogue, props, and scenery.

E = Students think about whether the author told a good story and decide if they would change any parts or elements if they wrote the book, thinking about the vocabulary word choices, text layout, chapters, and illustrations.

Topic: Estimation

G = These students round numbers to the nearest ten, hundred, thousand, ten thousand, hundred thousand, million, and dollar amount, following step-by-step models and written procedures. They are introduced to real-life estimation applications and decide if estimations are reasonable ones—e.g., if there could actually be about 150 students on a school bus—or tell the temperature or batting average to the nearest whole number.

A = These students independently solve multistep, real-life word problems using appropriate operations in daily situations, e.g., approximate the cost of items if they were shopping in a store, and estimate the change they would receive.

M = This group of students cooperatively creates its own word problems comparing estimated and actual answers using all four operations.

E = Students in this group also use estimation skills to solve multistep problems. In addition, they decide in which situations estimation skills would be beneficial, and evaluate which situations would require exact computations.

Topic: Map Skills

G = These students identify their geographic area on local maps, telling basic directions (north, south, east, west) and then intermittent ones (NE, SE, SW, NW). Students also learn about their country in relation to the different continents on a world map, locating and identifying nearby cities, bodies of water, bordering countries, and hemispheres.

A = This group of students applies map skills by finding the latitude and longitude of major world cities and uses a scale of miles to locate the distances between given locations.

M = After these students have demonstrated the preceding map skills, they create their own community and world maps with latitude and longitude grids.

E = These students compare political, cultural, and historical maps of geographic locations, noting the differences and how to interpret them (e.g., Mesopotamia compared to present-day Iraq). These students also evaluate the differences between cylindrical, conical, and flat-plane projections.

Topic: Forces

G = Students identify push, pull, balanced, and unbalanced forces through experimentation and demonstration. They also come to know what forces affect us in our daily routines. Forces for study include friction, magnetism, and gravity.

A = Students analyze and investigate the reasons simple machines can lessen the workload to make jobs easier. Daily environmental connections will be given.

M = Students identify specific forces in action at amusement parks. They also learn that a change in the state of motion, e.g., velocity, requires a *net force,* and that an object accelerates directly in proportion to the net force acting on it.

E = Students interpret data by evaluating different scientific experiments with varying hypotheses, materials, procedures, and conclusions to prove *forceful* concepts, e.g., if distance or weight/mass increases, so will the amount of force needed.

Grades 6–8 GAME Plans

Topic: Imperialism

G = Students note the historical time periods and world locations of imperialistic events and the countries involved, e.g., Ancient Rome, England, France, South Africa, India, Argentina, Germany, Italy, Japan, Ottoman Empire, United States. Information is gathered from approved online research sites, texts, maps, and available primary sources.

A = This group applies the knowledge by investigating how the motives of pride and power negatively and positively affect countries.

M = These students manipulate the knowledge by changing the historical scenarios, e.g., geographic locations, political climates, and then give hypothetical results. For example, if France had had no need for fur, would they have sent explorers to the New World? Or, if Julius Caesar had never lived, would the Roman Empire have expanded? If Germany's economic conditions had been better after World War I, would Hitler have been able to gain the same political momentum for his ideas?

E = Students critique the decisions made by the government of one of the imperialistic countries, evaluating short- and long-term effects on the peoples living there, bordering countries, and future generations.

Topic: Geometry

G = These students identify basic properties and terms involving polygons and other geometric shapes such as triangles, rectangular prisms, pyramids, and circles, noting similarities and differences, e.g., vertices, faces, angles, and measurements such as perimeter, circumference, surface area, and volume.

A = Students in this group apply the knowledge to prove or disprove geometric theorems.

M = This group manipulates the knowledge by constructing figures using Geometer's Sketchpad software to make perspective drawings, tessellations, fractals, and animated sine waves.

E = When this group completes all of the above assignments, they then evaluate how geometry is a form of communication and tell how societies have benefited from this geometric knowledge.

Topic: Your Body and You

G = Students study the body systems—circulatory, digestive, excretory, respiratory, skeletal, muscular, reproductive, nervous, and endocrine—and their interactions with each other. Through lab investigations, students gain knowledge by examining and categorizing cells under microscopes.

A = These students analyze the effects of drugs, alcohol, and tobacco on the body systems, diseases that may develop, and the body's immune system.

M = Students set up controlled and teacher-guided experiments to examine and document the effects of human activity on the body, e.g., pulse and heart rate during sedentary vs. more physical activities.

E = Students in this group evaluate the scientific promises to living beings offered by increased knowledge, e.g., nutrition, exercise, heart procedures, robotic limbs/bioengineering, epidemiologists combating and possibly eradicating cancer.

Topic: Research Reports

G = These students identify key words in individual research and then compile information on given issues and topics using texts, journal articles, and online sources.

A = With a peer, students cooperatively select and organize pertinent information to compose three paragraphs that include appropriate on-topic research facts and concepts, while including a bibliography of sources consulted.

M = After completing the two prior steps, these students expand this three-paragraph report into a five-page research paper, adding subsequent research with correct citations.

E = Students manipulate ideas presented by taking a position on the research, telling if they believe that the points presented are valid, slanted, or unbiased.

Grades 9–12 GAME Plans

Topic: Discrete Mathematics

G = With step-by-step modeling, direct instruction, online sources, and videos, students view examples that connect and interpret mathematics in everyday situations.

A = Students analyze decisions made while problem solving in noncontinuous situations, e.g., finite probability, graph theory, finite differences and recurrence relations, logic, mathematical induction, and algorithmic thinking.

M = Students connect information to interest-generated topics. Garfunkel (1988) gives examples, such as identifying the optimum percentage of fastballs that a pitcher should throw in the game of baseball.

E = Students collaboratively evaluate their reasoning, verbalizing how each variable or decision affects the final outcome. Students will also investigate and evaluate the evolving role of technology in discrete mathematics and their possible future careers.

Topic: Connecting Economics to World Governments

G = Students define and outline basic economic terms and principles, e.g., supply and demand, pricing, profits, risks, incentives, and competition.

A = After prior knowledge of economic terms is established, these students connect the principles to the context of past or present world examples, e.g., entrepreneurs in Fortune 500 companies, stock market decisions, trade embargos.

M = Students pair up with a partner to research and create an economical timeline for a country of choice, noting the changes over time, e.g., former Soviet Union/Russia, Cuba, Germany, Japan, Israel, Argentina, Vietnam, Iraq, the United States.

E = Students research and compare the living conditions in countries that have government-controlled economies versus those that have free enterprise.

Topic: Nutrition and Exercise

G = Students gather information about good nutrition and exercise choices from magazines, journals, texts, organizations, and online sources, e.g., healthy food choices, balanced diets, fat calories, appropriate daily physical exercises.

A = Students analyze food labels of similar products, e.g., different types of nacho chips, and decide which is a better nutritional or caloric choice.

M = Students figure out a sound way to lose or gain weight, based on portion control and calorie consumption. They also figure out the type of daily or recommended exercise required to either maintain weight, gain muscle mass, or appropriately lose weight.

E = Students evaluate their own nutritional and exercise choices, examining how these choices affect their moods and decisions in school, at home, and in their personal relationships. They evaluate whether their health decisions match up with their recommended BMI (Body Mass Index) and examine their overall well-being.

Topic: Writing a Thesis

G = Students learn components involved in formulating a thesis statement, e.g., intensive readings, examination and compilation of specific topics, evidence, and arguments.

A = Students analyze ways to formulate, refine, revise, and support or negate a thesis statement and decide whether their thesis is justified by their written discussion.

M = Students take their same topic and rewrite their thesis so that it expresses two different arguments or viewpoints, e.g., "Although having a disability is viewed by some as stifling, it can have a positive effect on creativity and personal growth," vs. "Despite the gains made by people with disabilities, society sometimes thwarts human creativity and stifles the personal development of individuals with disabilities."

E = Students partner with a peer and review each other's final thesis by conducting their own research and critically examining their research and conclusions, e.g., Does the thesis outline and refute counterarguments?

Developing Instructional Ideas

It takes time for some ideas to develop!

Photographers will tell you that they need that darkroom and the  right combination of chemicals for pictures to develop. In the classroom, the right combination of interventions develops students' minds. Educators can guide students on a path of learning with well thought-out *enlightening* lessons.

Effective educational instructional strategies are definitely still in their infancy. Many photographers today no longer use that darkroom, and instead use digital cameras. They can crop, enhance, play with the angles, and more, right on their computers. The world is booming with *developing* knowledge. Expectations are raised. Instructional practices implemented in today's inclusive classrooms for students with disabilities are quite different from those practiced in segregated schools and classrooms decades ago. Attitudes toward teaching students with disabilities to maximize their assets are developing in a positive way, too! Just because sensory, perceptual, physical, learning, or cognitive issues exist, does not mean that students with these needs cannot be included in educational and community landscapes.

Standards are now within everyone's grasp, including students with disabilities who are no longer out of accountability since their annual yearly progress is monitored as well, and their achievement of higher expectations is very much in the picture! The picture is enhanced every day as the *classroom photographers* ensure that students' ideas continue to develop under their educational auspices. Future instructional strategies with the right game plans will help us to continue to zoom in, to develop every student's maximum potential to live a productive, independent life!

5

Content-Related Strategies and Lessons

Chapter Highlights: This fifth chapter highlights curriculum concerns and proactive ways to improve understandings in the content areas of reading, writing, mathematics, science, and social studies.

Classroom Connections: Curriculum is matched with varied assignments that honor the strengths and intelligences of diverse students, encouraging students to develop more self-awareness about the ways they learn best.

Ways to Differentiate Attitudes: Even though teachers wish that students master the curriculum, without the correct mindsets and willingness to differentiate the presentation, students are set up for failures. This chapter emphasizes that yes, the curriculum is important, but educators' and students' attitudes certainly prevail and quite often influence and impact successes.

THEIR STRATEGIES, NOT OURS!

Sometimes, less is better! It's certainly true that many students need to have strategies modeled and instructed on the best ways to learn. However, if students are always given the step-by-step strategies and do not have the opportunity to independently apply the strategies or concepts, then they will never develop their own ways of figuring things out. Educators need to

- Guide, model, and concretize new concepts
- Observe students' independent applications
- Scaffold only if needed
- Encourage students to be self-confident and to reflect upon their output

- Support again as needed with appropriate accommodations and modifications
- Praise and offer constructive corrections
- Repeat the process and experiences to ensure retention and solidify learning

"PUT ME IN, COACH"

Sometimes, students with disabilities are anxious to *play a position on the field* known as the classroom that they may not be quite ready for. Here's where educators need to maximize students' abilities without setting them up for failures. The following questions come to mind. Your answer choices will vary and must be ones that you, your colleagues, and your students are comfortable with.

- Do you give a student with a lower cognitive level an assignment that is identical to the one that you gave the other students if you know ahead of time that it is way over his or her head?
- If a student hands in an assignment that is incorrectly completed, do you hand it back to him or her to be redone, or do you grade it accordingly to teach that student a lesson?
- If a student is behaving inappropriately during cooperative station work, do you remove that student from his or her group?
- Do you call on a student with special needs, if the child has not raised his or her hand?
- Do you correct a student who has given an incorrect response in front of the rest of the class, or privately?
- Do you take into account a student's effort and progress, or are your grades based solely on test-grade achievements?
- Do you ever give a student with special needs a parallel assignment?
- Do you have peers working together as teams to help each other?
- Do you let students *run the bases* by themselves?
- How often do you and your students *review the game plan?*

IT'S ALL IN THE PRESENTATION

Some fast food restaurants serve hamburgers wrapped in wax paper, and other more exclusive restaurants serve *chopped sirloin* on lovely decorated glass plates with some carefully positioned sides. The food names, consistency of the meat, prices, and ambiance of the restaurants are a bit different. The question here remains, which meal and taste is preferred by patrons? Analogously speaking, teachers may deliver somewhat similar content, but the process and instructional strategies often determine just how palatable the learning is to the students and consequently how well the students will *digest the concepts*. Some *nutritious* presentations and *FDA approved* recommendations are indicated in Table 5.1.

SPECIFIC CURRICULUM CONNECTIONS

The following lessons are divided into the subject areas of reading, writing, math, social studies, and science, with grade-level divisions for K–12 students. The

Table 5.1   FDA Approved Presentations

FDA Approved Presentations: *Favorable Delivery Approaches* From the Restaurant to the Classroom		
Restaurant	*Classroom*	*Implications & Results*
Give the patrons menus.	Determine the students' interests with inventories.	Offers empowerment with personal choices, increases motivation and concentration, helps students to *enjoy the meal!*
Allow patrons time to select an entrée.	Introduce lessons with appropriate instructional paces for students to practice and apply skills and concepts.	Varied ongoing activities set up in the classroom take into account individual levels and allow students to both accelerate and remediate their learning through stations, centers, individual research, art activities, and more individualization.
Offer an assortment of appetizers that appeal to different tastes.	Realize what precedes the lesson by determining students' prior knowledge, e.g., K/W/L charts.	Teachers can ascertain if students have solid or shaky knowledge of the vocabulary, concepts, and other references and then preteach accordingly.
Background music helps patrons enjoy their meal; some even stay longer and order more. Adding pretty décor to the restaurant helps too!	A soothing and pleasant classroom setting maximizes students' visual, auditory, and kinesthetic-tactile strengths.	Students learn best through their preferred modalities and intelligences, e.g., content-related lyrics to songs, active brain breaks, appropriate visuals to concretize abstract words and concepts, communication boards, talking Web sites.
Restaurant staff who respectfully treat their patrons courteously get higher monetary gratuities.	Develop collaborative and productive relationships between educators, families, students, administrators, and all support staff	When everyone is planning and sharing the *educational meal,* the academic and social progress is fruitful and valuable for all!
Restaurants that offer coupons to return through frequent dining programs are cost-effective ones that have repeat business.	Give consistent praise and recognition for students' strides and accomplishments with repetition and revisitation as necessary.	Increased student self-confidence with more productivity—it's a win–win for all!

lessons value multiple intelligences; cooperative learning, the merits of art, music, and dance; along with individual students' strengths and interests. The lessons actively allow students to learn by doing, manipulating the concepts, and formulating their own conclusions under teachers' directions. When possible the lessons are interdisciplinary, since connections to other subjects are a natural way to solidify the learning and link it to prior knowledge. For example, students need to know that writing exists beyond specific writing assignments; reading applies to every subject; and mathematics is an integral part of students' everyday lives, living outside the textbook, too! Yes, the lessons have objectives, but their main objective is to involve students in their own learning experiences to create lifelong learners who are active participants, not passive recipients of the knowledge.

The national standards are integrated in the lessons. Sources consulted include

NCTM—National Council for Teachers of Mathematics: http://nctm .org/standards/

The Kennedy Center ArtsEdge: http://artsedge.kennedy-center.org/teach/ standards.cfm

National Standards for Music Education: http://www.menc.org

NCSS–National Council for the Social Studies: http://www.socialstudies .org/standards/

NSTA—National Science Education Standards: http://www.nsta.org/ standards

NCTE—National Council of Teachers of English: http://www.ncte.org/ about/over/standards

Also, note that when worksheets are included, they are clutter-free and open-ended when possible. Their dual purpose is to act as study guides and a summation of the knowledge. Their main function is to encourage educators to figure out ways to teach the students the concepts beyond the readings, with higher-level thinking skills that jump off the page. *Teaching subjects* is an easier task than *teaching subjects to students*. Everyday dilemmas and curriculum concerns are presented in the lessons that follow, and some solutions are suggested as well. Most important, prepared teachers need to

1. Know their subject matter
2. Know their students' interests and levels
3. Know how to maximize and value students' strengths
4. Frequently assess progress
5. Enjoy what they do!

READING CURRICULUM CONCERNS THAT EDUCATORS NEED TO WATCH OUT FOR

- Poor fluency with inappropriate phrasing; slower or faster reading paces
- Students who are unable to apply phonetic patterns to decode written words exhibiting inaccuracies that lead to lower understandings; e.g., reading a word such as *interdependence* as *independence*
- Students who read by sight and are unable to recognize unfamiliar words out of context
- Frequent misunderstandings of written passages in nonfiction texts (e.g., science and social studies), literature stories, and written directions
- Difficulties in answering oral and written questions

Possible effects of reading difficulties on students:

- Displays of *feigning behavior*, which tries to conceal difficulties from teachers and peers, to fly under the *reading radar*
- Behavior/social difficulties due to reading frustrations
- School apathy, e.g., uncompleted reading assignments, frequent absences, and possibly dropping out of school when older (http://www.athealth .com/consumer/disorders/Reading.html)

Table 5.2 Appropriate Reading and Language Arts Accommodations

Appropriate Reading and Language Arts Accommodations, Adaptations, and Strategies for Lessons				
Concretize abstract concepts by preteaching vocabulary to improve prior knowledge, provide students with outlines of the lesson, e.g., help those students with hearing issues to follow along.	Use active classroom learning experiences with more visual, auditory, and kinesthetic-tactile activities to replace lectures, e.g., guided cooperative activities, stations and centers, *brainbreaks*, graphic organizers, books on tape with headphones.	Use peer tutoring and cooperative learning activities with instructions, guidance, and explanation of roles for peers.	Use direct skill instruction in phonics, fluency, reading comprehension, vocabulary development, word choices, and revision process.	Regularly check and monitor students' understandings, e.g., privately ask student to paraphrase a concept or schedule weekly conferences with the whole class to review or expand readings and writings.
Physically rotate about the classroom to provide individualized instruction, guidance, and organization, e.g., check to see if students are following oral directions.	Grade on content, not just the appearance of the writing. To be sensitive to those students with dysgraphia and other fine motor issues, you can also ask students to dictate thoughts.	Increase praise, communication, and collaboration with the student and home; communicate at eye level to a student in a wheelchair.	Use uncluttered, larger font, student-friendly worksheets with extra visuals that explain written words and new vocabulary.	Use repeated practice of reading and language instruction in small doses in class and at home, e.g., daily oral language, writer's journal, DEAR (drop everything and read) time, combined with guided instruction and teacher modeling.

Increase use of technology, e.g., interactive white boards for note taking. Use Web-based skills practice, e.g., www.funbrain.com, word prediction, speech-recognition programs, electronic dictionaries, http://www.franklin.com.	Provide opportunities for guided and independent practice and application of language skills and new vocabulary introduced; provide students who speak another language background information about the readings in their primary language.	Allow students to track their progress, e.g., number of correct words read, grades on reading tests, genres read and written.	Connect readings and writings with other disciplines and students' interests and strengths, e.g., music, art, math.	Gradually introduce and vary types of comprehension questions to include higher-level critical thinking skills, e.g., inferences, cause–effect.
Incorporate games and other *fun* activities with letters and words, e.g., puzzles, word searches, www.puzzlemaker.com, Scrabble, Boggle, Pictionary.	Use visuals and videos that explain concepts, www.unitedstreaming.com, www.brainpop.com, Usborne books, content-related pictures.	Use preferential seating to minimize distractions, avoid behavioral concerns, and maximize attention for those with learning, visual or hearing needs.	Decrease fine motor requirements for some students, e.g., provide a scribe, copy of another student's notes, or access to lessons on a teacher Web site.	Allow students to use writing templates, or refer to a list of frequently misspelled words or transitional words.

The purpose of the following reading section with vignettes and lessons is to circumvent the apathy, frustrations, and difficulties and replace them with more teacher awareness, preparation, and instructional ideas to increase students' reading skills across the content areas and outside the classroom, too.

Curriculum Connection: Columbus Did Not Fly Planes!

While reading a passage in the social studies textbook about explorers, one student said, "Columbus took his planes to Queen Isabella." Now, as far as I know, Columbus and all of his contemporaries were well grounded. The correct sentence was, "Columbus took his *plans* to Queen Isabella." The point here is what a difference a letter makes!

Reading comprehension is affected by poor decoding. Quite often, weak word analysis and shaky phonetic skills interfere with students' understandings.

Students with stronger oral comprehension skills, whose brains are not wired to automatically read, often miss out on content lessons if they are required to gain and demonstrate their knowledge exclusively through heavy text readings. As Sousa (2007), points out, reading is not a natural ability. Neuroimaging has established differences in the way students with dyslexia respond to both spoken and written tasks. Reading requires the coordination of three neural networks of visual processing (orthography), phoneme recognition (phonology), and word interpretation (semantics). Not everyone's brain is wired the same way, yet appropriate reading interventions that build phonemic awareness for literary successes assist learners who struggle to read. The *Columbus scenario* is a common one! Direct skill instruction will circumvent phonetic reading disorders from negatively impacting upon students' comprehension skills. Students need to be aware of how to decode unfamiliar words, by breaking words into syllables across the content areas. Appropriate interventions include increasing students' metacognition of written words and the significance each letter holds. This part-whole word concept needs to be consistently reinforced. Teachers can use the following passage and reproducible to emphasize the difference one letter can make upon students' comprehension skills and the benefits of breaking words up into their syllables.

Did Co-lum-bus Have Planes or Plans?

Nav-i-ga-tion and ex-plor-a-tion yield-ed the dis-cov-er-y of new ter-ri-to-ry! Co-lum-bus was nev-er at an air-port! The Ni-na, Pin-ta, and San-ta Mar-i-a sailed a-cross the At-lan-tic O-cean with the fi-nan-ces from the Queen of Spain. Oth-er-wise he nev-er would have set sail! She liked his plans!

Reproducible 5.1

How to Spell, Not Spill!

If a letter makes a difference, how do you get a student to improve encoding (spelling) skills? Many students do not pay attention to details, or even notice the difference between similar-looking words. This exercise asks students to note what letter exists in the first word, but not the second. The point is to concentrate on details, in this case individual letters. This *skill* will then *spill* over to the spelling!

Table 5.3

First Word	Second Word	Missing Letter
Example:		
world	word	l
house	hose	
sight	sigh	
watch	thaw	
praise	spare	
speak	sake	
flies	self	
point	pint	
three	tree	
fray	fry	
flimsy	filmy	
closet	close	
slender	sender	
loose	lose	
string	sting	
least	last	
scare	scar	
pleading	leading	
friend	fired	
spied	dips	
dealt	lead	

An Informal Reading Assessment

(Refer to Appendix C for the Word Recognition and Comprehension Reading Survey.)

If teachers are to help students, one of the best ways is to properly assess and dissect their reading errors. Teachers need to ask

- Is the error related to a grapheme (written representation of a sound) or meaning?
- Is the student a sight word reader, or does he or she sound out words by syllables?
- Is there an error pattern? (e.g., consistently mispronounces digraphs or medial vowel pairs)
- Does the student's rate of reading interfere with his or her comprehension? (e.g., reading too rapidly or too slowly)
- Will the student substitute words in context that are close to the real word's meaning? (showing that he or she is comprehending, despite mispronunciations)
- Are the student's errors significant ones that interfere with understandings? (e.g., car for cat vs. bug for insect)
- Are the comprehension errors sequencing ones, related to facts or the main idea, or do they involve higher-level thinking, such as making inferences or drawing conclusions?
- Does the student omit words or sentence lines while reading?
- Does the student self-correct often?
- Are there outside-the-classroom factors that interfere with the student's reading? (e.g., emotional issues)
- Does the student's interest, attention, or correct responses wane at certain times of the day?
- What motivation does the student have?

Table 5.4

Type of Error	Possible Codes
Insertions	+
Mispronounces	−
Omissions	O
Substitutions	S
Finger Pointing	FP
Reversals	R
Intonation/Fluency	I/F
Self-Corrects	SC
Duplications	D
Nonpronunciations	N
Hesitations	H

Sentence Pair 1

What student read: *I like red bricks about my horses.*

Correct sentence: *I like to read books about houses.*

What could be going on:

Student is inserting and omitting words (my, to) and has difficulties with medial sounds and consonant blends (bricks for books and horses for houses). This student also has trouble with vowel pairs (red for read). This student is not reading for meaning since the errors are significant ones that interfere with his or her comprehension. Maybe this student likes horses and that's what he or she was thinking about as words were read.

Sentence Pair 2

What student read: *I accept that odd property is behind where she knew it saw.*

Correct sentence: *I expect that old prophecy is beyond what he knew it was.*

What could be going on:

Student may be reading too quickly and guessing at words. Student is substituting similar-looking words that have completely different meanings. Prepositions, verbs, adjectives, and pronouns are interchanged. Visual perceptual issues may be present (reversal—saw as was), along with other reading errors.

What Teachers, Children, and Families Can Do

- Talk about your favorite characters and events from books, television shows, and movies that you have seen or read together.
- Play rhyming and word games, e.g., songs, Scrabble, Boggle.
- Write and read letters, words, and stories together in magazines and newspapers, or compose letters or postcards to relatives and friends.
- Retell familiar stories from books read, or from movies and television shows seen.
- Make reading an enjoyable event and a time to bond.
- Translate thoughts to words on paper while relating to students' interests, e.g., writing a story about video games or skateboarding.
- Have students match pictures with words, sentences, paragraphs, and stories.
- Act out characters in stories from nursery rhymes to literature books.
- Play charades with vocabulary words, pantomiming nouns, verbs, adjectives, and adverbs.
- Make children aware of the types of errors they display, but praise accomplishments and strides, too.
- Allow students to use line markers to keep their place if they tend to skip lines when reading.
- Encourage students to pay more attention to details using drawing and perceptual activities such as matching, tracing, completion, copying, sketching.
- Publish student-created phonetic picture dictionaries of initial and final sounds in words from pictures found in computer clip art or magazines, or drawn free hand.
- Be aware that reading trepidations can be displayed as apathy. Reach the student by offering much praise and encouragement for progress as well as achievements.
- As an adult, model good reading habits, too!

Programs to investigate for direct daily training with word decoding, syllabication, structural analysis, reading comprehension, and study skills:

Achieve 3000: http://www.achieve3000.com/home.php
Wilson Language Program: http://www.wilsonlanguage.com
Books on Tape: http://www.simplyaudiobooks.com, http://www.rfbd.org, http://booksontape.com
Scholastic Read 180 Intervention Program: http://teacher.scholastic.com/products/read180
Skills Tutor: http://www.achievementtech.com
Reading Recovery: http://www.readingrecovery.org
Academic Skills: http://www.studyisland.com
Scientific Learning Fast for Word: http://www.scilearn.com

Curriculum Connection: How to Prevent Being Lost in the Woods

The Sign of the Beaver, by Elizabeth George Speare, is a historical fiction book that takes place in colonial America in the eighteenth-century territory now known as the state of Maine. It's written for students aged 9–12, but the example from this book can be scaled up or down for students in older and younger grades. The *woods analogy* is about connecting students to their reading by having the compasses point to themselves!

One passage in *Sign of the Beaver* refers to how the Native Americans marked their woods with the signs of their clan; in this case, it was a beaver. That way it was known which people were allowed to hunt, fish, gather berries, tap maple syrup, and more in certain territories. It was their *turf,* so to speak. The Native Americans believed that no one really owned the land, that it was their collective hunting grounds. It was their *address.*

Now, to connect students with the learning, I asked one boy, "Where do you live?" He promptly and rotely rattled off his street address. "Aha," I said, "that's your sign, where you live. You don't carve it on trees, but that's how people know that your house belongs to your family, and where your mail is sent." His eyes then opened wide as he made the connection, and without any words necessary, he understood the analogy.

This particular book, written in a time period totally unfamiliar to students, can hold more meaning if they compare and contrast it with their own frame of reference. Comprehensions become clearer, lessons enlivened, and retentions solidified.

Whenever possible, make connections to students' lives; this prevents them from literally and figuratively becoming *lost in the woods!*

How to Book It!

When teaching reading, teachers need to be aware of selecting books with

- Varying genres, e.g., poetry, narrative, biography, science fiction, nonfiction, mystery, fantasy, realistic fiction, historical fiction, expository

- Illustrations that correspond to written thoughts and concepts
- Vocabulary and language appropriate to instructional levels
- Width of white space between lines on the page
- Number and size of printed words and lines on each page
- Amount of multisyllabic words
- Book's organization, e.g., chapters, headings, highlights, index, table of contents
- Portrayal of people with disabilities as, neither superheroes nor as weaker individuals, unable to accomplish tasks
- Pluralistic and global themes
- Authors and illustrators from a variety of cultures
- Content-related literature, e.g., historical fiction, *The Egypt Game*, *Sign of the Beaver*, *Out of the Dust*, *The Fighting Ground*, *Night*

The following books and worksheets give specific reading connections with appropriate K–12 literature and reading content relevant to social, academic, and functional skills and levels.

READING LESSONS FOR GRADES K–12

Alexander Goes to School (Grades K–3)

Books can be used to connect to subject areas across the curriculum. Reading is more than words on a page; it's about multiple concepts presented and the thoughts they inspire in students. The tricky part is inspiring each student to personalize the reading.

This following cooperative lesson connects to several different subjects, including math concepts, map skills, animals, transportation, and sounds. Use your discretion as to how many assignments students should complete. These activities can also be set up as stations around the room, with numbers and directions placed on index cards that students collect as they go. The cooperative element encourages more interpersonal skills. If students need more direction, the teacher can walk them through each station as the class collectively completes the assignments.

Inclusion Tip: Placing directions around the room on index cards allows kinesthetic learners a chance to move about while learning.

For these activities, you will need the following materials:

- Multiple copies of *Alexander and the Terrible, Horrible, No Good, Very Bad Day*, by Judith Viorst
- Index cards

- World map
- Crayons or markers
- Drawing paper
- Dictionaries
- Thesauruses

To complete the activity, do the following steps:

1. Ahead of time, set up eight different "stations" around the room. Make copies of the *Alexander Goes to School* reproducible, cut apart the eight assignments and glue them to index cards. Put a stack of index cards for

assignment #1 at the first station, a stack for assignment #2 at the second station, and so on, for all eight stations. Make sure you have an index card for each pair of students in your class.

2. Pair up students with partners. Then read aloud to students the book, *Alexander and the Terrible, Horrible, No Good, Very Bad Day.*

3. When you're finished reading, send out student pairs to each station. Each pair must collect an index card with one of the numbered station directions on it. They then cooperatively answer each of the numbered assignments before moving on to the next station.

Alexander Goes to School Questions

Teacher directions: Cut apart the station assignments and glue them to index cards. Make sure you have an index card for each student pair.

Table 5.5   Alexander Goes to School Questions

1. The story has foods such as cereal and gum. List three more foods from the book.	2. Alexander wants to go to a place called Aus-tral-ia. Aus-tral-ia is a large land form called a con-ti-nent. Find three more con-ti-nents on a world map and list them.
3. Alexander talks about the number 16. Write five ad-di-tion prob-lems with a sum of 16 (12+4). Then try to write five sub-trac-tion problems with a dif-fer-ence of 16 (18–2).	4. Alexander's teacher said he sang too loudly. Think of and list at least five more loud sounds you hear in the world around you.
5. A sailboat and a car called a Cor-vette Sting-ray are in the book. List at least five other types of trans-por-ta-tion that are used to travel in the water, on land, or in the sky.	6. Alexander talks about Mickey Mouse. Think of your favorite animals and give them first names that have the same letter. For example: *Betty Bird* or *Cool Cat.*
7. *Terrible, horrible, no good,* and *very bad* are all words that mean the same thing. These kinds of words are called syn-o-nyms. Words that have opposite meanings are called an-to-nyms. Use a dic-tion-ar-y, the-sau-rus, or com-put-er to find five words that are antonyms of *terrible, horrible, no good,* and *very bad.*	8. Draw two pictures from the book that show your favorite scenes. Make sure your pictures have cap-tions (a sentence under the picture) that de-scribe the scenes.

Amazing Grace and Me (Grades 2–4)

The three R's (reading, writing, and arithmetic) are important; however, students should also experience character education as part of the curriculum. Topics such as cultural acceptance and prejudice should first be introduced at formative ages, in a way that does not preach, but informs and even entertains!

This next lesson centers around a favorite children's book, *Amazing Grace*, by Mary Hoffman and Caroline Binch. It tells the story of a very imaginative little girl who loves to act out the parts of different characters, such as Hiawatha, Mowgli, and Aladdin. While trying out for a class production of Peter Pan, she learns she can be anything she wants to be.

This interdisciplinary activity capitalizes on students' interests while teaching about historical figures, map skills, and research skills. It also hones reading and listening skills while inspiring more caring, culturally savvy citizens. Overall, that's a win–win situation for all and correlates with numerous global standards!

Reproduce and distribute the *Real or Make-Believe?* reproducible to students. Tell students to check off each name they hear as you read aloud the book, *Amazing Grace*. Then invite student groups to use an atlas, encyclopedia, computer, or other resource to research when and where these real and make-believe people lived and what they did. Have students explain why they would or would not like to be each person.

Inclusion Tip: Teachers need to circulate and monitor cooperative groups to ensure that everyone understands the directions and assignments and is on task.

Reproducible 5.2

Name _____ Date _____

Real or Make-Believe?

Check off each name as you hear it in the story. Then research each person and fill in the appropriate columns on the chart.

Table 5.6

People ✓	Real	Make-Believe	Where? or When?	Would you want to be this person?
Joan of Arc				
Anansi the Spider				
Lady from Troy				
Hiawatha				
Mowgli				
Aladdin				
Mary Hoffman or Carolyn Binch				
Doctor Grace				
Peter Pan				
Captain Hook				
Wendy				

Answer the following questions:

1. Do you like being yourself?

2. Have you ever pretended to be someone else?

3. Do you think anyone in this world is better than anyone else?

4. What does this book's message tell us about using our minds?

CONTENT-RELATED STRATEGIES AND LESSONS

CONTENT-RELATED STRATEGIES AND LESSONS   **167**

Reproducible 5.3

Grades 4–6 Vocabulary Development: Examining Words

Student directions: Words are incredible since they can have dual meanings, synonyms, antonyms, and more. Words can even share the same base or root word, prefixes, and suffixes. Review the following chart, define the words, name the type of relationship (using the a–e code given), fill in the analogies, and then write some sentences telling what you have learned about these words.

Table 5.7   Word Definitions

Tell the Words/Definitions & Relationships: a. <u>Synonyms</u>—same meaning b. <u>Antonyms</u>—opposite meanings c. <u>Homonyms</u>—words that are spelled and sound the same but have different meanings d. <u>Homophones</u>—words that sound alike but have different spellings and meanings e. Shared base word, prefix, or suffix	What I Have Learned About Words Challenge: Can I complete these analogies?
cents—sense	1. Cents is to sense as pleas is to _____.
wait—weight	
shy—demure	2. Compassionate is to benevolent as similar is to _____.
unicycle, bicycle, tricycle	
draft—draft	3. Approximate is to exact as minute is to _____.
circumvent, circumnavigate, circumference	
pleas, please	4. Unicorn is to unicycle as triangle is to _____.
colossal—minute	
approximate—estimate	5. Impudent is to polite as outgoing is to _____.
impudent—polite	
graphite—graphic	6. Geometry is to geographers as photosynthesis is to ___ _____.
compassionate—benevolent	
photosynthesis—photography	
diverse—similar	7. Thyme is to time as affect is to _____.
similar—comparable	
affect—effect	Name _____

Copyright © 2008 by Corwin Press. All rights reserved. Reprinted from *Embracing Disabilities in the Classroom: Strategies to Maximize Students' Assets*, by Toby J. Karten. Thousand Oaks, CA: Corwin Press, www.corwinpress.com. Reproduction authorized only for the local school site or nonprofit organization that has purchased this book.

Lessons From *Old Yeller* (Grades 6–8)

Each year, I choose to *reinvent the wheel*. What I mean by that statement is that I don't always teach the same way, using identical materials, manipulatives, or literature lessons. Yes, I do follow the curriculum standards and IEPs, and I have high expectations for my students, but each year I work with another group of students. That means that the students I meet possess different academic, cognitive, behavioral, social, perceptual, and physical needs and interests. Since the students are not clones or replicas of the prior year's students, why would I use identical materials year after year? This particular year, we had fun with the novel, *Old Yeller.*

Now, those of you who know the novel are well aware that it's not a happy, fun story, but my students and I had a blast for the two months when we read, reviewed, and thoroughly explored this book. First, I compiled a packet of materials that included activities in encoding, decoding, and comprehension skills for the novel. Immediately after we read each chapter, we wrote summaries that outlined the major points. We continually identified parts of speech, syllable types, new vocabulary, and prefixes and suffixes to increase proficiencies with language skills, context clues, and structural analysis. We illustrated scenes and graded the book at various intervals. We researched eastern Texas and learned about cattle drives. We even cried together when we realized the heifer's and Old Yeller's fate due to the hydrophobia (which we needed to look up in a dictionary).

Why choose *Old Yeller* as our novel when it was a total tearjerker? Well, the students loved anything that was about dogs. Many of them had dogs as pets and given three books to choose from, they collectively decided on *Old Yeller.* After we completed reading the book and summarized each chapter, we then decided to write our own abridged version. We jigsawed the book into thirds, dividing *Old Yeller's* chapters into the beginning, middle, and end. We also divided the class into three groups, with each group collectively responsible for writing their third. Each group proofread their section and then exchanged their part with another group who did a peer review, checking for organization, content, accuracy of facts, spelling, punctuation, and word choices. As a final edit, the class worked together to proofread all three parts, with the teachers as the supreme editors. When we were satisfied with the final product, the abridged retelling of *Old Yeller* was duplicated for the class and then bound together as a book. Two weeks were allotted for the writing and editing, but due to enthusiasm and thoroughness, we needed three weeks instead!

So, were we done? Of course we were not. It was the end of the school year with hot weather steaming up in an unairconditioned building with students who were definitely in a *June, it's almost summer, no school soon* mood! We then decided to turn the story into a script and act out the play. We auditioned for parts and turned our abridged version into a narrative script. We had a narrator who called out the scenes; together we made props, pantomimed the action, and had a technology crew who videotaped the whole skit for an I-movie. Actually, the technology crew first had to learn how to take different camera angles, use the zoom, and even add the sound effects. It was an awesome experience for all, and one of my favorite teaching units! I even designed a rubric using http://rubistar.4teachers.org/, which the students used after they viewed their video to rate themselves in the categories of collaboration with peers, voice volume, enthusiasm, listening to others, effective pauses, speaking clearly, posture and eye contact, preparedness, videography, and knowledge of the content.

Through *Old Yeller,* we accomplished the following objectives:

- Improved reading comprehension to understand the plot, sequence of events, and cause–effect relationships
- Honed language skills while writing and revising the summaries and scripts
- Learned keyboarding skills on the computer, editing skills, and how to use language tools, e.g., thesaurus, spell check
- Gained socialization skills by cooperatively reading, writing, revising, acting out the story, making performance decisions, and cohesively organizing all
- Increased presentation skills for an audience, e.g., eye contact, rate of speech, staging, body language
- Gained proficiencies with technology tools, e.g., digital camera, zoom, pause, to record the play
- Improved self-awareness by reviewing taped performance, given a set rubric, e.g., content, loudness, videography

All in all, I think *Old Yeller* will hold a special place in our hearts always!

The purpose of the following table on *Canterbury Tales* is to help students neatly organize the information presented. Quite often, the written presentation directly influences the understandings. The middle school–high school lesson on *Beowulf* explores cause–effect relationships to ascertain deeper understandings, rather than using a direct line of questioning. The last reading lesson on *Night* also offers additional ways to explore comprehension with connections to other curriculum disciplines, research skills, and multiple intelligences. The purpose of these next three lessons is to extend the knowledge beyond the book's pages and connect concepts to students.

Reproducible 5.4

High School Lesson: *Canterbury Tales* **by Chaucer**

Table 5.8

Student Directions: Write some details from each pilgrim's story. Review and print out the Middle English Glossary to help you understand some terms in your readings (http://www.librarius.com/gy.htm). As an option, listen to the book on audio or watch the DVD to gain further understandings to help you complete this frame. An example of details from a tale is shown for the knight. On the reverse side of this paper, try to invent and describe your own pilgrim, giving his or her story/tale. Your pilgrim can live in the past, present, or future; be creative!

Knight	Action packed with battles; speaks of chivalry with two knights; Arcite and Palamon dueling over Emily's affections. Love is valued!
Squire	
Canon's Yeoman	
Prioress	
Second Nun	
Monk	
Friar	
Merchant	
Clerk	
Man of Law	
Franklin	
Cook	
Shipman	
Physician	
Parson	
Miller	
Manciple	
Reeve	
Summoner	
Pardoner	
Wife of Bath	
Chaucer	

Reproducible 5.5

Middle School–High School Lesson: If...Then...for *Beowulf*

Directions: Look at the examples given for numbers 1–3 and then fill in your own.

1. If Grendel had not devoured Hrothgar's sleeping warriors, then this story would not have told of Beowulf's deeds, or _____.

2. If Beowulf had lacked perseverance, then Grendel might still be alive, or _____.

3. If the setting had been the frozen tundra, then Beowulf would not be able to travel on the sea, or _____.

4. If Beowulf had not severed Grendel's right arm, then _____.

5. If Grendel's mother had not killed Aeschere, then _____.

6. If Hrothgar had not believed in Beowulf, then _____.

7. If Unferth had been a nicer person, then _____.

8. If Beowulf had not become the King of the Geats, then _____.

9. If Queen Wealhtheow had not allowed Beowulf to leave, then _____.

10. If Wiglaf had not been by Beowulf's side, then_____.

11. If this epic poem had never been part of Anglo-Saxon literature, then _____ _____.

12. If I were Beowulf, then _____.

Source: http://www.awerty.com/beowulf2.html

Some students with differing reading levels could read this easier version: *Beowulf: A New Telling,* by Robert Nye (5.5 Reading level)

Reproducible 5.6

High School Lesson for *Night,* by Elie Wiesel

Directions: Complete number 1 and then choose three more assignments from numbers 2–10.

1. Identify the victims, perpetrators, and rescuers in *Night.*

Table 5.9

Victims	Perpetrators	Rescuers

2. Tell about the politics of these countries during *Night's* setting (early 1940s); identifying the leaders and their philosophies:

Table 5.10

a. Romania
b. Germany
c. United States
d. Japan
e. England
f. Italy
g. France
h. Russia

3. Make an illustrated timeline of the events portrayed in *Night.*

4. Write a poem you would like to share with Elie's family.

5. If you lived at this time, explain which country you would choose to live in. (3 paragraphs)

6. Compare the events that occurred in 1944 with happenings in other countries since then. Do you think history repeats itself? (Venn diagram or essay is acceptable)

7. Write a speech that supports religious freedom.

8. Create a map of Europe in 1944.

9. Compose a song or dance that expresses your thoughts about this book.

10. Compare and contrast Elie's personality traits to someone that you know, telling how they are similar and different people. (Venn diagram or essay is acceptable)

WRITING CURRICULUM CONCERNS: WRITE ON!

Writing is a form of communication that allows students to send instant messages on the computer, transmit text messages to their friends, answer essays and open-ended questions, release inner thoughts, express their knowledge, and more! Good writing includes proper organization with transitional words, along with correct spelling, punctuation, grammar, voice, and sentence fluency while holding the audience's interest. Writing is a way to introspect, entertain, persuade, and inform! As teachers, we can help students view this written expression as a pleasurable rather than a tedious task by offering *student friendly* strategies. Pencils, paper, and proper mindsets are only some of the writing tools needed. Writing is definitely more than students counting the words on a page, which has a period at the end!

Students with fine motor issues or varying cognitive and emotional levels can all reap writing rewards. Language, physical, decoding, and encoding issues are circumvented with available software and technology that helps students to better communicate and refine their ideas. Writing strategies that offer remediation on students' instructional levels will encourage students in the process of communicating their ideas on paper. As with reading, self-reflection is a crucial ingredient. (See page 269 in Appendix C for a writing self-reflection/documentation form.)

It's up to us as educators to encourage students to write. This encouragement needs to begin from an early age, and then be refined in the middle and upper grades. The following K–12 lessons offer suggestions on how to draw the student into this writing process, without the student viewing writing as a task *fit for a criminal serving time!* Writing is fun, but somehow that's a well-kept secret that students need to be privy to as well! The following K–12 writing lessons offer ways for students to express themselves, paraphrase what they read, think about technology, and then revise elements of stories read.

The K–4 alphabetical list can be referred to throughout the year, when students are asked to write on a personal-choice topic. More advanced students can list words that tell final consonants, or even two or three letters at a time for consonant blends or trigraphs, e.g., *c* and *r* for crayon or *s, t,* and *r* for street. Students can draw their own pictures, find computer clip art, or write words representing each letter. Some students may need to scribe their thoughts to a peer or an adult for the written words or sentences. Other students can be given a pile of pictures, which they can then place by correct beginning letters. The lesson for Grades 3–5 concentrates on writing, but crosses over into all content areas. Students need to learn how to paraphrase and understand written instructions in reading, mathematics, science, social studies, art, music, health, physical education, world languages, and life, too! In Grades 6–8, the lesson asks students to become cognizant of topic sentences, supporting details, organization, capitalization, and punctuation by dissecting their written pieces. It offers a word box with *technology words* to jump-start some students in the process. The lesson for Grades 9–12 connects reading with the writing by having students evaluate literature from a variety of genres and cultures and then write their own version by changing one of the elements in a structured five-paragraph essay. All of these lessons value thinking skills and using writing as a form of communication and expression. Students need to be taught the *right* way to *write, right* away as a school *rite!*

Reproducible 5.7

Grades K–4: Lesson for Expressive Writings

Student directions: Write a word or draw a picture by each letter of something that you like that begins with that sound. Write sentences that tell more about some of the words you have chosen.

Table 5.11

a	b	c	d	e
f	g	h	i	j
k	l	m	n	o
p	q	r	s	t
u	v	w	x	y
z	My sentences:			

Reproducible 5.8

Grades 3–6: Interpretation of Verbal Messages and Written Directions

1. Circle all word choices that help you to understand the lesson better.

   a. listening with attention   b. writing notes   c. playing at my desk

2. Write a sentence that tells about how you learn best during classroom lessons.

   _____

   _____

3. Write a sentence about sounds you hear that <u>stop you</u> from understanding and how you deal with it.

    _____

4. Write a sentence about where your eyes are during a classroom lesson when the teacher is talking.

    _____

5. Tell why reading and understanding written directions are important. <u>Paraphrase</u> the paragraph in the box below; in other words, use your own words!

   _____

   _____

   _____

> Listening to the teacher is vital because it's a way that students are able to learn new information. If you hear or read a vocabulary word that you never saw before, it's okay to investigate more by looking it up in a dictionary, online, or asking questions. If you want to succeed in school, then you as the student hold the key!

Reproducible 5.9

Grades 6–8: Write About Technology

Student directions: Write three paragraphs about how technology continually affects your life.

Use some of the following word choices or your own words. Review this table before you write your paragraphs. Afterwards, rate your writing by filling in each of the 10 parts below. Give specific sentences/examples from your paragraphs that fit each of the 10 descriptors.

Table 5.12

My paragraphs have	Examples From My Paragraphs
1. Topic sentences in each paragraph that tell the main ideas	
2. Supporting details that elaborate on those main ideas	
3. Organized sentences that flow into each other (with transitional words)	
4. A variety of nouns, verbs, adjectives, and adverbs with no boring or overused words	
5. A specific message and awareness of an audience	
6. Correct punctuation with ending marks, commas, quotations, and more	
7. Appropriate capitalization for proper nouns and adjectives and sentence beginnings	
8. Words spelled correctly. If you are not sure of some words, consult a dictionary or computer spell check.	
9. Sentence variety, e.g., apposition, no choppy sentences. Use different beginnings, e.g., no "I" award!	
10. Good conclusion with loose ends tied up and *gift wrapped* for the reader!	

Word Choices

technology	Web sites
questions	eventually
data	transportation
education	industry
software	innovative
first	video games
afterwards	science
consequently	trade
Internet	discovery
ultimately	effective
e-mails	learning
information	future
interactive	to sum it up
graphics	pace
animation	applications
communication	searches
research	business
computers	

Reproducible 5.10

Grades 9–12: Writing Lesson

Student directions: Read one of the following plays or stories. Then, after you have filled in the boxes, write your own version that changes at least one of the elements. If it's a narrative or autobiography, you can also change the person who is telling the story. A minimum of five paragraphs is required.

Table 5.13

Story/Play & Author	Characters	Setting	Plot	Resolution
Barrio Boy, by Ernesto Galarz				
A Tale of Two Cities, by Charles Dickens				
The Joy Luck Club, by Amy Tan				
Having Our Say, by Sarah and Elizabeth Delaney				
The Great Gatsby, by F. Scott Fitzgerald				
One Flew Over the Cuckoo's Nest, by Ken Kesey				
The Color Purple, by Alice Walker				
The Glass Menagerie, by Tennessee Williams				
Black Swan Green, by David Mitchell				

MATH CURRICULUM CONCERNS: MATHEMATICS MATTERS, TOO!

Numbers surround us. Just as reading has its letters and its place in the world, math definitely has its own place, values, and certainly *counts,* too! Whether students are comparing prices of items, using a calculator, counting out change, telling time, or solving quadratic equations, they must learn that mathematics is an *integral* part of their world and always will be.

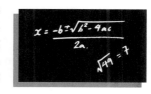

Mathematics is much more than an isolated subject. It connects to the world and allows students to transfer this type of logical thinking to other subject areas such as following steps in scientific experiments, drawing logical conclusions, understanding inferences in abstract readings, and sequencing thoughts in writings.

Students with dyscalculia may have difficulties with numerical reasoning, operations involving mental computations, understanding basic facts, mathematical symbols, telling time, or even opening up their locker with the right combination of numbers. However, with the correct instruction, scaffolding, and encouragement, teachers can help students with dyscalculia unlock their strengths to improve their mathematical skills!

As with reading and writing, the goal with mathematics instruction is to increase the baseline knowledge on an instructional level that does not frustrate or intimidate the students, but helps them to understand and apply concepts. That means not just for the day or unit, but for life! Once the concept is theirs, it needs to remain in their working memory. Mathematical concepts spiral, and without basic understandings, students will sink below the number line and achieve negative results, if the basic knowledge is not there. The idea is to provide direct instruction with modeling, guided applications, manipulatives, and connections to real-life situations and interest levels. Without breaking the phonetic code, students will have difficulties in all of their readings in future grades. Without understanding the basic language of math, the mistakes and frustrations will spiral as well!

Researchers talk about math anxiety and how students' lack of self-confidence interferes with their performance, not allowing them to concentrate on tasks at hand or filter out distractions (Cavanagh, 2007). Through friendly, inviting, and of course *numerous* ways, educators need to erase this math anxiety, especially when students are introduced to unfamiliar concepts and procedures. Mathematics is a huge part of our world, and students can understand this in everyday, fun classroom activities that go beyond the textbook assignments. The following K–12 lessons hope to achieve that goal!

Laying Down Foundations for Grades K–2

Before more difficult math skills are learned, students in primary grades need to experience early successes so that they will have positive attitudes about mathematics. Learners with special needs may have difficulties understanding visual cues, too much auditory information or multiple steps, and abstract facts. Memory, literacy, attention, discrimination, and motor issues can interfere with students' abilities to master, retain, and apply concepts. An activity such as the next one

Table 5.14   Appropriate Math Accommodations, Adaptations, and Strategies for Lessons

Concrete manipulatives: algebra tiles, Wikki sticks, place-value charts, area counters, unifix cubes, Cuisenaire rods, counting chips, playing cards, dice, chopsticks to show angles	Example cards, outlining steps, with gradual weaning off the cards to internalize concepts	Peer tutoring and cooperative learning activities with direct roles, instruction, and guidance	Mnemonic devices, *Please excuse my dear Aunt Sally* (PEMDAS); order of operations	Calculators with direct skill instruction and worksheet practice on correct usage and explanation of calculator functions
Individualized instruction	Web-based skills practice, e.g., www .aplusmath .com, www .coolmath4kids .com, www .mathforum.org	Alternate scope and sequence	Uncluttered worksheets	Repeated practice in small spiraling doses
Increased technology, e.g., interactive whiteboards for notes, geometer's sketchpad www.keypress .com, www .visual fractions.com	Opportunities for independent practice and application with frequent praise for math strides	Informal assessments to monitor students, track their progress and effectiveness of instruction	Connecting math with literature and other disciplines, e.g., *Tiger Math* by Nagda & Bickel to teach graphs, math journal	Connecting to higher-level logic and critical thinking skills, e.g., plexers and think-a-grams www.math-n-stuff.com/logic .html
Games and other *fun* ways to handle numbers, e.g., *soduko*, www .soduko-online. com, talking *factor frenzy* multiplication game, www .learning resources.com	Animated videos that connect math to life, e.g., *Donald Duck in Mathmagic Land* http://dep .disney. go.com/ educational/ store/	More visuals to explain and help visualize processes, e.g., draw equations	Interest-based functional and student-created word problems, e.g., double or halve your favorite recipe	Integrate educational music, www .math-n-stuff.com/ logic.html, multiplication rap. Ask students to create their own songs, too!

has the teacher ask questions while students identify, sort, and count the box of shapes. The following are some student directions for this *shapely picture prompt:*

1. Color the shape that is different.

2. How many shapes did you color?

3. How many shapes are not colored?

4. What shapes are in the box?

5. Write and solve an addition problem that shows the circles added to the triangle.

6. Write and solve an addition problem that shows the triangle added to the circles.

7. Write and solve a subtraction problem that shows the circles subtracted from the total number of shapes.

8. Write and solve a subtraction problem that shows the triangle subtracted from the total number of shapes.

9. Is the total number of shapes in the box an even or odd number?

10. What do you see in the classroom that is also in the shape of a circle?

11. How many sides does the triangle have?

12. Can you copy this box with shapes on a separate piece of paper?

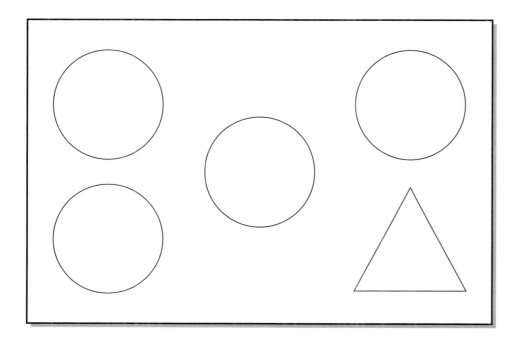

Lesson for Grades 2–4: Everything Has Its Place!

Students with learning differences often have difficulties with perceptual skills, such as discriminating written numbers, counting, one-to-one correspondence, and ordering and comparing by size and amount. Horizontal and vertical alignments require direct instruction with a solid understanding of place value. Adding larger numbers will never be mastered if students do not have conceptual understandings of just what those bigger numbers or larger words represent. Concrete learners especially need to understand exactly what the difference is between the ones, tens, and hundreds columns. How can students keep their columns straight if they are not taught the place value of each column one at a time? This page illustrates that. Once when my students were not getting the concept, I used a *high tech tool*, the abacus, to demonstrate place value, and they finally understood it, *one, two, three!* The point is, *back to basics* works, too!

First step: Solve the problem across (hor-i-zon-tal-ly)→

$5 + 3 = 8$

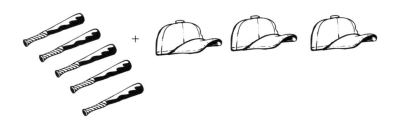

Second step: Write it going down (ver-ti-cal-ly)↓

$$\begin{array}{r} 5 \\ + 3 \\ \hline 8 \end{array}$$

Now you try it!

First step: $7 - 2 =$
(Hint: Place an **X** on 2 footballs.)

Second step: Write it going down (ver-ti-cal-ly)!

Teacher note: Students add horizontally first and then rewrite and solve each problem vertically on lined paper. Some students may need horizontally lined paper to be held sideways to keep their columns straight with the vertical lines. In addition, assorted manipulatives help students to add and subtract, both vertically and horizontally. They can use set amounts of chips or other counters to concretize the value of numbers. The point is to make the connection that equal values will be obtained, no matter how you write it! Also, have students highlight or circle the + and − signs before they begin each problem, to avoid careless errors.

More Place Value Practice

Teacher note: The same rules apply here. Now students add larger numbers, writing them horizontally first and then vertically. Lined paper turned sideways works best here, too. Some students may need more guidance as shown below with the boxes, at first plugging in the numbers in these number frames. Remind students to highlight signs as they gain and lose yards. Model regrouping and borrowing with chalkboard examples.

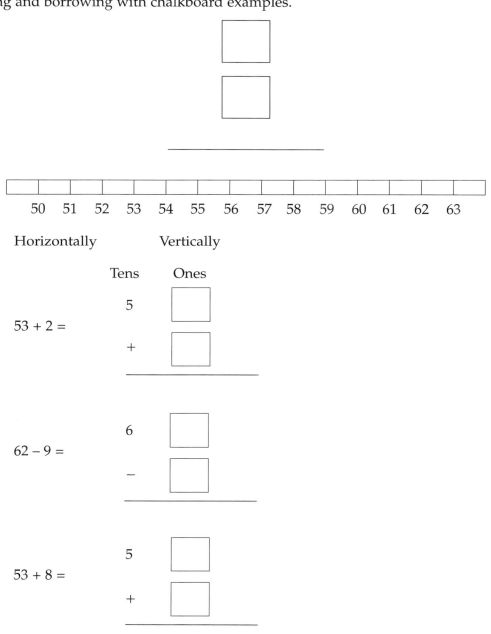

Reproducible 5.11

Math Lesson for Grades 3–5: Permutations and Combinations

Student directions: Permutations and combinations can apply to the different ways that numbers can be arranged and grouped. In using permutations, the order matters, while with combinations, order is not important. With this exercise, you are to use and correctly order all numbers in the set. That's what factorials are all about. For example, using the set of numbers, 1, 2, 3, the factorial would be written as 1 x 2 x 3 = 6, which means that the numbers 1, 2, and 3 can be arranged in six different ways. Let's illustrate this using the numbers 1, 2, and 3.

They can also be arranged as

1, 3, 2	3, 1, 2
2, 3, 1	3, 2, 1
2, 1, 3	

Try finding different sequences for the set of numbers 1, 2, 3, 4, 5
The factorial here would be 1 x 2 x 3 x 4 x 5 = ____ different combinations.

Table 5.15

1	2	3	4	5

Reproducible 5.12

Math Lesson for Grades 4–6: Probability

Model problem: Have you ever heard the weather report when it says that there's a 50% chance of rain? Just what does that mean? Well, it means there's an equal chance that it will rain or not rain. A 25% chance would mean it's not probable that it will rain, while an 80% chance makes rain highly probable, with an excellent chance that you'll need your umbrella. 0% is no chance of rain, while 100% chance of rain means that you'll be soaked without an umbrella! Read the A–H examples below and then convert them to fractions, decimals, and percents. Place your answers in the table.

Table 5.16

	Fraction	*Decimal*	*Percent*
A			
B			
C			
D			
E			
F			
G			
H			

Place answers in fractions, percents, and decimals in the columns where they belong, next to the corresponding letters for these situations:

    a. You buy one raffle ticket where 20 tickets in total were sold.
    b. You buy 10 tickets where 10 are sold.
    c. You buy 12 tickets out of 24 sold.
    d. You left your money at home.

There are 12 books on a shelf of which 3 are mystery, none are historical fiction, 7 were written by a woman, all of the books were written in the twenty-first century, and 6 are 100 or more pages in length.

    e. What are the odds that you will not pick a historical fiction book?
    f. How probable is it that the book you choose will be written by a woman?
    g. What are the odds that the book you pick will be a mystery one?
    h. What are the odds that your book is under 100 pages?

Reproducible 5.13

Math Lesson for Grades 5–8: Increase Computational Skills

Directions: Try solving these problems, working across from left to right and placing your final answers in the boxes below. Some problems will be easier than others, and some may be harder to figure out. Check the accuracy of your answers with a calculator to see which type of problems you need more help with. Then go to the site www.aplusmath .com to create your own worksheet to practice the skills you need to sharpen. You can even print out your own answer key and decide how many problems will be on each page. For example, you may need to practice multiplying one digit by two digits, dividing by two-digit numbers, adding fractions, using the correct order of operations, or subtracting decimals. These are written horizontally, but you can use a separate piece of paper to solve them vertically. Show your work on the scrap paper. The idea is to be your own teacher to improve your computational skills!

Table 5.17

5 + 9 + 7 =	293 – 18 =	786 + 487 =	1,000 – 657 =	40,769 + 236,879 =	98,309 – 467 =
9 x 6 =	58 x 7 =	908 x 17 =	430.2 x 7.6 =	72 ÷ 8 =	96 ÷ 12 =
67 ÷ 8 =	465 x 764 =	136 ÷ 2 =	8,078 ÷ 9 =	80.5 ÷ 5 =	80.5 ÷ .5 =
$2/3 + 1/3 =$	$7/8 - 5/8 =$	$3/4 + 1/2 =$	2.07 + 78.9 =	87.08 – 6.5 =	$98.65 +.27 =
$5 - 5/8 =$	$1/3 + 3/4 + 1/2 =$	5 × (2 × 9) × 4 =	(3 – 7) × 6 + (6 + 5) × 4 =		

Okay, What Happens After McDonald's Serves Cheeseburgers?

Quite often, students are dependent upon math's many tricks, such as Does McDonald's Serve Cheeseburgers? or Daddy, Mother, Sister, Cousin, Brother, which stands for the steps in long division: divide, multiply, subtract, compare, and bring down. Well, when should the cheeseburgers stop being served and the division process be committed to memory? When should students start learning their multiplication facts and stop depending upon charts? When should students stop counting upon their fingers to add or subtract? Eventually, the math has to become theirs, which will not happen if the teachers do not gradually fade out the math crutches, e.g., using multiplication charts for basic facts. It's almost comparable to memorizing words, without ever breaking the phonetic code!

Educators need to use their best discretion on when they are helping vs. limiting students' potentials to get better at knowing their mathematics facts or internalizing the processes and operations. When will students be ready to *fly solo* without the math tricks, but be equipped with the conceptual knowledge? Teachers' interventions need to be given on an *as needed basis.* Giving a student example cards with steps written on each one to get him or her started in learning a new process such as simplifying improper fractions is fine, but should the student always use the cards, or be gradually weaned off them? It goes back to that scenario of when a man is stopped on the street by a woman and asked, "Can you tell me how to get to Carnegie Hall?" And the response he gives her is, "Practice, practice, practice!" The point is that she doesn't really need the physical directions, but the guidance on how to be better at what she does. Math is like music in many ways, with its own notation system and the counting of numbers rather than beats. The more practice, the better it sounds with *immeasurable* applause!

Reproducible 5.14

Math Lesson for Grades 9–12: Solving Word Problems—Understanding the Language of Math

Every word counts!
Read these sporting scenarios:

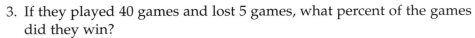

1. If the basketball team won 7/8 of its games, what percent of its games has it won?

2. If the basketball team won 3/4 of its games, what percent of its games has it lost?

3. If they played 40 games and lost 5 games, what percent of the games did they win?

4. If they played x number of games each week, how many games did they play in 8 weeks?

5. If the team had 12 players and the same 5 players had court time, what percent of the players were probably disgruntled each week?

6. If Player #1 scored s number of shots and Player #2 scored four times as many shots as Player #1, write an algebraic representation of the total number of shots for both players.

7. If Player #4 is n years old and Player #5 is 2 years younger, express the age of Player #5 in terms of Player #4.

8. If the coach called for four practices each week for 3½ months, how many practices were called?

9. If one team won by 12 points, then 8 points, and then 6 points, what's the average or mean number of points the team won by for the three games?

10. If a basketball team makes 55 out of 80 attempted shots from the field, what is their shooting percentage?

Table 5.18

<u>My Answers</u>: After you have solved these basketball problems on scrap paper, place the final answers by the correct number below.				
1.	2.	3.	4.	5.
6.	7.	8.	9.	10.

OTHER CURRICULUM LESSONS

Science Lesson for Grades K–2: A Heavy and Light Lesson

This lesson acknowledges and anticipates the varying abilities that exist within an inclusive classroom. Cooperative assignments reinforce both *heavier* and *lighter* learning activities! Appropriately assign students to groups as partners, trios, quartets, or quintets. Model and explain all to the whole class or smaller individual groups as needed.

Objective: Students will cooperatively predict and then classify single items as light or heavy and then do the same in varying combinations with other objects. Student groups will share findings with the class.

Academic and Social Skills: Receptive and expressive language, identification, classification, prediction, organization, fine motor skills, language arts skills, graphing, social reciprocity, team building, combining objects, counting skills, creating equations, measurement skills, concepts of light and heavy, charting, scientific inquiry, ordering.

Concept: Items with different size, mass, and density have different weights.

Procedure: Each group of students will predict which objects they think will weigh the most and which ones they think will weigh the least and then check their predictions by using the equal arm balances. Afterwards, the whole class will meet as a group to share and graph their results and find the lightest and heaviest equations! Teachers can distribute prediction charts or ask students to make their own by folding a piece of paper in half and writing their predictions on one side and the actual weights on the other. More advanced groups can also independently use the equal arm balance to discover which combinations of objects are balanced. Some groups with more learning needs can be given only two objects to compare. Students can rank object weights by using numbers such as 1 for the lightest and 10 for the heaviest.

Assessments: Teachers observe groups' interactions and record social behaviors as they circulate and assist. Final results sentences, pictures, equation findings, light–heavy rankings, graphs, and class participation to oral questions are used for assessments and accountability.

Revisitation/Follow-Up Activities: Continued experiments balancing and ranking the weights of different objects.

Table 5.19

Cooperative Roles
Goodies Getter: Collects the materials needed
Namer: Describes the properties of the materials.
Chooser: Picks which items to combine and classify as light or heavy
Talker: Leads the discussion with his or her group and then shares findings with the rest of the class
Writer/Artist: Writes a simple sentence or draws pictures showing what his or her group discovered

Table 5.20

Materials
Equal arm balances for each group
Pipe cleaners or Wikki sticks
Nontoxic clay
Different coins: pennies, nickels, dimes
School supplies: crayons, pencils, paper clips, erasers

Table 5.21

P = I think	Weight: L to H

Table 5.22

List objects of balanced weights in the left and right columns	
I think these objects will =	**these objects**

Reproducible 5.15

Science Lesson for Grades 3–6:
Matter and Changes in Your Day!

Study the chart below. Then read the sentences to decide whether a physical or chemical change has occurred. Place a check mark in the correct column.

Table 5.23

Different Reactions: a. _Matter is anything that takes up space and has mass._ b. _Reactions or changes can be physical or chemical._	_Physical Changes:_ _Different shape_ _Different size_ _Different color_	_Chemical Changes:_ _Atoms rearrange_ _Different properties from the original substance_
1. You wake up in the morning and brush your teeth.		
2. You get dressed.		
3. The bread you were going to eat is green with mold.		
4. That fried egg smells delicious!		
5. You pour milk on your cereal.		
6. Uh-oh, the toast is burnt!		
7. You drink fresh orange juice your dad squeezed.		
8. You hear the construction crew outside hammering nails to fix your neighbor's roof.		
9. Your sister is mowing the lawn.		
10. Ahh! You smell leaves burning.		
11. You want to ride your bike to school, but the chain is rusted.		
12. When you get to school, you break your pencil.		
13. Your teacher melts butter on the popcorn she gives the class as a snack.		
14. You fold your papers before putting them in your backpack.		
15. You arrive back home and start your homework, but the dog eats it!		
16. Now it's time for bed. You lay down on nice, clean sheets!		

Source: Karten, T. (2007c). _Inclusion activities that work! Grades 6-8._ Thousand Oaks, CA: Corwin Press.

Reproducible 5.16

Science Lesson for Grades 4–6: Planting Words

Writing is a form of expression and a way for students to demonstrate what they've learned across the curriculum. Expository writing in the content areas is vital!

Student directions: Think about what you know about each object below. Then ask yourself, *What would these objects say to each other?* Write your words in the speech bubbles below. Use quotation marks around your words.

1. What would this plant say to the gas, carbon dioxide (CO_2)?

 *CO₂*

2. What would the sun say to this plant?

3. What would a ladybug say to a plant?

4. What would a plant say to the soil?

Science Lesson for Grades 6–8:
Think, Pair, Collide, Move, and Grind

Teacher note: The following activities have the concepts leap off the page and *erupt into solid understandings.* Some vocabulary words in subject areas are not within students' prior knowledge base. This science/reading lesson breaks up a unit on plate tectonics into smaller plates. First, students kinesthetically demonstrate the vocabulary. Next, they read more about plate tectonics, focusing on vocabulary words in context. This type of organization helps learners concentrate on the key points without reading an inordinate amount of information. Afterwards, students have an excellent study guide!

Types of Boundaries:

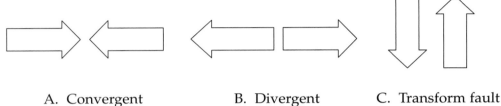

A. Convergent
   boundary

B. Divergent
   boundary

C. Transform fault
   boundary

A. Plates colliding into each other

B. Plates move away from each other

C. Plates grinding past each other

Student directions:

1. With a partner, act out these plate movements.

2. Find another pair, and as a quartet act out the boundaries again.

3. Now, get together as a class and converge, diverge, and transform!

Reproducible 5.17

All About Plates (not the ones in the kitchen!)

Student directions:

1. First, read each paragraph.

2. Next, fill in the letters that correctly complete each plate tectonics sentence. Use choices from each word box below the paragraph.

3. Then, use these filled-in pages as your study guides.

The plate tectonic theory talks about the Earth's outermost layer, called the *lithosphere.* The separate plates look as if they are one big jigsaw puzzle that has been separated into land masses. There are seven large plates that move at different speeds and in different directions. The plate boundary is where the two plates meet. The three types are convergent, divergent, and transform fault boundaries.

The plate tectonic theory talks about the Earth's outermost layer, called the _____. The separate plates look as if they are one big _____ that has been separated into land masses. There are _____ large plates that move at different _____ and in different _____. The _____ is where the two plates meet. The three types of boundaries are convergent, divergent, and transform fault.

Table 5.24

a. lithosphere	b. plate boundary	c. jigsaw puzzle
d. speeds	e. seven	f. directions

Reproducible 5.18

Divergent boundaries: The liquid rock that seeps upward to fill the cracks is called magma. Earthquakes occur near the fault. When magma reaches the surface, volcanoes form. When these divergent boundaries cross the land, rift valleys form. An example of this is the Rio Grande. The Mid-Atlantic Ridge is an example of when a divergent boundary crosses the ocean floor.

The liquid rock that seeps upward to fill the cracks is called _____. Earthquakes occur near the _____. When magma reaches the surface, _____ form. When these divergent boundaries cross the land, _____ form. An example of this is the _____. The _____ is an example of when a divergent boundary crosses the ocean floor.

Table 5.25

g. volcanoes	h. Rio Grande	i. rift valleys
j. fault	k. magma	l. Mid-Atlantic Ridge

Convergent boundaries are places where the plates collide into each other. Mountains and volcanoes form where plates collide. Earthquakes repeatedly occur at the faults, which are fractures or weaknesses in the earth's crust.

Convergent boundaries are places where the plates _____ into each other. _____ and _____ form where plates collide. _____ repeatedly occur at the faults which are fractures or weaknesses in the earth's crust.

Table 5.26

m. collide	n. earthquakes
o. mountains	p. volcanoes

Transform fault boundaries happen when plates slide past each other. The San Andreas Fault in California is an example of a transform fault boundary.

Transform fault boundaries happen when plates ____ past each other. The _____ Fault in California is an example of a transform fault boundary.

Table 5.27

q. San Andreas	r. slide

Source: http://www.cet.edu/ete/modules/msese/earthsysflr/plates3.html

Science Lesson for Intermediate and High School: Experiment Design

The following outlines more about Bloom's Taxonomy, and gives a classroom application on how to develop better critical thinking skills. Students need to choose a scientific topic or issue to be resolved and follow the steps below. Cooperative groups plan their experiment together. Students are allowed 4 weeks to complete this long-term, teacher-approved project with intermittent teacher review and guidance to ensure understandings and progress. Students meet, plan, and complete requirements in class, at the library, and at home.

Knowledge:

1. Identify your topic.
2. List materials in your experiment.
3. Define vocabulary.

Comprehension:

1. What are you doing?
2. List the steps:

First, _____

Next, _____

Later, _____

After, _____

Finally, _____

> Science Topics to Explore
>
> Buoyancy
> Ecosystems
> Natural resources
> Technology
> Weather
> Phases of the Moon
> Friction
> Light
> Solar energy
> Chemical changes
> Plants
> Nutrition
> Recycling
> _____

Application:

1. Conduct the experiment.
2. Record data:

What was done?

What was seen?

Analysis:

1. Think about what your results mean.
2. What are your conclusions?

Synthesis:

1. Create a picture, graph, model, chart, diagram, poem, song, dance, news article, or PowerPoint presentation about the topic and experiment.
2. List some predictions about what would happen if you changed the procedure or any of the variables.

Evaluate:

1. Were you satisfied with the results?
2. What did you learn?
3. Criticize or defend the experiment.

Elementary Social Studies
Geography Lesson: Serving Up Knowledge

Movement gets students out of their seats and thinking on their feet!

"Serve up" some knowledge by doing the following activity.

1. Write the following words about the United States on paper plates: North America, Canada, Mexico, Pacific Ocean, Atlantic Ocean, Gulf of Mexico, Washington DC, Philadelphia, South America, New York, Fifty, Thirteen, Mississippi. Spread out the plates around the floor. (To increase difficulty, add more statements and "paper plate" answers.)

2. Divide students into teams who stand in a circle and look at the paper plate choices as you read aloud the statements below.

3. Invite team members who know the answer to raise their hand. Choose a student to jump on the paper plate answer. If the student is correct, his or her team gets to keep the plate.

4. Read these statements, one by one, until you are finished. The team with the most paper plates wins!
   - The United States is on this continent.
   - This country borders the United States to the north.
   - This country borders the United States to the south.
   - This body of water is on the East Coast of the United States.
   - This body of water is on the West Coast of the United States.
   - This body of water is to the south of the United States.
   - This city is the capital of the United States.
   - This city is home to the Liberty Bell.
   - This city is home to the Statue of Liberty.
   - This is the number of original colonies in the United States.
   - This is the number of states currently in the United States.
   - This is the longest river in the United States.

5. Afterward, invite students to review world geography by establishing north, south, east, and west directions in the classroom (like a large compass rose). Ask students to review world continents and large bodies of water by holding/placing paper plates in the correct geographic location in the room.

Table 5.28   Varied Assignments That Value Students' Strengths Across the Curriculum

World Languages: Ask students to translate a book report, or answer science, social studies, or math questions into the language they are learning or one spoken in their home, e.g., Spanish, Japanese, Russian, Italian, Chinese, French, Arabic, Hebrew, and more. ESL students will be sent the message that their language is (in this case), not secondary! Coordinate your grading with the language teachers, allowing the student to receive credit and recognition for both subjects.

Musical Understandings: Ask students to create a song, musical composition, or dance that relates to their learning. If it's a song, the lyrics need to match the concepts and vocabulary. If it's a musical composition, then it needs to reflect and relate to the content, e.g., book's mood, conflict, setting, characters. If it's a dance, the movements need to kinesthetically relate to and demonstrate the curriculum concepts learned.

Art Reflections: Students can draw a storyboard that sequences historical events, economic conditions, scientific concepts, or math word problems, e.g., show how to solve geometric proofs, algebraic equations, and more!

Research Proficiencies: Students are asked to further investigate a subject by obtaining additional facts, details, and background information at the library, including correct citations for books and Internet sources in their research. Requirements can range from a 5-paragraph essay to a research or position page paper.

Director Assignment: Students can collaboratively write and direct their own curriculum plays showing their knowledge in subjects or topics such as world history, chemistry, biology, disabilities, and others. Their understanding of concepts will be demonstrated through the dialogue, writings, props, scenery, and more. This is a good opportunity for positive social interactions and for those students with higher bodily-kinesthetic intelligences or interpersonal intelligences to improve their verbal-linguistic intelligences, too.

More concrete learners: Students can *pair with a peer* who can mentor and guide the student through the activity, allowing the student to perform functional tasks under peer's and the teacher's supervision and guidance, e.g., sorting books, self-help pictures, or even a parallel, but meaningful academic or social assignment or activity, e.g., reading a train schedule, reciting his or her phone number, ordering from a menu, counting change, reading sight words on road signs, interpreting social skills pictures that depict appropriate behavioral and social interactions.

The Value of Stations and Centers in Elementary Lessons

Students with learning, attention, and behavioral differences often exhibit difficulties with reading comprehension, word decoding, mathematical reasoning, computation, or peer social interactions. In reference to instructional styles, many students with and without disabilities understand and retain concepts best when learning is presented outside the *all heads facing forward*, lecture-style format. Allowing students bodily-kinesthetic opportunities to move about to learn proactively circumvents auditory processing, attention, and motivation issues. Teachers then become more the facilitators of the learning than the disseminators! Centers and stations offer opportunities for *disguised* learning practice, application, and demonstration of skills across the curriculum.

Inclusion tips: If students have visual or auditory challenges, add more kinesthetic-tactile elements such as content-related objects and manipulatives to concretize the abstract (actual magnets, inflatable map globes). In addition, peer coaches can describe the environment and help with lesson navigations, communications, and directions for students with physical, sensory, behavioral, and varied learning needs.

The following five stations, although generic in nature and not requiring repeated teacher preparation or additional student instructions, value diverse curriculum topics and students' intelligences. The best part about the stations and centers is that they are not assigned but are student-selected, creating more motivation and ownership of student learning experiences. If prior knowledge is shaky, group work and further research strengthens that weaker knowledge base. Stations and centers allow students in the earlier grades and up to learn to work together cooperatively to complete an assigned task, thereby developing appropriate lifelong skills, which will be applicable in future academic, social, community, and work experiences. Centers also value alternate forms of assessments with students being graded on academic content and social performances. Give students a rubric with expectations and grade requirements to review. Teachers can circulate around and offer assistance as needed. The classroom can be set up year round with materials for the centers, e.g., art supplies by the *Picture This Station,* graph paper for the *Word Station,* posted recommended content-related computer sites by the *Research Station.* The final product is then presented to the class, allowing students to practice oral presentation skills, e.g., appropriate eye contact, proper volume and rate of speech. Students often ask if they can use their textbook for more information. The answer is, of course, "Yes, you may!" Skills in reading, writing, mathematics, content areas, and creative expressions match curriculum standards with literacy, inquiry, conceptual, and social improvements. The next table presents a few curriculum possibilities; the connections are unlimited, while the potentials for increased understandings are just as vast.

Table 5.29   Sample Curriculum Connections Across the Grades

	K–4	*5–8*	*9–12*
Research Station Research primary sources, online computer Web sites, texts, and library books. Students in higher grades cite sources in a bibliography format.	Music: Students use the computer or teacher-created tapes to listen to, create, and learn about different sound effects, patterns, and musical instruments (even taped assemblies of the school band will work!).	SS: Students investigate primary and secondary sources to find out more about the Truman Doctrine; Martin Luther King Jr.'s speech, *I've Been to the Mountaintop*; JFK's speech, *Ich bin ein Berliner.*	Geometry: Students use the computer to create, describe, and investigate vertex-edge graphs and computer algorithms, e.g., software programs, computer art tools.
Teacher Station Students create tests with multiple choice, open-ended questions, essays, and other formats. Point values of questions are decided.	Math: Addition and subtraction problems are created with students using pictures, counters, or other set representations to create test problems on correct sums and differences.	Art: Students create a *picture test* with questions asking for demonstrations of complementary colors, different shadows, intensities, and hues.	Physics: Students design a test with a variety of questions, e.g., multiple choice, essay, fill-ins, about daily applications for the principles of light, heat, electricity, and magnetism.
Picture This Station Illustrations, diagrams, clip art, or different mediums represent main concepts in the curriculum. Pictures are accompanied by brief explanatory text.	Science: Students draw environmental pictures with captions or create dioramas after a nature walk outside the school with a variety of tactile elements, e.g., Wikki sticks, sand, grass, leaves, rocks.	Math: Students draw pictures or find clip art to solve given word problems involving whole numbers, fractions, and decimals.	Chemistry: Students illustrate equations with images of compounds, e.g., $C_6H_{12}O_6$ (picture of sugar), or create clay and pipe cleaner representations of neutrons, protons, and electrons in elements listed in the Periodic Table.
Word Station Word acrostics, stories, crossword puzzles, word searches, and debates are created with students pantomiming key vocabulary words.	Writing: Given the prompt words, *first, next, later, after,* and *finally,* students create stories and then write acrostics about characters in a book they have read. They also pair up and pantomime vocabulary words to each other.	Math: Students pantomime the place value of decimals up to the millionths place, moving about to be decimals, points, and whole #s. Math text glossary is then used to create word searches, fill-ins, and decimal acrostics.	SS: Students use vocabulary words in a debate about civil liberties in an age of increased security. Students then create a computer-generated crossword puzzle and word search from this online site from discovery's school: www.puzzlemaker.com
Performance Station Content-related skits, jingles, songs, dances, video games, or commercials.	SS: Students create a rhyming song about classroom rules. Older grades can create a jingle about checks and balances and the three branches of government.	Science: Students demonstrate the laws of motion through three skits that show the knowledge of reaction and action forces, inertia, acceleration, momentum, and mass.	Health: Students act out a play with a moral about the positive and negative effects of nutrition and exercise choices on their daily decisions and the lifestyles of others.

6

Instructional Differentiation and Sensitivities That Respond to Students' Behavioral, Social, Emotional, and Perceptual Needs

Chapter Highlights: Behavioral, social, emotional, and perceptual needs are highlighted in this sixth chapter in relation to self-advocacy and classroom scenarios.

Classroom Connections: Information is given about how to connect sensory strategies with students' visual, auditory, and kinesthetic-tactile strengths. Emotional dynamics for individual students and groups in the classroom are explored.

Ways to Differentiate Attitudes: The chapter reviews how attitudes to maximize abilities are influenced by educators' and students' self-determination, motivation, and metacognition.

Table 6.1   Appropriate Behavioral Accommodations, Adaptations, and Strategies

Compile and post a list of positively stated behavioral expectations, rules, and specific hierarchical rewards and consequences with the class. Use lists and accompanying visuals on the charts for more concrete learners.	Use active classroom learning experiences with more kinesthetic opportunities to allow positive channeling of hyperactivity, e.g., *brainbreaks*, class errands, stretching, classroom stations.	Encourage peer awareness of appropriate behaviors and acceptable language with classroom interactions, e.g., visual social stories, positive peer photos, *catch you being good* program.	Direct social skill instruction in natural classroom environment, e.g., cooperative roles, *social rubrics*, teaching about body language.	Regularly acknowledge and try to establish more intrinsic motivation for students' positive social strides, e.g., personal attention, saying *thank you, good for you,* and *congratulations,* increased student metacognition.
Understand and note the reasons or function for the behavior, e.g., what preceded the student's actions, functional behavioral analysis—attention, boredom, student comments, academic misunderstandings.	Value appropriate affects with courtesy, politeness, and respect for all students.	Increase praise, communication, and collaboration with the students, administration, and families for consistency and enforcement of acceptable behavioral rules.	Always be in control with calmness; confidence; and, if appropriate, humor, but never sarcasm!	Know students' outside interests and try to motivate them with lessons that connect to their lives to maximize attention, e.g., inventories, class discussions, writer's journals, art projects, content-related lyrics.
Establish personal connections with the students, sharing your own experiences.	Like the student, but dislike the negative behavior.	Allow students to daily and weekly track their behavioral progress on a mutually agreed-upon rating scale, varying complexity based on cognitive levels.	Connect academic content with other disciplines, strengths, and intelligences of students.	Use preferential seating to minimize distractions, avoid behavioral concerns, and maximize attention.

ATTENTION-GETTING LESSONS

Attention is the gateway to learning. If a teacher doesn't have a student's attention, no learning takes place. Giving students assignment choices makes a student-centered classroom. The student must be attending to the task at hand, and the easiest way to get this attention is through the perception of choice and control. (Nunley, 2003)

Choice and Control Examples

- "Respond to 5 of the following 8 essay choices."
- "Decide which learning station you'd like to complete: teacher, research, picture, word, or performance."
- "Cooperatively choose a current events topic you'd like to explore more."
- "Pick the genre you'd like to read or write about."
- "Follow the outlined directions for the completion of the environmental science research project. You may choose your own topic from the table of contents in our textbook."

The general idea here is that students are learning, but at the same time they are involved in the process by personalizing their assignment. This way learners have more of a stake in the completion of the project since their attention is increased with assignments that have built-in individualized components. Ownership of the learning is not solely in the hands of the teacher, but is shared with students to increase their attention to the task. Adding family involvement then increases and values the learning even more. Learning connections to a child's life is a formula that includes teachers, students, and families.

Clearly, social and emotional skills strike a chord with students in terms of what they believe they need to thrive in high school and in the future. (Beland, 2007)

TEACHERS + STUDENTS + FAMILIES = LEARNING

INSTRUCTIONAL YESSES AND NOES

Slowing the pace of instruction not only contributes to students' lagging attention but misbehavior and lack of skill acquisition as well. (Heward, 2003)

Yes, educators need to respond to students' needs.

Yes, repetition is essential, but boredom is not equivocal with learning.

No, we can't be everything to every child.

No, you can't always teach to 100% mastery.

Yes, step-by-step instruction can help, but it's not for every student.

Yes, differentiation of instruction addresses learners' needs.

No, it's not solely about academics, but connecting to the whole child.

Yes, it's about students listening, responding, and wanting to learn.

Yes, it's about learning how to teach in ways to reach each student!

Yes, you can maximize potentials when you differentiate positive from negative attitudes!

SYNTHESIZING THE PART INTO THE WHOLE

Dissections and Connections

The skills involved in some curriculum objectives need to be dissected and served on *palatable learning plates.* At the same time the learning is dissected, it also needs to be connected to students' lives with appropriate accommodations for students with disabilities. Not an easy task, but not an impossible one either, if you possess an attitude that says, *I'll figure out how to reach ALL of my students!*

The following are some specific curriculum grade-level objectives for students with varying abilities that try to dissect, connect, and accommodate:

Table 6.2

Curriculum Topics/ Concepts/Objectives	Dissections: Skills Involved	Connections to Students and Accommodations
Grades K–2 a. Demonstrate left-to-right directionality in picture books and their own writings	a. Be able to repeatedly scan/ write across a printed line, without skipping words or lines.	a. Students kinesthetically move their bodies and/or hands, imitating written text, such as moving from the left to the right side of the room and back across again. Let students follow a flashlight beam with their eyes. Some students can use a tracking guide, such as a thin ruled line to keep pace with the readings. Provide students with a tracker to use in their home environment, too.
b. Solve simple addition and subtraction picture word problems	b. Know values of numbers. Listen to clue words, e.g., altogether, how much more or less than. Needs to differentiate + and − signs.	b. Use concrete classroom objects in the lesson to have students physically and concretely represent subtraction and addition word problems. Highlight and say signs and numbers in written problems.
c. Identify the difference between living and nonliving objects	c. Comparing and sorting objects, prior knowledge, observational skills.	c. Use a Venn diagram or concrete large hula hoops to list and place findings. Include actual photographs of living and nonliving organisms to sort. Ask students to identify and list living and nonliving things with their families in their home environments, too.
Grades 3–5 a. Identifying and sticking to the main idea and supporting details in readings and writing	a. Being able to understand the big picture or *umbrella topic* that the other ideas fall under.	a. Give a common analogy that relates to students' lives, e.g., if you are writing a story about breakfast, explain why including a line about the movies is inappropriate. Review writing models.

(Continued)

Table 6.2 (Continued)

Curriculum Topics/ Concepts/Objectives	Dissections: Skills Involved	Connections to Students and Accommodations
b. Comparing and estimating the value of decimals	b. Knowing the place value of whole numbers and decimals. Being able to visually read numbers with and without decimals.	b. Relate decimals to money. Students can hold lined paper vertically to use columns for neater place value. They can even act out the value of decimal points, moving themselves to indicate different values, e.g., 1.2 vs. 12. Give out math coins that the students need to total. Relate values to actual concrete objects.
c. Demonstrating understandings about landforms	c. Discriminating different landforms, reading a map legend, identifying meanings of unfamiliar vocabulary, e.g., elevation, basin.	c. Create raised relief maps with teacher- or student-created clay models for students to feel the difference between terms such as a valley, hill, plateau. Ask students to identify landforms they have seen in movies or on trips they have taken.
Grades 6–8 a. Students will read a variety of genres to gain vocabulary comprehension skills	a. Word decoding skills, grade-level vocabulary, knowing the meaning of cause–effect, connotations, denotations, paraphrasing, and ingredients of effective summaries.	a. Relate learning to students' interests and culture, e.g., *Quinceanera* for Latino culture, *Chicken Soup for the Teenage Soul, Sports Illustrated for Kids.* Use high interest, age appropriate, but lower level readings if necessary. Obtain digital and Braille copies if needed.
b. Understanding of human body systems	b. Ability to identify and match organs with systems and to connect their functions in relationship with another system.	b. Relate study to personal or family health and nutrition choices. View Web sites, e.g., http://library .thinkquest.org/5462/
c. Symbolism in art and music as related to different cultures	c. Knowing that there is more than meets the eye with symbolism expressed in music and art. Understanding that the abstract relates to unseen concepts.	c. Allow students to create their own artwork and musical pieces freehand, with an instrument or on the computer with varying media, clipart graphics, and musical sound effects. Invite families to share music and art from their own cultures.
Grades 9–12 a. Knowledge that many civilizations were a product of cultural invention and diffusion	a. Understanding the difference between direct, indirect, and forced diffusion.	a. View videos and online sites that depict present and past civilizations. Read historical fiction and act out published or student-created plays to increase understandings through dialogue.

Curriculum Topics/ Concepts/Objectives	Dissections: Skills Involved	Connections to Students and Accommodations
b. Develop a concept of the transformation of energy, knowing that energy cannot be created or destroyed, only changed from one form to another	b. Ability to describe energy types: mechanical, heat, nuclear, electrical, light, sound, chemical, and electromagnetic.	b. Relate and act out everyday situations, e.g., playing a violin (mechanical) to show sound energy, turning a lamp on (electrical) to show light, playing a video game (changing electromagnetic energy into sound and light energy). Students can keep an energy diary for the week.
c. Creation of a resume	c. Organization, sequencing, proofreading, computer technology skills, self-awareness of interests.	c. Establish a *dangling carrot* for the resume with students understanding the significance of a resume's appearance for postsecondary job choices and college applications.

Think of some of your own curriculum dissections, connections, and accommodations.

Table 6.3

Curriculum Topics/Concepts/ Objectives	Dissections: Skills Involved	Connections to Students and Accommodations

There are no better words than:

"Aha, Now I Know!"

When students declare their knowledge, there is no better *pedagogical natural high!* Some students will rephrase their understandings into questions to clarify uncertainties. Others will shout out, "Oh, I get it now!" The students who sit quietly, hoping not to be noticed, are the ones who need to be questioned to solidify the concepts. It's at this point that teachers need to understand students' body language. Students who inattentively fidget or avoid eye contact are sending out blaring messages. It may not always mean that they don't care about the learning; it could be that their *internal switch* is turned off. To avoid saying that they are not getting it, they just don't listen or they pretend to listen. Remember that this is not always a conscious effort, but sometimes is a matter of classroom survival or learned routines from prior years that automatically reoccur.

The *classroom wattage* definitely varies, as shown by these examples:

Classroom Wattage

10 watts:

"I hear what you are saying and can repeat the lesson word for word, but just what does it all mean?"

30 watts:

"I kind of know what it means, but just in case you are wondering, I'll nod my head so you'll think I'm totally on target and you won't call on me."

60 watts:

"When you are showing me a model, I get it, but then when I have to do it on my own or for homework, I forget some of the steps, concepts, and details."

75 watts:

"This stuff is hard to understand. I'm trying, but I still have some gaps. It's not just about applying myself, since I am trying my best. At least I understand 75% of the lesson."

100 watts:

"I definitely get it! I'm glad that the teacher has those centers set up around the room for me to work on that ongoing cooperative project. Just because I get the lesson, doesn't mean that I should have to always tutor the other kids who don't. I don't mind helping out sometimes, but when I work on my center project, I can learn even more!"

FOLLOWING ROUTINES AND DIRECTIONS

Teachers often make assumptions that their directions have gotten through. But the disconnect is that the student often doesn't get it. His or her interpretation is really different. (Standen, 2006)

Quite often, in teachers' haste and desire to get through curriculum mandates, they think students are on the right track, but when assessments are graded, the news is not always so comforting. This can be circumvented by

- Asking students to intermittently paraphrase directions, steps, or procedures;
- Checking for understandings before students start assignments and at set intervals for long-range assignments;
- Adjusting the volume and pace of your voice, e.g., sometimes the softer and less rushed-sounding voice commands more attention;
- Assigning peers as study mentors to clarify and assist students with assignments, if they are willing to assume that role;
- Modeling expectations with a concrete rubric and samples of completed works;
- Repeating and rephrasing directions using less complicated vocabulary;
- Asking students to evaluate their progress against a checklist of requirements;
- Requiring students to keep a journal of the steps they've completed;
- Letting the students draw pictures, illustrations, or diagrams of their steps;
- Demonstrating your own enthusiasm for the learning material by using positive body language and exciting activities that help the learning leap off the page;
- Praising the asking of questions with a risk-free environment that values relevant dialogue without the teacher being the sole disseminator of the knowledge;
- Encouraging the students to continue applying the learning and skills through revisitation and meaningful interdisciplinary activities;
- Ongoing self-help skills and more metacognition of personal, social, and academic skills.

CLASSROOM COMMUNICATION

Communication involves more than saying the words, but understanding and applying the word meanings as well. This becomes more complicated for students with disabilities when language, cognitive, social, behavioral, and physical levels interfere with intended messages. Many students know what they want to say, but the words chosen are not always the correct ones to reach their audiences. Some students cannot physically speak their intelligent thoughts the same way as their peers, but can be more *introspectively articulate* than a student with no interfering physical issues. Students who are hearing impaired may speak differently, but their body language or eye contact may even shout a louder message than their words. Students with lower cognitive levels sometimes have larger smiles and more to say than a student with an IQ in the gifted range. Aside from verbalizing, students can express their thoughts by nodding, pointing, and even sorting objects. It's up to educators, caring professionals, knowledgeable support staff, families, and students with and without disabilities to establish and maintain comfortable, receptive environments in which there is acceptance of and support for all. All student interactions and different ways that students respond to the curriculum and others are part of that comfortable environment. No one in the classroom should have a monopoly on communication. Here are some terms and concepts that are important to understand:

1. Receptive language refers to the ability to understand what is being said.

2. Expressive language is when students communicate thoughts.

3. Pragmatic language involves social skills, e.g., classroom conversation, cooperative groups, talking with peers, playing a game.

4. Speech is an oral form of language, but nonverbal skills are an integral part of communication, too.

5. Augmentative communication and assistive listening devices are beneficial technology options for some students.

6. "Language is a code made up of rules that include what words mean, how to make words, how to put them together, and what word combinations are best in what situations." (http://www.asha.org/public/speech/development)

7. Clarity is when you enunciate and can be understood by others.

8. Voice quality includes your intensity, inflections, and intonations.

9. Fluency refers to pace or rate of speaking.

10. Language disorders can affect communication with oral and written thoughts and may lead to misunderstandings in reading, writing, mathematics, and other content areas with listening and comprehension affected.

11. Students need instruction on how to understand and appropriately give commands and requests, e.g., understanding a message's tone or when the intended message is not directly stated but must be logically inferred.

12. Students with communication disorders will often miss out on social cues in classroom, family, and community settings.

13. If students have difficulties filtering out background noises, first practice in a quiet environment, and then gradually add sounds.

14. Auditory closure involves filling in and predicting information from the classroom and conversations. Again, practice step-by-step with reflective inferences, modeling, and support as needed.

15. Use more external tools, e.g., communication notebook, digital recorder, language checklist.

16. Direct skill instruction under the auspices of speech/language pathologists strengthens skills in memory, cognitive reorganization, and language enhancement with receptive and expressive language skills improved.

17. Embed communication skills in classroom routines.

Teaching verbal behavior, a functional analysis of language described by B. F. Skinner (1957) using applied behavior analysis (ABA), has helped many students with autism who have cognitive and language delays learn functional communication. Verbal behavior includes, but is not limited to, speech, sign language, picture exchange, and other forms of augmentative communication. Some terms include *echoic* (vocal imitation), *mimetic* (motor imitation), and *manding* (requests, e.g., command, demand; used for desired items, information, assistance, and more). Production of language then leads to desired effects/positive reinforcement. One way for language to develop is through natural environment training (NET). The term *motivative/establishing operation* (MO/EO; Michael, 1984) refers to conditions of deprivation and satiation that temporarily make certain related behaviors more important and likely. If a student is deprived of something, then that student is more likely to mand for what he or she wants. If something undesired occurs, or causes pain or discomfort, then the child is more likely to mand as well to remove the unpleasant stimulus. Another operant is the tact, verbal behavior under the control of the nonverbal environment. It includes nouns, verbs, adjectives, pronouns, relations, and more (derived from the word, con*tact*). It is vocabulary in the form of expressive recognition and labels. *Intraverbals,* verbal behavior controlled by other people's verbal behavior, are a major component of conversational language. This involves the exchange of information, such as when a student says something that is then reinforced with an appropriate response. Intraverbal responses occur without the concrete objects that are spoken about being physically present, which makes the language much more abstract. Teaching students to mand, tact, echo, and provide intraverbal responses, using prompts and rewards, is part of helping some students with autism and others with communicative needs to develop language.

Source: Adapted from *What Is Applied Verbal Behavior?* by Christina Burk, MA, from www.ChristinaBurkABA.com. Material interpreted by Toby Karten and used with permission of Christina Burk.

IMPROVING BEHAVIOR

Some additional studies concerning behavior and social skills reveal the following:

Gresham, Sugai, and Horner (2001) provided several recommendations for improving the effectiveness of social skills interventions for students with autism spectrum disorders (ASDs). Their recommendations included increased hours of intervention, providing instruction in the natural environment as opposed to pull-out programs, specific matching of the intervention strategy with type of skills and deficits exhibited, and consistency with allegiance rather than abandonment of interventions over time.

Studies from the University of Nottingham found that students with autism are able to interpret animated facial expressions by using sophisticated digital imaging rather than using static images:

> The conclusions of previous research are largely based on methods that present static photographs to participants. Our study indicates that a more accurate measure of the abilities of those with autism can be obtained through the use of sophisticated digital imaging techniques with animated facial expressions. (Back, Ropar, & Mitchell, 2007)

Bellini, Peters, Benner, and Hopf (2007) conducted a meta-analysis of 55 single-subject design studies and discovered that the school setting provides a fertile ground for delivering effective social skills programming. However, they also mention formidable obstacles such as the limited teacher training on how to implement social interventions, along with the quality and quantity of available resources. Overall, the best social skills training occurs in students' natural classroom settings as opposed to alternate locations that do not allow for generalizations and everyday application of the social skills learned.

In addition, behavioral interventions for students with disabilities need to be proactive ones. Teachers who give students a reason to attend, with engaging lessons, often deal with less misbehavior or inattention. That means thinking about what would interest your student, and giving students that connective hook, rather than spewing out information students need to know because it will be on the test! In addition, looking around the room through the eyes of a child often will reveal possible distractions, which can be eliminated through choice seating or even removal of extra visuals from the walls. Positive, respectful, and well-organized classrooms proactively support students' behavioral, social, and emotional needs through modeling, praise, consistency, and more teacher preparation. Here are some behavioral classroom suggestions:

- Establish rules and consequences together with students.
- Encourage and organize integrated play groups for younger students.
- Post rules and expectations.
- Apply rules consistently.
- Reward appropriate behavior with individual behavioral plans and in groups for less competition.
- Observe and record behavior of individual students and cooperative groups.
- Encourage teamwork with assignments for more positive social interactions.
- Understand the reason for misbehavior (functional behavior assessment [FBA]), e.g., antecedents such as lack of attention or misunderstanding of lesson's concepts.
- Conduct weekly reflective class meetings.
- Teach thinking skills for social problem solving.
- Model and demand a respectful environment.
- Be fair; dislike the behavior, not the child!

These books and Web sites offer additional emotional, behavioral, and social resources:

When Sophie Gets Angry—Really, Really Angry, by Molly Bang

Sometimes I'm Bombaloo, by Rachel Vail

The Social Skills Picture Book: Teaching Play, Emotion, and Communication to Children With Autism, by Jed Baker

The Social Skills Picture Book for High School and Beyond, by Jed Baker

Smart Discipline for the Classroom: Respect and Cooperation Restored, by Larry J. Koenig

Positive Classroom Management: A Step-by-Step Guide to Helping Students Succeed, by Robert Giulio

Classroom Management That Works! Research-Based Strategies for Every Teacher, by Robert J. Marzano, Debra Pickering, & Jana S. Marzano

More Inclusion Strategies That Work! Aligning Student Strengths With Standards, by Toby J. Karten

Shouting Won't Grow Dendrites: 20 Techniques for Managing a Brain-Compatible Classroom, by Marcia L. Tate

Dr. Mac's Behavior Management Site: http://www.behavioradvisor.com. Behavioral interventions with online teacher exchange of ideas and strategies

ProTeacher: http://www.proteacher.com/030001.shtml. Offers behavior, classroom management, and discipline plans

Carol Gray' Social Stories: The Gray Center for Social Learning and Understanding: http://www.thegraycenter.org

VISUAL, AUDITORY, AND KINESTHETIC-TACTILE STRATEGIES

Some students with exceptionalities have difficulties responding to and processing sensory information. At times, they are either oversensitive or undersensitive to information coming in. An occupational therapist (OT) often serves students with sensory interventions with programs that include *purposeful playtime.* If a child is overaroused, the therapist uses things like low lights or gentle touches to help him or her deal with upsetting or startling sensations such as sudden loud noises, e.g., a fire drill. If a child is undersensitive, the OT helps the child to be more alert to his or her surroundings and incoming sensations, e.g., through pulling or lifting. These types of sensory difficulties can be evidenced in children with and without developmental delays.

Some studies have also revealed an atypical EEG for certain students when they are exposed to input from two things simultaneously (Carey, 2007).

To be specific, autism spectrum disorders (ASD) are challenging for the classroom teacher and the student due to the diverse needs and sensory issues faced by the student. (Daily, 2007)

Temple Grandin (Grandin & Johnson, 2005), a renowned speaker with autism, tells of her visual sensory strength:

I almost never remember words and sentences from conversations. That's because autistic people think in pictures; we have almost no thoughts running through our heads at all. Just a stream of images. (p. 10)

The following rebus highlights that there are indeed ways of reaching and communicating with students through different sensory channels.

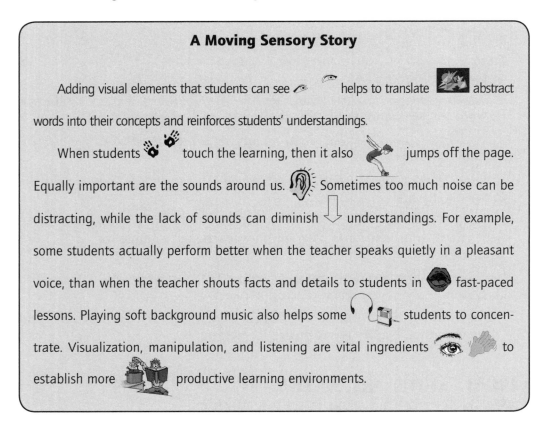

A Moving Sensory Story

Adding visual elements that students can see helps to translate abstract words into their concepts and reinforces students' understandings.

When students touch the learning, then it also jumps off the page. Equally important are the sounds around us. Sometimes too much noise can be distracting, while the lack of sounds can diminish understandings. For example, some students actually perform better when the teacher speaks quietly in a pleasant voice, than when the teacher shouts facts and details to students in fast-paced lessons. Playing soft background music also helps some students to concentrate. Visualization, manipulation, and listening are vital ingredients to establish more productive learning environments.

PUTTING IT ON THE TABLE

This *place setting* involves areas beyond the academics, placing academics on the table, too! Educators who plan to not only teach but also reach their students, need to know about their students' lives. The *other stuff* has an impact upon school achievements and affects the students' general demeanor and progress. This list is a mere tip of that  *educational iceberg* of proactive factors that may surface, helping educators avoid social disasters of *Titanic proportions* by setting the table with

- Establishment, encouragement, and coordination of daily school and home routines with children being privy to all
- Communication and coordination with families to help motivate students
- Being certain that students eat balanced diets
- Teaching the *hidden curriculum,* to help students understand social or behavioral issues, e.g., the unwritten or unspoken school rules like classroom procedures, or acceptable dress, appropriate language to teachers, peers, lunchroom staff, bus drivers, and more

- Teaching of pragmatic language with cooperative learning activities
- Treating students beyond their labels, as people first
- Knowing when to *raise the learning*, e.g., letting students use manipulatives such as Wikki sticks to form geometric shapes and mark their place, using writing templates in content areas of science or social studies if they are not ready to free write yet, writing letters and words in salt trays
- Aligning objectives with students' levels on informal and formal tests; having assessments and grading include observations and classroom performances
- Rewarding of learning strides as well as achievements
- Realistic communication with students about their progress and needs
- Minimizing of frustrations and negativity by not concentrating upon weaknesses, but maximizing competencies, strengths, and opportunities
- Helping students generalize and apply the learning
- Letting students explore the learning through play and cooperative study groups
- Offering discovery opportunities across content areas
- Blending of constructivist-behaviorist philosophies in the blender to achieve a recipe worthy of being called the perfect *"educational daiquiri"*
- Making RTI about *living the research*
- Appreciating *global learners*, but trying to help the *galactic learners* achieve effective realistic landings that focus their attention on the concepts and facts
- Honoring creativity and understanding the students who hear the different drummers and happily march to the tune, but diffusing the academics into their repertoires as well!

IT'S ALL ABOUT CHOICES: DEMOCRATIC EDUCATION

Education is a bit like politics, but on a smaller scale. Democratic education offers students with and without disabilities who live in the United States and many other countries the opportunity to maximize their capabilities to circumvent having personal limitations or disabilities interfere with their learning.

We live in an incredible age of open communication, with people able to share ideas and strategies in countless ways. This amazing age also has made the world much smaller, with increased mobility across continents. Yet views and laws regarding how education should be delivered differ the world over. Some countries only allow teachers to instruct what the government says is appropriate, while other countries reinvent or delete aspects of history. Some nations train their young children to be soldiers before they are young learners. Others do not see the need for students with disabilities to have access to the same education as their peers without disabilities, nor do they offer the services to allow these children to maximize their potentials.

In contrast, the facts and concepts presented in democratic educations—wherever they may occur in the world—acknowledge the principles of learning and then allow and encourage students to become divergent thinkers, ready to make a positive impact upon the world, regardless of their differences.

Democracies on smaller individual classroom and school scales honor choices in the learning environment, with universal designs that maximize

Table 6.4

Democratic School Choice Comparisons		
No Choices	*Giving Bad Choices*	*Offering Good Choices*
No direction by the teacher or administration may lead to unstructured learning with little or no consistency, few opportunities for collaboration, and curriculum underdevelopment. Ultimate outcome could lead to regression and underproductivity. Schools with little or no educational access offered to students with disabilities are robbing their own communities and societies of the *unopened gifts* diversity yields!	An autocratic classroom may be a quieter one, but teacher and administrative dictates are often rotely obeyed, and not internalized by staff and students. Schools and societies who deny their young learners and citizens with disabilities the same basic and equal educational opportunities as their other citizens have quieted the many voices of their communities and nations.	A democratic learning environment allows students and teachers to have responsible voices to construct classroom/ school rules, establish professional development, communicate needs, and further the learning. Schools that offer students with disabilities the appropriate educations with the necessary accommodations and modifications enhance everyone's lifestyles and futures.

everyone's assets as indicated with this chart. The basic idea is to honor equal participation, with both leaders and educators who facilitate and guide but do not dictate. Democratic education offers freedom in thinking for students with and without disabilities.

WELCOME TO THE WORLD!

Yes, the world exists as it does, and that includes the *school world* as well! Whether a student boards a plane and crosses into another time zone, or enters a different neighborhood school or classroom, that student takes him- or herself along as he or she approaches that new environment. That's the only constant that students with and without disabilities can count on. As students mature, they must deal with every situation, even the ones they do not choose, which then become part of their world.

There is no *educational chisel* that allows students to reshape their classroom if they do not like the circumstances presented. On one hand, empowerment is wonderful. Yet on the other hand, acceptance is even more of a valuable lesson. Just as there is no template for inclusion, there is no universal classroom template. Students will meet teachers with a wide range of personalities, varying instructional styles, classroom management rules, testing procedures, expectations, and numerous grading systems.

Students with emotional, behavioral, and social differences may think that some teachers are simply unfair. These students may very well be right! However, here's where reality lands: That's just the way it is sometimes. *Welcome to the world!* Families and well-meaning professionals often try to change things around to remove a student from interacting with Mrs. Ima Notnice or Mr. U. N. Fair, but can that always be done in the real world? Will all of life's obstacles always be removed for students with disabilities, or will they sometimes need to deal with people and things that cannot be changed?

Of course, in an ideal world, unfair practices would not exist, but if a cross-section of occupations were surveyed, it would reveal the inequities that occur in environments outside the school as well. Students with and without disabilities must learn to control the one factor that they can, which is themselves and their reactions to classroom decisions and expectations. Self-determination and learning about self-advocacy is the way that the world can become an even more welcoming one for students with and without disabilities. If they are taught from an early age to believe in their capabilities, then they will be better able to handle the sometimes *uncontrollable world!*

Self-Determination

> Development of knowledge, skills, and beliefs that lead to self-determination is an important consideration throughout the life span from the preschool through the retirement years. (Field, Sarver, & Shaw, 2003)

Without self-determination, school learning occurs on a dead-end street! Without the application and reflection, why bother with teaching or learning skills? With self-determination, learning extends beyond the school years. With self-determination, disabilities are the background, with abilities in the foreground!

Field and Hoffman's (1994) model of self-determination identifies key components of self-determination:

1. Know yourself
2. Value yourself
3. Plan
4. Act
5. Experience outcomes
6. Learn

The table on the next page applies these six principles to academic and social school scenarios. When I showed a student with Asperger syndrome the following table, he affixed his own thoughts to personalize the table's comments even more. For example, when he said, "No, I don't have a lot of friends," he qualified it by adding, "but I'm working on that." He even admitted the importance of staying positive and focused. He summed it up by saying, "Yeah, that's just the way it is sometimes, but I'm learning!"

Throwaway Words to Replace With Positive Self-Talk

"I can't!" becomes "I can!"

"I'm stupid!" becomes "I need to learn more."

"I'll never do this!" becomes "I'll try harder!"

"It's tough!" becomes "How can I understand this?"

"I give up!" becomes "I'll keep pedaling the bike!"

"This is so unfair!" becomes "What can I do to improve this situation?"

Table 6.5

Self-Determination Principles	Academic Scenarios	Social Scenarios
Know yourself	"I really do not understand this stuff about subjects and predicates." vs. "I *guess* I got it."	"I don't have a lot of friends." vs. "The whole class is mean."
Value yourself	"Maybe I can figure it out another way." vs. "I'll never get it!"	"I think that I am a good person." vs. "There's something wrong with me."
Plan	"I'll review it when I get home or maybe I can ask the teacher or my friend in class for some help." vs. "Who has time for this? It's just not important!"	"I need to talk to the guidance counselor in school about this." vs. "Who cares? That's just the way it is!"
Act	"Mr. Blank, could you explain that again?" or "What extra work can I review to understand sentence parts?" vs. "Maybe I'll get lucky on the test!"	"Wow, that counselor gave me some good advice on how to act with other kids." vs. "I'll just stick to myself."
Experience Outcomes	"Wow, sure glad I got some additional help!" vs. "I can't believe I failed, I hope there's a curve on this test!"	"Glad I'm not sitting alone at lunchtime anymore!" vs. "Those kids are still creeps for making me sit by myself!"
Learn	"Next time, I'll ask for help when I don't understand something." vs. "That test was unfair!"	"Now I understand what I need to do." vs. "I can't understand why nothing ever changes!"

The next two tables, 6.6 and 6.7, both titled "Social Stories to Illustrate Cause–Effect Relationships," are similar in content, yet different. Both tables delineate the importance of visuals, along with terse and direct points. Some students with shorter attention spans, perceptual issues, weaker decoding skills, or lower cognitive levels cannot extract the main idea when there are too many extraneous words. The second table has the general gist intended, without the unnecessary elaborative words that are present in the first table. Compare the two tables and then think about this point the next time you design a worksheet or assessment. The boxed visuals and fill-in assessments are also designed to be clutter-free, but *kid friendly*—simply stated, yet effective! The point is to sometimes *get to the point!*

Table 6.6   Social Story to Illustrate Cause–Effect Relationships

1. I wake up in the morning because I set my alarm clock the night before.

2. The first thing I do is brush my teeth and wash my face for proper hygiene.

3. Then I check the weather report in the newspaper, on television, or the computer to decide what clothes are appropriate to wear.

4. I eat a good breakfast, so I have more energy during my day.

5. Then I pack up my schoolbag and take all my homework from the day before, so I can be prepared in class. I take my lunch too!

6. I arrive at the bus stop 5 minutes before the bus is due, so I do not miss my ride to school.

7. When I walk into the school, I smile at teachers and other classmates because it's nice to share cheer with others.

8. Then, I unpack my bag and focus on the chalkboard and listen to announcements about morning assignments and daily activities, so I am prepared to follow the schedule.

9. I raise my hand when I have questions. I'm ready and willing to learn more and more each day, so I can become whatever I choose to be!

Source: Adapted from Karten, T. (2007a). *Inclusion Activities That Work! Grades K–2.* Thousand Oaks, CA: Corwin Press.

Table 6.7   Social Stories to Illustrate Cause-Effect Relationships—Abbreviated Version

1. I wake up in the morning because I set my alarm **clock** the night before.	2. The first thing I do is **brush** my **teeth** and **wash** my **face.**	3. I wear the right **clothes** for the weather.
4. I eat a good **breakfast.**	5. Then I pack up my **schoolbag.**	6. I go to the **bus stop.**
7. When I walk into the school, I **smile.**	8. Then, I unpack my bag and look at the **chalkboard,** and **listen** to the announcements and the teachers.	9. I **raise my hand** when I have questions or need something.

Source: Adapted from Karten, T. (2007a). *Inclusion Activities That Work! Grades K–2.* Thousand Oaks, CA: Corwin Press.

Reproducible 6.1

Student directions: Look at the boxed pictures of the cause-effect social story if you need help to answer these questions. Answer them by yourself, with a peer, or with an adult you respect and trust.

1. If I didn't set the alarm, then _____.

2. When I don't brush my teeth, _____.

3. If I am not dressed properly, _____.

4. Without breakfast, I feel _____.

5. When I forget my homework, _____.

6. If I am late to the bus stop, _____.

7. If I am grumpy in school, _____.

8. When I don't listen to morning instructions, _____.

9. When I am *ap-a-thet-ic* about school (not caring), then _____.

Pictures help us to learn to sequence and organize our thoughts into a written story.

Could you try to write or illustrate your own story with drawings or clip art?

Table 6.9

Source: Karten, T. (2007d). *More Inclusion Strategies That Work! Aligning Student Strengths With the Standards.* Thousand Oaks, CA: Corwin Press.

The Perfect Cup of Coffee

Some of the strategies recommended for *special* learners include slowing the pace, repetition of concepts, and step-by-step instruction. This is accurate, but only some of the time! *Overslowing* or *underpacing* can also cause inattention. Students who are forced to follow the instruction for extended periods of time do not process well through auditory channels with too many lectures, and then they become bored out of their minds or might even act out. Learners of all abilities need to be challenged by performing tasks that stimulate their critical thinking process, which is not always accomplished by oversimplifying the content. It's like adding more hot water to a freshly brewed pot of coffee. Sometimes less is better.

In most cases, it is best to evaluate the task and somehow separate the student's competencies from the completion of the academics, as delineated in the next chart. This next chart, *What I Think About Some Lessons I Heard in Class Today,* is intended for student self-assessment to increase their listening awareness. Younger students or those who think more concretely can dictate responses to teachers or parents. Remember that dilution often dilutes mastery and makes for a lousy cup of coffee!

Pacing is not racing!

Reproducible 6.2

What I Think About Some Lessons I Heard in Class Today

Table 6.10

	Circle the rating, **E**, **M**, or **T**:
Name _____	**E** = Easy "I understand this."
	M = Medium "Not sure about this topic."
Subject _____	**T** = Tough "No clue what's going on!"
	My plan:
Topic_____	If I circled E: *"Since I understand this,*
	_____
	_____
Text Pages and/or Assignment:_____	_____*."*
_____	
Date_____	If I circled M: *"Since I am not sure about this topic,* _____
Other Comments, Thoughts, or Plans:	_____
	_____*."*
_____	If I circled T: *"Since I have no clue what is going on,* _____
_____	_____
_____	_____*."*
_____	

ROLE-PLAYING

We all have roles in our lives, some more than others. You may be a parent, daughter, son, sibling, educator, dancer, artist, athlete, coach, student, and more. We all wear many hats, juggling responsibilities, priorities, and whatever additional *beanbags* are tossed our way. Performance is usually contingent upon factors such as complexity of tasks, time of day, interests, prior experiences, intelligences, and background knowledge. Students with and without disabilities who fall under educators' auspices are no exception in the fast-paced world they inherit.

Sometimes students are dragged to that soccer game, dance recital, or food store, when they'd rather be doing something else. Many students with disabilities do not know how to successfully juggle their many roles and responsibilities. Some are faced with inherited situations. They'd like to be successful students, but maybe there are different levels of support. Sometimes, no one at home can help solidify shaky academics. Perhaps some students need to get a job after school to support their family. Other students with disabilities may have medical, physical, and social issues that interfere with the school agenda.

Disability roles are intricate ones. If a task is too complex, some students with disabilities would rather assume the role of being a bored or disinterested student than admit that they do not understand the complexity of some required tasks or assignments. Differing prior experiences or the lack of background knowledge may result in some students displaying *acting out* behavior. Whether this is a conscious or unconscious decision does not matter because the results are the same. Teachers must realize what the reason for the misbehavior is and *nip it in the bud*, before this role develops *thorns* that negatively impact upon the student, his or her peers, teachers, and families.

Roles involve the demands of others. The way that people look at them influences how some students and adults with disabilities behave. *Juggling roles* is tough, whether you are a child or adult, and whether or not you have a disability as defined and labeled by others! This next graphic organizer asks students to think about themselves in terms of their many roles.

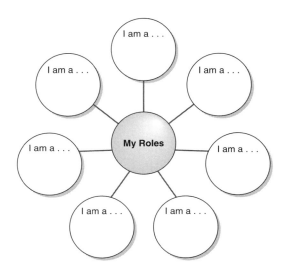

SOCIAL NAVIGATION

A *scale* of emotions will hopefully translate to "Every good boy (and girl) does fine!"

E ntering school can be overwhelming for students with and without disabilities.

G etting the other kids to like you may be more important than what the teacher is saying.

B eing different is not always the way to make friends.

D iscipline is a hard thing to manage for kids and adults of all ages.

F ollowing the social rules sometimes requires direct skill instruction!

Students often have agendas that differ from the rest of their classmates. Some students' realities at home differ from the norm, too. Often students with autism, Asperger syndrome, bipolar disorder, oppositional defiant disorder, attention deficit disorder, obsessive compulsive disorder, and some emotional disturbances have different ways of seeing the world. Yet these students are expected to follow the identical school rules and somehow *fit in*, and make friends with their peers. For students living in safe environments who have good role models with encouraging family support that reinforces school policies, the social, emotional, and behavioral navigations and decisions become easier accomplishments. But even some students with such supports have hard times, too.

Students with and without disabilities need to be taught that it's okay to be different, but it's not okay to think that your differences make you better or inferior to someone else. Students with disabilities need to be taught the *hidden curriculum* of what's acceptable and what's not appropriate in varying situations and environments. When students accept each other for who they are, minus the bullying that some students think helps them establish their superiority, then guiding them onto the road of being happy with who they are and making a few friends along the way becomes an easier task. It's not always about being the most popular, but it's certainly not about letting students *step on* each other. When students accept themselves and get on well with their peers, then classrooms can gel, with everyone being a contributing factor and a team player. Maybe some students will be peer buddies, mentors, or social navigators for students with lower social, emotional, behavioral, or cognitive needs. This type of mentoring definitely begins in the classroom under the appropriate character education programs.

Colleges are now seeing many students with emotional issues as part of their population who would never before have stepped upon the campus:

The transition from high school to college, from adolescence to legal adulthood, can be tricky for any teenager, but for the increasing number of young people who arrive on campus with diagnoses of serious mental disorders—and for their parents—the passage can be particularly fraught. (Clemetson, 2006)

This preceding statement brings much to light, but this following list, partly compiled from the National Alliance on Mental Illness (NAMI, www.nami.org), helps us to realize that social differences do not translate to people with inabilities, but people with incredible potentials! Maybe schools can tap into students' minds and help tomorrow's children one day join this list of achievers whose social, emotional, and behavioral needs differed from the norm, but did not hinder their expressions of greatness. In many cases, the impact that these people have had upon society is truly remarkable.

Some Famous People With Emotional, Social, and Behavioral Differences

Virginia Wolfe	Lionel Aldridge
Abraham Lincoln	Isaac Newton
Judy Garland	Tipper Gore
Janis Joplin	John Forbes Nash
Ludwig van Beethoven	Tennessee Williams
Edgar Allan Poe	Vivien Leigh
Vincent Van Gogh	Charles Dickens
Ernest Hemingway	Marilyn Monroe
Winston Churchill	Patty Duke

To sum up this social section, it is important to realize the following:

Through understanding others we understand ourselves and vice versa. (Cumine, Dunlop, & Stevenson, 1998)

This understanding starts in the early grades and continues beyond when students realize postsecondary choices, such as technical careers, college, and whatever decisions they make to lead productive and socially interactive adult lives. It's always more than just about the academics, but how the student is reacting and gauging the learning, environment, others in the classroom or school, and his or her own feelings of confidence and self-worth. Students are definitely influenced by their understandings of more than just the curriculum. More constructive positive social school experiences are the seeds that will flourish in adult lives, as evidenced by this quote from an anonymous source:

Students will remember how we treated them long after they forget what we taught them.

The next chapter speaks more about choices, collaboration, the impact of factors inside and outside the school environments, and future possibilities for students with disabilities.

PART III

Schools, Families, and the Future

7

Increasing Disability Awareness: Promoting Positive Attitudes for Families and All Communities

Chapter Highlights: This chapter highlights the importance of community, family, and administrative supports. Discussion includes the *other agendas* and how they often positively and negatively influence student performances.

Classroom Connections: Quite often, outside familial and community factors come into play and affect classroom dynamics. This chapter investigates ways to maximize the best instructional and social approaches; collaboration; and communication with students, school staff, and families.

Ways to Differentiate Attitudes: When partnerships are formed, collaborative attitudes improve and multiply students' achievements.

Families of students with and without disabilities are the important catalysts who ensure and propagate more positive educational outcomes for their children. Increased academic and social performances are evidenced when students have *double support* in both the school and home environments.

The following research and perspectives from experts in the field validate the home–school connection to help students maximize their school successes.

Getting Adults on Board With Students by Tying a Bond Between School and Home Environments

Forming a solid, trusting relationship with your child's teacher is the key to a successful inclusive-classroom experience. (Greenspan, 2005)

Factors such as academic confidence, homework completion, increased attendance, improved motivation, and better behavior are influenced [by] supportive families who are involved in their children's educational experiences. (Examining Family Involvement in Support of Youth with Disabilities, 2005)

Parents are effective intervention agents because they can increase the number of hours of interventions that children receive and they can intervene throughout the child's life span. (Sousa, 2007)

Often children with disabilities feel a sense of control instead of a sense of support from their families. Instead, families should be given adequate support, including public support, so that they could offer more independent care to their family members with disabilities. (UN News Centre, 2007)

FAMILIES, WE NEED YOUR HELP!

Without connecting what takes place in a classroom with the home environment, the learning is never anchored to students' lives. Parental/family perspectives often reinforce or negate the progress of students with special needs. Sometimes other *familial agendas* can interfere with a student's school concentration and the completion of in-school and homework assignments. School staff can connect with parents and families via communication through home notes, e-mail, phone calls, classroom visits, report cards, conferences, and more. Communities that offer more resources and services to children with disabilities allow student opportunities for increased independence, higher self-confidence, self-esteem, and emotional support. Often, teachers are not privy to the dreams, hopes, and sometimes frustrations that parents and caregivers experience with children in home environments or the other burdens families might share. In addition, families may need to vent or unburden themselves by emotionally sharing stories with others in similar situations. Many support groups are available for parents and caregivers of students with disabilities. These groups can help adults bond, consult with, and comfort one another. Overall, valuing students with disabilities and their families as integral and contributing people is the way to go! When all adults are on the same game board, then students with and without disabilities are the ones who advance and become winners!

Teachers Helping Families

Lend parents materials for use to implement one of their child's IEP goals, send home learning activities with instructions, materials…communicate with [a] class newsletter…plan workshops…attend parent meetings. (Dardig, 2005)

Help families develop the knowledge and skills to make decisions in the best interests of their children and family. Families of children who are deaf have told us…[they need teachers to] be supportive, understanding, and encouraging. (Sebald & Luckner, 2007)

Families Helping Families

Parents who had gone through a parent mentoring program reported significantly greater positive coping skills and had made greater progress in addressing their problems than did a group of parents who did not participate in the program. (Spitz, 2005)

Families Helping Students

The Individuals with Disabilities Education Act of 2004 wants parents to have meaningful opportunities to participate in the education of their children at school and at home. (Sec. 601 [c] [5] [B])

Families Helping Teachers

Good collaboration and communication with students' families can strengthen the connection between school and home and create a commitment to learning. (Salend & Sylvestre, 2005)

Students Helping Families and Themselves

When students bring home assignments and communicate what happened during their day, then families are not left in the dark, but enlightened on how to help. (Karten, 2005)

Families Helping Students Help Teachers Help Them

If meaningful parent involvement remains a largely unfulfilled promise, the goal of having an effective, high-quality teacher to instruct every student is equally elusive. (Furger, 2005)

Communities and Agencies Supporting Families

It's difficult for parents of children with disabilities to find appropriate health care for their children. Between inadequate transportation, high medical costs and doctors who don't take Medicaid, some children with disabilities can't access the health care they need. (Hunsberger, 2006)

In a perfect world, there would be no such dilemmas, but even though services for students with disabilities and their families have improved, more advancement is always necessary!

Everyone needs to realize that

1. You can describe syndromes, not individual children.

2. Labels are serious things.

3. Children within the same disability group have heterogeneous characteristics.

4. Experts need to be consulted, and many of those experts are the families.

5. More is accomplished when adults (families, community agencies, administration, teachers, all school staff) and students themselves focus on strengths and increased communications and collaborations to build up competencies.

The level of family support for education given to middle school and high school students with disabilities was examined in a 10-year study by the National Longitudinal Transition Study-2, sponsored by the U.S. Department of Education. The sample consisted of 9,230 students who were aged 13 through 17 and receiving special education services, with 82% of the families responding (Newman, 2005).

Some of the findings of the families who responded include the following:

- 80% reported regularly talking with their children about school.
- 76% of the families reported helping with homework at least once a week.
- 20% of the families provide homework assistance as often as five or more times per week.
- Approximately 75% of the families attend school meetings and conferences.
- About a third of the families surveyed wanted more involvement in the planning and decisions made concerning their children's IEPs.

The survey also determined that lower levels of family involvement result in more negative youth behaviors. In addition, students who are African American have families who are usually more involved with helping at home, but are less likely to attend IEP meetings or be involved with the school. The importance of parent groups to provide more information, strategies, emotional bonding, and continued focus at home and school was also revealed. However, ironically, research has found that only one quarter of schools offer support or parent groups to families of students with disabilities. Fewer than half of schools report offering parents of students with disabilities consistent weekly or monthly information about curriculum or instruction (Schiller et al., 2003). The survey also discovered that more invitations and additional school efforts are necessary for the families of students with emotional disturbances or mental retardation to be involved in school-based events and activities. If families are to be partners, then schools need increased proactive measures to allow families to share the knowledge and be equipped with more tools to support educators' efforts. More collaboration will benefit all!

This next quote sums it up best:

We must do everything in our power to protect the rights of persons with disabilities, using families to achieve this goal. (UN News Centre, 2007)

Additional Resources for Information and Family Support

Understanding All Minds: Differences in Learning: http://www.all kindsofminds.org. Mel Levine, MD, is a developmental pediatrician who founded All Kinds of Minds in 1995 with Charles R. Schwab to translate the latest research on how children learn into programs, products, and services that help students struggling in school become more successful learners. This Web site offers help to families, educators, clinicians, and kids to understand and manage learning issues.

The National Association of School Psychologists: http://nasponline .org. Has resources and information for families and educators.

Charles and Helen Schwab: http://www.schwablearning.org. Family-friendly resources, support, and latest educational practices about learning disabilities.

Learning Disabilities Online: http://www.ldonline.org. Web site that offers information and links on learning-related issues.

Harvard Family Research Project: http://www.gse.harvard.edu. Latest professional information, research review, and best practices advocated.

Building Partnerships Between Families, Schools, and Communities: http://www.bridges4kids.org/. Offers resources and information to families of children with disabilities on concerns about education, legislation, and services.

Center for Effective Collaboration and Practice: http://cecp.air .org/families_broad.asp. Offers information and research about effective practices for children and youth with emotional and behavioral problems.

Kid Support: http://www.kid-power.org. For families with cerebral palsy and other disabilities.

National Resource Center for Parents with Disabilities—Through the Looking Glass (TLG): http://www.lookingglass.org/parents. TLG provides information, training, and consultation to parents and family members with disabilities and professionals nationally and internationally. It offers assistance and guidance on parenting with a disability to parents and families with physical, visual, hearing, intellectual disabilities, and other medical conditions.

Asperger Syndrome Education Network (ASPEN): http://www.aspennj .org. Provides families and individuals whose lives are affected by autism spectrum disorders (Asperger syndrome, pervasive developmental disorder-NOS [not otherwise specified], high-functioning autism) and non-verbal learning disabilities with support, education about the disorders, and advocacy for appropriate education.

AD/HD Information Library: http://www.help4adhd.org/en/living. Offers parenting advice to parents and families of children with AD/HD.

The Arc of the United States: http://www.thearc.org. This organization is committed to the welfare of all children and adults with mental retardation and their families.

United Cerebral Palsy (UCP): http://www.ucp.org. Information on cerebral palsy and advocate for the rights of persons with any disability. UCP's mission is to advance the independence, productivity, and full citizenship of people with disabilities.

Family Resource Website: http://family-friendly-fun.com/index.htm. Fun, health, special needs, and family life with disabilities. Offers activities and resources.

TASH: http://www.tash.org/index.html. International association that promotes inclusive communities through research, education, and advocacy.

Internet Special Education Resources: http://www.iser.com/. Offers information for parents, family members, caregivers, friends, educators, and medical professionals who interact with children who have disabilities.

The Center for Family, School, and Community—Education Development Center: http://www2.edc.org/fsc. Designs professional development programs that improve teaching and assessment, enhances the leadership capacity of district and school administrators, engages families in their children's education, and assists with community-building efforts.

The Council for Exceptional Children (CEC): http://www.cec.sped .org. Teachers, administrators, students, families, paraprofessionals, and related support service staff are provided with professional development and resources to improve educational outcomes for individuals with exceptionalities, students with disabilities, and/or the gifted. CEC advocates for best practices in the classroom, communities, and legislation.

Hearing Loss Association of America, Self Help for Hard of Hearing People (SHHH): http://www.shhh.org

The American Foundation for the Blind (AFB): http://www.afb.org

COMMUNITY ACTIONS AND REACTIONS

The ultimate goal is for persons with disabilities to live independent and productive lives. This includes nondiscriminatory treatment in schools and communities. Community integration involves access to legal systems, health care, employment, recreation, sports, and more. Communities that value the strengths of all its members are offering maximum integration potentials for children with disabilities when they are younger and for their transition into adulthood. When open arms are offered, negative and counterproductive disability attitudes are put aside.

Students with disabilities and their families are often aware of the condescending attitudes and unwanted stares they may receive from others. The more integration there is, the more acceptance is possible! Why can't a boy who is in a wheelchair go kayaking with his Boy Scout troop? Students with limited vision can be artists, too! A teenager with Down syndrome can be the prom queen, while students with learning differences most certainly can qualify for the honor roll! Societal doors are now open even wider for children with disabilities to maximize their potentials so they can achieve not only the same results as their peers, but have opportunities to maybe even surpass them! Hopefully, one day soon, differences associated with disabilities will be viewed as ordinary in schools and communities.

Honoring present and possible contributions of students with disabilities communicates a strong message. *Subtracting* the skewed views *adds* up to an accepting community that *multiplies* and accents the positive, instead of *dividing* and separating students. Thrusting preconceived opinions about disabilities on others hurts a child or adult who may already feel like less than a whole person. The next table offers a mathematical analogy about attitudes toward disabilities that hopes to *exponentially erase illogical negativity*.

AGENDAS BEYOND

Administrative leadership and guidance for teachers instructing students with special needs requires more than expelling data at teachers and telling them we need to raise students' test scores. Teachers also need to realize how legislative demands influence many administrative decisions. This trickles down to classroom decisions that involve

- Ongoing financial and academic commitments to staff
- Encouraging collaborative relationships with common planning time
- Investigating and promoting research-based interventions
- Developing subject-based teams
- Encouraging professional-based learning communities
- Respecting teachers' needs and experiences
- Focusing on growth rather than teacher conformity
- Listening to the data, but not letting the data control the curriculum
- Acknowledging students' strengths, e.g., music, art, more physical movement
- Honest communications meant to help each other and bridge students' skills
- Modeling a *team mentality* with parity for all staff
- Teachers and administrators having respect for each other's days and conundrums

We want teachers to habitually examine their beliefs and practices and then move toward affirming, modifying, or changing them as necessary to help all students learn. (Kise, 2006, p. 15)

Table 7.1

Disability Operations	Possible Computative Results
	Decide which computations you'd like to implement in your classrooms and communities!
Addition of the facts	More informed classroom decisions and community involvement with teachers and community members who are knowledgeable about different disabilities. Teachers can find ways to differentiate peer attitudes. It adds up to a better *educational equation* with the addition of students with disabilities to all lessons and extracurricular activities. Communities can develop and maximize the competencies of children with disabilities by proactively adding everyone to the agenda with inviting attitudes, supports, and resources to accommodate differing physical, emotional, and developmental needs with sensitivities, resources, and support available for full inclusion of students and their families.
Subtraction of skewed views	Better outlooks by all when the negativity is removed and replaced with positive views in communities and schools. Subtraction is the obverse property of addition, meriting and advocating the deletion of all put-downs!
Multiplication of the positive attitudes	Receptive teachers, school staff, supportive families, and community members who instill feelings of self-confidence within students with disabilities and their families multiply the academic and social experiences!
Division of students and families	Societal losses when students and their families are divided, separated, or excluded from peers, learning, and future potentials for school and community integrations. Everyone in society is entitled to full participation with cohesive school and community attitudes that spell out acceptances and maximum opportunities for inclusion!

Administrations who offer continuing and pragmatic professional development to their staff are valuing and respecting teachers' experiences. This can be accomplished through the implementation of the following:

a. Teacher-generated professional development topics at school and district levels with appropriate in-services and workshops offered on staff development days. Independent professional study related to specific, ongoing student and teacher needs with districts offering teacher credit and recognition for continuing education hours

b. Grade-level study groups to handle curriculum concerns as they impact educators' classes. Then allow these groups to share key findings with other staff members, e.g., teacher blogs, educational reading groups, committees to adopt a new textbook, conducting staff development workshops

c. Curriculum groups to plan ways to differentiate instruction but still honor the content standards

d. *Ability teaching groups* that share success stories and promote an *I love teaching* attitude to replace the sometimes nightmarish stories shared in the faculty room

e. Monthly time slotted into scheduled faculty meeting for cooperative teachers to plan upcoming lessons and to discuss students' progress

f. Promoting consistent collaboration, cooperation, and collegial respect

g. Of course, offering food at faculty meetings—this allows teachers to *digest* everything better!

TOASTING TEACHERS

Clink! Clink! Congratulations are in order; the children with disabilities you have included in your classrooms have achieved measurable academic and social gains. You deserve to be toasted! Now what is the reward these teachers receive for their countless hours of *doing the right thing,* attending conferences and planning sessions, and giving those extra hours to match the needs of the children who are assigned to their care? Quite often, the reward is that the administration and instructional support teams say that these teachers get to do it all over again next year!

The teachers who refuse to make accommodations and modifications and try their best to do an unacceptable job are told that they will not have students with disabilities included in their classes. Now which group is the winner here? The teachers who are not instructing students with disabilities in their classrooms are certainly the ones who are missing out. The students with disabilities and their teachers are on the winning team!

However, the following focus questions need to be discussed in many school districts:

- Is the practice of repeatedly assigning students with disabilities to the same teachers a beneficial one?
- Will the teachers who give 150% each year eventually burn out?
- How can other colleagues be trained to *step up to the plate* to be teachers of all students?
- Should teacher requests from families of students with disabilities always be honored?
- Can we find a fine line between *toasting teachers* and *burning the toast?*
- How can supervisors and administration support all of their teachers and related staff to better educate, accommodate, and accordingly modify instructional strategies to serve the needs of all children?
- How can in-services and more staff development benefit school personnel?
- What specific type of training and support do educators, related staff, and students need to maximize students' assets?

- How can a team mentality be brought to all of the staff?
- How can all students with disabilities achieve social, behavioral, emotional, and academic gains in inclusive classrooms?

ACKNOWLEDGE THE PACE: PRESS THE PAUSE BUTTON!

Teachers are a unique breed of people in terms of their daily schedules and work conditions. Very often, educators are accustomed to existing in a *classroom vacuum.* For the majority of their day, some teachers only converse with students whose ages can range from 4 years to more than 50 years younger than they are! Students with disabilities present unique challenges that often require 1,000% attention. An educator's day can be a hectic and fast-paced one! On the whole, teachers sometimes just need to be allowed to *press the pause button*—to chill, reflect, and breathe *like a grown-up!*

Entering a teacher's classroom, some of these daily frustrations are often evident. The speech/language pathologist or another professional can walk into the classroom to try to chat or communicate his or her concerns, but the conversation isn't a flowing one, since it is interrupted by whatever is happening at that given moment. Quite often, school districts allow educators a half an hour to eat; go to the bathroom; and then, if there's time, wash their hands, too! Whew! Prep times are often spent making copies, organizing the next lesson, speaking to a coteacher or colleague, calling a parent, making a personal phone call to arrange a doctor's appointment, conferencing with a supervisor, and whatever else that particular day may present.

Administrators who acknowledge this conundrum can then acknowledge this hurried pace by treating the educators as professionals and offering them a chance to *press the pause button* with more planning time, additional resources, and more recognition:

- Spontaneous coverage if there's a substitute available in the district or building
- Additional planning time with colleagues during the day
- Teaching the lesson to the class while the educator has release time
- Extra opportunities for in-service days and planning sessions
- More funding for resources from the school budget
- Extra smiles and praise!

8

Future Horizons for People With Disabilities

Chapter Highlights: The purpose of this last chapter is to emphasize that positive approaches include the right attitudes by all. The importance of matching learning to life, developing and continuing ideas, and capitalizing on everyone's strengths is highlighted.

Classroom Connections: Discussion of realistic teaching, feedback, social strides, and academic mobility.

Ways to Differentiate Attitudes: When commitments are made to students' potentials, then additional gains become evident. Maximizing and differentiating attitudes include respect for all.

COMMITMENTS TO STUDENTS' ACHIEVEMENTS

Competent students translate into productive employees and citizens. Bright horizons for individuals with disabilities can exist if students are taught at an early age that everyone has similarities and differences. It's okay that abilities differ, as long as attitudes *toward* abilities do not limit and prejudge potential capabilities.

If for no other reasons than selfish ones, treating students with disabilities the right way and educating them beside their peers benefits society as a whole. Future health care costs and disability payments are lowered when students are taught at an early age to be independent and productive. Under educators' auspices, future independence and lifelong productivity and competencies are attainable goals that are well worth reaching!

Education is crucial for peers, communities, teachers, family members, caregivers, and students themselves. Teachers and all persons in school settings need to encourage and teach students how to believe in themselves, regardless of the sometimes negative messages or attitudes of others. Students with disabilities need to distinguish condescending attitudes from constructive criticisms and move forward from that point onward. Growth is essential, while put-downs are counterproductive, not only for the person or student with the disability, but the whole community as well. A person with a disability becomes society's issue and a family's burden when he or she is not given the tools, strategies, and access to the same opportunities afforded to the child's school contemporaries. We *positively* need to concentrate on the *positive!*

Karen Flippo, the chief executive of the National Association of Councils on Developmental Disabilities, has stated, "There is a misconception that people with disabilities can't work" (DeFord, 2006). IDEA has guaranteed public school access for students with disabilities, but that has not always translated to higher adult employment rates. Formal education training and sensitive perceptions about disabilities for students with and without disabilities begin in school systems, and then extend beyond the school years, into productive employment choices.

We as educators must be committed to students' achievements. This involves not only increasing academic achievements, but also applying school learning and earlier training to productive career choices for students of all cognitive, emotional, and physical levels.

Some recent changes in career and technical education (CTE), formerly called vocational education, include emphasizing hands-on applied learning with reforms that are recognizing the crossover potential between CTE and academic classes. Offered courses range from auto welding to culinary arts and robotics! Since the Perkins Act was reauthorized, which in part requires that education in academic and technical skills be provided for students with disabilities, schools that receive funding must have state-approved programs that align with high-skilled, high-demand, and high-wage jobs (Gustin, 2006).

Structural and attitudinal barriers still exist, but Tony Coelho, chairman of the President's Committee on Employment of People with Disabilities, poignantly sums it up with the following quote: "Finally, those of us with disabilities must believe in ourselves. A positive mindset and self-advocacy can be our most powerful assets. Success is contagious. Day by day, one person at a time, we are tackling the barriers blocking the road to employment."

Companies such as Microsoft, Dell, IBM, Albertsons, McDonald's, JC Penney, Coca-Cola, DuPont, Toys "R" Us, Lowe's, and Marriott are to be commended for their consistent support of individuals with disabilities in the job market. All of society benefits when individuals with disabilities can maximize their assets through gainful employment opportunities. Quite often the accommodations needed in the workplace are minor ones such as adjusting the height of chairs, tables, or the towel dispenser in the bathroom. Having hands-free phones, enlargement of the print on office memos, adjustable work schedules/hours, or voice synthesizers are examples of accommodations someone with a disability may need to succeed on the job. Other more severe disabilities may require supportive employment with job coaches and community-based service providers to teach and train individuals with appropriate and ongoing support.

Some online sites to assist individuals with disabilities with employment include the following:

The Job Accommodation Network: www.jan.wvu.edu

Hire Disability Solutions: http://www.hireds.com

United Cerebral Palsy: http://www.ucp.org/

Just One Break: http://www.justonebreak.com

AFB Career Connect: http://www.afb.org

Hearing Loss Association of America: http://www.shhh.org

Disability Work: http://disabilitywork.com

The following table outlines possible careers from A to Z and some descriptions of those careers for students in upper elementary and intermediate grades. It encourages students to investigate and learn more about different job possibilities. It attempts to connect students' futures to the very school subjects they are taking now, encouraging them to realize that careers and job choices are not exclusively decided when they are older. It's all part of a journey from the early school grades and onward as students transition academically and emotionally throughout the grades!

Matching Learning to Life

Table 8.1

Occupations from A–Z	Something about it	More I learned	School subjects that would help a person in this career or occupation
Archaeologist	Digs deeply for evidence		
Barber	Has style		
Chef	Combines ingredients		
Disc jockey	Communicates to an audience		

Occupations from A–Z	Something about it	More I learned	School subjects that would help a person in this career or occupation
ENGINEER	Applies science to life		
Firefighter	Handle hot issues to heroically save lives		
Hairdresser	Keeps schedules, listens to clients, and offers style		
Interior decorator	Plans and designs home décor and furnishings		
Journalist	Writes and communicates the news and world events		
K–9 Officer	Teaches discipline and trains his or her companion for multiple purposes		
Lawyer	Handles people's objections, researches laws, defends and prosecutes		
Mechanic	Knows how the parts make up the whole, step-by-step, fixing cars, trucks, buses, trains, planes, and more		
Nurse	Cares for others in need in hospitals, homes, and other facilities		

(Continued)

Table 8.1 (Continued)

YOUR CAREER OUTLOOK *Occupations from A–Z*	*Something about it*	*More I learned*	*School subjects that would help a person in this career or occupation*
Other occupation I would choose			
Podiatrist	Helps people to put their best foot forward		
Queen	Relates to her subjects		
Roofer	Starts with the top☺		
Sanitary engineer	Takes away unneeded items in neighborhoods		
Surgeon	Dissects details to diagnose, operate, and heal people		
Tailor	Makes alterations and cleans clothes		
Undertaker	Cares for the deceased and their families who grieve		
Veterinarian	Doctor for animals		
Web designer	Communicates information online with computer sites		
X-ray technician	Takes pictures of the insides of people's bodies		
Youth director	Guides young students		
Zoologist	Works in animal care, habitat management, data analysis		

Students and adults can review the following sites for more general information about types of careers:

Careers and Education: http://www.careersandeducation.com, http://disabilitywork.com

JOB: Just One Break: http://www.justonebreak.com

Career and Technical Education: http://www.ed.gov/about/offices/list/ovae/pi/cte/index.html

HEATH Resource Center—Online Clearinghouse on Postsecondary Education for Individuals with Disabilities: http://www.heath.gwu.edu

Positive Steady Growth

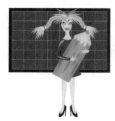

Schools are not about excelling at every subject or getting 90–100% on each assessment. They are about the journey. It's about the growth students with all ability levels can and will achieve. When educators, students, families, and administrators adapt and apply the attitude that this is an *evolutionary process,* much more will be accomplished.

Students with varying emotional, physical, cognitive, and sensory levels are at times frustrated if they do not achieve the same grades as their peers. Families are at times discouraged and disappointed to see their children struggle. Teachers and administrators want to see students obtain yearly progress, yet at times progress is so gradual that it cannot be seen or measured, or it may occur after that particular marking period has ended! Seeds will grow and flourish. However, watching and hurrying seeds along does not change their need for the right conditions and the time to mature. It is sometimes about the virtues of patience and perseverance. Schools are the students' incubators!

A recent newsletter article I wrote, "Children and Butterflies," which follows, compares this whole school journey to the stages of a butterfly. Each stage or step must be mastered, without any omissions. Students with disabilities go through their own metamorphoses. We need to stick to the educational course as well, yet let the *butterflies* be free to soar!

Children and Butterflies

The colorful butterfly emerged, and with a charming natural poise soared into the accepting sky, gracing the world with its presence. People may forget that at first this magnificent butterfly was an egg, then a crawling caterpillar, and a pupa before it became that magical butterfly. As we proceed into the school years, we can learn many lessons from the butterfly. It's all about stages. Students with special needs are a bit like that butterfly, gradually evolving into the young adults they will become, prepared to grace the world with their presence. Educators, families, assistants, related staff, administrators, legislators, and the students themselves are the catalysts in this evolutionary process. With the proper interventions, environments, experiences, and mindsets, students with exceptional needs will also experience successful metamorphoses.

It seems like an easy ideal scenario, but as we can all attest to with our own stories, it's not always that simple. That swinging pendulum of discriminatory attitudes, fluctuating practices, and bureaucratic demands sometimes interferes with and may even thwart the flight of that delicate butterfly. If we succumb to the negativity, the flight will not only be delayed, but permanently postponed.

How wonderful it is that expectations for students with special needs have been raised! They are no longer out of the *accountability radar*, but are now required to meet, reach, and even surpass the standards with the application of research-based interventions. This requires more staff development with personnel who are equipped and trained with the knowledge and strategies. We as a profession need to help students with exceptionalities show what they know by focusing upon their strengths. Improvements in academic, social, physical, and perceptual skills are most definitely part of a process that, as depicted with the butterfly example, will occur in stages.

If there was a magical *educational wand* to make this progress happen quickly, we'd all order several dozen of those wands from the latest **We Say It Works** catalog. As we know, there are no wands, but there are research-based interventions that have proven, effective track records. An occupational or speech therapist, special education teacher, general education teacher, guidance counselor, learning consultant, administrator, family member, and those in the community are watching the butterflies soar. It's a great time for education and the exceptional learners who will soon soar to higher acclaims than we could have ever imagined just a few decades ago!

Let's continually prepare for and share the successes together. We need to respond to the issues with the knowledge, strategies, and interventions to help all exceptional children to soar to new heights! In the interim, here's to *educational entomology!*

Realistic Teaching, Feedback, and Academic Mobility

Help is fine, but help should not define students with disabilities. Independence is gained when students are taught strategies and are then able to appropriately apply them in the correct situations. Teachers who share this knowledge with students and families allow for academic mobility through realistic feedback.

The trick is not getting the kids into support classes, but how to get them to leave [them]. (Matthews, 2006)

Let's stop looking for disabilities and just teach the children what they need to know. (Delpit, 2006)

This includes

- Teaching study skills
- Raising expectations
- Helping students to recognize their strengths and realize that they are not average or below average in all areas
- Giving students and families time and reassurance

- Encouraging students and families to make a commitment to school
- Increasing students' and educators' self-awareness and self-determination to be a master of the curriculum
- Differentiating student comments with specific constructive feedback
- Teaching students how to be independent
- Supporting families with resources and strategies to help their children

Negativity about students' abilities and discouraging attitudes thwart growth. Educators, administrators, students, families, and communities can be the fans and coaches who realistically praise and encourage students with disabilities to possess positive attitudes about past, current, and future successes and opportunities. Even when students, adults, families, or even educators make the *wrong play,* there's a huge lesson to be learned there as well. The answer remains: positive, steady growth for all!

R-E-S-P-E-C-T

Aretha Franklin sang it loudly and clearly! We're all in this game together. When we give each other emotional and academic support, then a great deal of progress can be accomplished. Quite often, teachers, administrators, families, and students become distracted and sidetracked by other agendas that take them off the educational course. It's not about personalities; it's about respect.

Respect for

1. People: students, families, teaching colleagues, support staff, administrators

2. Curriculum: content to be taught

3. Strategies: how to reach and teach the students (It's not just about the curriculum.)

4. Abilities: believing in what students can do

5. Strengths: yours, mine, ours, and theirs!

6. Education: research-based or peer-reviewed interventions

7. Past: where students have been

8. Present: current levels

9. Future: endless possibilities!

Universal Design for Learning (UDL) Stamps for Achieving Educational Success

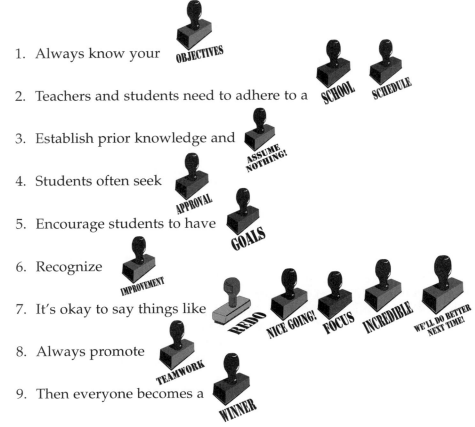

1. Always know your   OBJECTIVES

2. Teachers and students need to adhere to a   SCHOOL   SCHEDULE

3. Establish prior knowledge and   ASSUME NOTHING!

4. Students often seek   APPROVAL

5. Encourage students to have   GOALS

6. Recognize   IMPROVEMENT

7. It's okay to say things like   REDO   NICE GOING!   FOCUS   INCREDIBLE   WE'LL DO BETTER NEXT TIME!

8. Always promote   TEAMWORK

9. Then everyone becomes a   WINNER

The Application

All of those educational UDL stamps advocate obvious strategies, yet even professionals with years of experience sometimes forget to consistently apply them, myself included! It's not intentional; it happens or sometimes *doesn't happen* in the course of a school day. Strategies such as establishing prior knowledge, using task analysis with more difficult concepts, or implementing concrete and kinesthetic approaches to solidify the abstract are not consistently applied to every lesson. Anxious teachers who move on to the next unit may create a *learning shuffle,* with too many concepts thrust upon the class. The concept of *less is better* then becomes lost! Students with disabilities in classroom settings are sometimes the unfortunate recipients of this de-application of the instructional strategies.

Instructional strategies that are consistently applied advocate the best teaching practices. We as educators just sometimes forget to *practice what we preach.* While presenting a workshop on inclusion almost a decade ago, I mentioned that diversity is a huge issue in our schools. *Sidebar: Surprise! Diversity is still a big issue!* I affirmed to the audience how educators' visuals, illustrations, and literature should represent and honor the contributions of people from a variety of cultures. Many of the professionals in the audience strongly agreed. Then I moved on to the topic of collaboration and compared coteaching and collaboration to a marriage. My overheads depicted pairs of people working together, such as George Burns and Gracie Allen, Laurel and Hardy, and Felix and Oscar from the *Odd Couple.* I was going for the humor here, but forgot to apply what I had just mentioned about cultural diversity. Were the photos I showed to my audience culturally diverse ones? Definitely not! I forgot to practice what I preach and was thankfully reminded of this by a participant's evaluation comment. Consequently, for the next presentation my collaboration visuals included the Cosby family, the Supremes, John Lennon and Yoko Ono, Lucy and Ricky Ricardo, and the Simpsons, too!

Reaching for the Stars

It would be wonderful if one day there were no arbitrary boundaries or hidden yet preconceived societal mores. Corporations need to hire more people with disabilities, giving them opportunities to display their competencies. Students need access to the same knowledge. Society as a whole, nationally and globally, needs to improve its way of thinking. One fifth of the population in the United States has a disability, while 70% of all the potential workforce with a disability are not working (www.census.gov, www.ilr.cornell.edu/edi/ disabilitystatistics/). These statistics disproportionately cry out for changes! ADA gives workers opportunities and accommodations, yet schools must begin with rigorous educational training that allows students with disabilities to be viable and competent adult workers.  Disability sensitivities and appropriate academic courses in school settings are where the changes can and must begin.

In conclusion, there are no conclusions but the ones we believe. Possibilities for maximizing students' assets are as endless as the number of stars in the sky. How beautifully we can help them to shine!

Appendix A

Differentiating and Assessing Attitudes With Ability Awareness Rubrics

Rubrics can be used as scoring scales and a description of expectations in a variety of subjects or assignments. The following rubrics try to gauge attitudes toward students with disabilities. Teachers distribute rubrics to their students, outlining requirements for assignments. Well, how about rubrics for teachers, too? This first rubric asks teachers and school staff to reflect upon their own attitudes toward students with disabilities. Indeed it is true that students will remember how you treated them, long after they forget what you taught them! Attitudes live on a *street of mutual respect* among school staff, families, peers, community members, and students themselves. Where do you fall on these following rubrics?

Dis*ability* Awareness Teacher/School Staff Rubric
(Circle one choice in each row)

Lower Expectations (LE) 1 point for each circled in the column below	Minimal Expectations (ME) 2 points for each circled in the column below	Exceeds Expectations (EE) 3 points for each circled in the column below
Thinks that students with disabilities are in some way not as capable as students without disabilities	Thinks that students with disabilities can have limited achievements, but are still not comparable to those students without disabilities	Thinks that a student with a disability is just as capable or may have even more competencies than peers without disabilities
Focuses on the students' weaknesses. Thinks difficulties will hinder classroom progress with academics and peers	Aware of students' weaknesses, but thinks students can achieve a few academic and social strides	Concentrates on students as individuals, looking beyond the disabilities toward student strengths. Teaches students compensatory strategies to achieve school successes
Automatically deletes more difficult assignments for classified students	Allows the student to try some activities, but has lower expectations	Exhibits high expectations for all students, establishing prior knowledge to determine instructional levels
Sees the students' disabilities in the foreground, without realizing that the disability is just one part of an individual's makeup	Knows that students with disabilities have individual personalities, but thinks that the disability is the primary focus	Teaches and communicates with individual students, using people-first language and behaviors that focus on the student, not the disability
Thinks students with disabilities will not achieve levels of independence and need only functional skills in school settings. Thinks their instruction interferes with the learning needs of students with higher levels	Wants to help students with disabilities, but thinks that the classroom modifications are actually harmful since they will enable the student, thereby not allowing them to eventually achieve an adult level of independence	Believes that students with disabilities will lead productive, independent lives as members of the community when given the proper accommodations, supports, and training in school settings
Believes that students with disabilities need to be educated in separate settings with different curriculums from peers without disabilities	Thinks some students with disabilities can be mainstreamed into regular education classes for certain subjects, but does not want to make adjustments in their lessons and grading	Gladly includes all students with disabilities in classroom lessons, adopting a mindset that the general education classroom should be the first viable placement option with appropriate supports in place

Scores:

6–10	Reevaluate your attitude
11–14	Better
15–18	Congratulations, you get it!

Source: Adapted from Karten, T. (2007c). *Inclusion Activities That Work! Grades 6–8.* Thousand Oaks, CA: Corwin Press.

Disability Awareness Parent and Guardian Rubric (Circle one choice in each row)

Lower Level of Acceptance (LA) ↓ 1 point for each circled in the column below	Medial Level of Acceptance (MA) ← → 2 points for each circled in the column below	High Level of Acceptance (HA) ↑ 3 points for each circled in the column below
Thinks their child is a burden, resenting the interference child presents to their family dynamics and other social relationships	Realizes extra responsibility their child demands. May isolate other family members and social contacts	Acknowledges the unique needs their son or daughter presents and embraces their child as an integral contributing family member
Skewed view of child's current performance level	Accepts child's current performance level	Accepts child's current performance level and envisions future potentials and strides
Blames self and others for child's lack of successes, with a level of hostility toward school personnel	Complacent about child's performance level and indifferent toward school personnel	Supportive of child's current level and appreciative toward school personnel's efforts. Partners with teachers
Ashamed of child and somewhat guilt ridden	Indifferent about child	Proud of son or daughter
Actively looking for a *cure*	Hoping for a miraculous change or reversal	Acceptance of disability and ways to attain future strides
Shattered self-esteem	Fragile self-esteem	Good self-esteem
Disinterest or disengagement in child's life with some avoidance of parental/ guardian involvement	Performs necessary parental/ guardian tasks to maintain child's health and daily needs	Thinks of innovative and positive ways to perform parental/guardian tasks to joyously be part of child's life

This is a complicated rubric to conceive since no one can imagine what it's like to be the parent or guardian of a child with a disability. Levels of support and degree of severity of each disability will most often influence parental/guardian attitudes. Again, it's difficult to be on the outside looking in on other people's lives without experiencing the daily agenda, complications, interruptions, and triumphs presented. It is hoped that by using this rubric, many self-reflective insights will be gained by families.

Scores:

7–10	Need more help with adjustments
11–14	You are dealing with situations
15–21	Total acceptance and an embracing attitude

Disability Awareness Student Rubric
(Circle one choice in each row)

Poor Self-Image (PSI) *1 point for each circled in the column below* ↓	*Fair Self-Image (FSI)* ←——→ *2 points for each circled in the column below*	*High Self-Image (HSI)* ↑ *3 points for each circled in the column below*
Refuses to try new learning activities	Scared to try new learning activities	Eager to attempt new learning activities
Strongly influenced by the way others think or act toward them, feeling inadequate most times	Somewhat influenced by how others act, usually wanting to please others	Aware of how others act toward them, but confident in own abilities
Thinks about self as a failure because of differences and limitations	Realizes differences and limitations interfere with progress	Proud of achievements despite existing differences, wants to circumvent limitations
Isolates self from others, fears rejection	Aware of others, but shy	Thinks it's okay and worthwhile to become involved with others
Puts self down for academic and social failures	Sometimes upset by academic and social failures	Understands life's *ups and downs* and learns from experiences
Wishes things would change	Wants to be better	Realizes and accepts own levels of achievements
No independence exhibited	Tries some tasks on his or her own	Eager to forge ahead to be independent, asking for guidance as needed

Scores:

    7–11   Think more of yourself!

    12–16   You're on the right road!

    17–21   You're the top!

Dis*ability* Awareness Peer Rubric
(Circle one choice in each row)

Lousy Outlook (LO) ↓ *1 point for each circled in the column below*	*Fair Outlook (FO)* ↔ *2 points for each circled in the column below*	*Mature Outlook (MO)* ↑ *3 points for each circled in the column below*
If I'm friends with *that kid*, people will think I'm weird!	I guess I could talk to *that kid*, but only in school!	I think I'd like *that kid* to be my friend!
I have no time to help someone like that! No way is he working with me on this project. He'll mess it up!	I understand that she has difficulties, so I'll try to help her sometimes. Just don't make me do it all of the time.	Everyone needs help sometimes, including me! She can definitely work with me on this project and add her thoughts.
How could anyone look or act like that? She's strange!	It's not right to poke fun at someone because of what he or she can or cannot do.	I'm going to stop those mean kids who are teasing that boy or girl, just because he or she is different
I feel sorry for that kid. What a lousy life!	I wonder if I could help that kid!	I admire that kid's courage and perseverance.
I hope that *weirdness* never happens to me!	I'm curious about what happened to that kid and if that could affect me.	It's not about me!

Scores:

5–7   Just what are you thinking?

8–11   Getting better

12–15   You're a true friend!

Disability Awareness Community Rubric
(Circle one choice in each row)

NIMBY Attitude (not in my backyard) 1 point for each circled in the column below	IMBYS Attitude (in my backyard sometimes) 2 points for each circled in the column below	WIMBY Attitude (welcomed in my backyard) 3 points for each circled in the column below
No way do I want that family living next door to me!	I guess it's okay if they move here, but just don't expect me to be best friends with them.	Glad to have you as my neighbor!
My kids are not playing with that weirdo!	I guess I could be nice to him and talk sometimes.	Why don't you invite that nice boy or girl to your birthday party?
How could they have that slow person making hamburgers and expect me to eat that food?	I wonder if he's really qualified for that job?	How wonderful that he's gainfully employed, independent, and a productive member of society.
I understand the disabilities where you can't walk or talk right, but I think that people with mental or emotional problems don't belong in society.	Well, I guess *they* are part of society, too.	We all have strengths and weaknesses and differing abilities. No one in society has more value than or is superior to another.
How can they ever expect to function by themselves?	How can we help them function?	People with disabilities can definitely learn to maximize their assets and function independently.

Scores:

> 5–7   Low sensitivities
>
> 8–11   Some understandings evidenced
>
> 12–15   Admirable mindset!

Appendix B

Reviewing Inclusive Lessons

Students/ Dates	Assignment/ Expectations	Accommodations	Results

Lesson Plan Format

Topic: _____

Lesson Concept: _____

Objective: _____

Desired Goals: Social/Academic/Emotional/Behavioral/Social/Physical/Cognitive:

_____

Baseline Knowledge: _____

Motivating Activity: _____

Visual/Auditory/Kinesthetic-Tactile _____

Sensory Elements: _____

Critical/Creative Thinking Skills: _____

Interpersonal Activity/Cooperative Roles: _____

Curriculum Connections: _____

Possible Accommodations: _____

Parallel Activity: _____

Anticipated Roles of

General Educator: _____

Special Educator: _____

Instructional Assistant: _____

Student: _____

Peers/Family/Specialists/Related Services/Administration:

_____

Adult/Peer/Self-Assessments: _____

Closure: _____

Revisitation dates: _____

Source: Adapted from Karten, T. (2005). *Inclusion Strategies That Work! Research-Based Methods for the Classroom.* Thousand Oaks, CA: Corwin Press.

Accommodations and Resources to Embrace DisABILITIES

Accommodations for students with . . .	Learning Needs	Emotional/Social/ Behavioral Needs	Physical/Perceptual/ Sensory Needs	Teacher/Student Concerns and Online Resources
Above-Average Skills	Individualized and independent assignments with realistic and attainable goals.	Lessons need to match maturity level and be age appropriate despite students' higher intelligence.	Dependent upon students; observe and assess accordingly.	Ongoing classroom assignments/centers set up that honor students' advanced levels. www.cectag.org www.nagc.org
Asperger Syndrome	Structured instruction with routines clearly explained and consistently followed, e.g., lists, graphic organizers, classroom rules.	Guided social skills training during cooperative assignments.	Limit distractions, yet honor other kinesthetic-tactile & visual presentations.	Can perseverate on own interests, need to be drawn back into lessons with more reflection. www.asperger.org
Attention Deficit/ Hyperactivity Disorder	Step-by-step presentations in a structured environment with organization/study skill instruction.	Need monitoring and reinforcement for positive behavioral/social interactions.	More chances to move about through *active learning*.	May be on medication to control impulses; be aware of possible side effects. www.chadd.org
Auditory Processing Needs	Accompany verbal instruction with written models and appropriate technology.	Same opportunities as peers.	Increase eye contact with students when giving oral directions.	May need additional wait time to respond. www.ncapd.org/php/
Autism	Functional vs. more advanced academics dependent upon cognitive levels.	Social stories with hypothetical, yet realistic role-playing of everyday encounters with peers and adults.	Tactile stimulation with concrete examples of abstract concepts; usage of more visuals.	Link students with peer mentors as role models in inclusive environments. www.autism-society.org

(Continued)

Accommodations and Resources to Embrace DisABILITIES (Continued)

Accommodations for students with . . .	Learning Needs	Emotional/Social/ Behavioral Needs	Physical/Perceptual/ Sensory Needs	Teacher/Student Concerns and Online Resources
Communication Disorders	Clear, explicit directions for academic assignments with more visual aids, e.g., visual dictionaries, videos, computer graphics.	Inclusion in all social class groups; be aware of frustrations.	Face student when speaking and talk in conversational tone; ask student to paraphrase understandings.	Collaborate with speech/ language pathologists. www.asha.org
Conduct Disorders	Consistent, structured class environment with rules outlined and enforced.	Behavioral/social contracts with more student metacognition—proactive approach to deter negative effect on classroom dynamics.	Check students' perceptions, e.g., diary, log of thoughts, student–teacher conferences.	Communicate with parents of students; behavioral strides with school–home coordination. www.nmha.org www.nimh.nih.gov /
Deafness/ Hearing Loss	Optimize students' abilities, e.g., more visuals for vocabulary, outlines, copies of teacher's guides and lessons.	Opportunities to effectively socialize with peers in class and extracurricular activities.	Match technology with individual student needs, e.g., PECS system, interactive board for easier note taking.	Be aware of individual preferences, e.g., total communication, speaking, lip reading, finger spelling, and/or signing. www.agbell.org www.shhh.org www.deafchildren.org
Depression	Allow alternate assignment if you think academic performance was negatively influenced by emotions at time of observation, instruction, or evaluation.	Have available *feel good* emotional outlets, e.g., intersperse exercise, art, or music with learning.	Encourage more metacognition for students to accurately reflect on perceptions and trigger points, e.g., graph daily moods.	Monitor quieter students who reach out in *silent ways*, e.g., writings, art, absences, self-care, dress. www.nimh.nih.gov

Accommodations for students with . . .	Learning Needs	Emotional/Social/ Behavioral Needs	Physical/Perceptual/ Sensory Needs	Teacher/Student Concerns and Online Resources
Developmental Disorder	Patient, repetitive, concrete learning presentations with concentration on functional academics.	Age-appropriate activities, direct social skill instruction, e.g., social stories.	Check with school nurse for possible medical concerns.	Introduce learning with high expectations for all students. www.devdelay.org www.thearc.org www.aaidd.org
Dyscalculia	Step-by-step kinesthetic approach with real-life connections.	Try to focus on other strengths to bypass math weakness, e.g., draw or write a math story.	Do not penalize students for number reversals; allow and teach usage and functions of calculators.	Have students record and graph his or her math strides. www.dyscalculia.org/ www.ldinfo.com
Dysgraphia	Maximize and utilize technology, e.g., from pencil grips to word prediction programs.	Encourage written communication by not penalizing students for illegible thoughts.	Ease fine motor strains by allowing alternate responses, e.g., express thoughts in dance or pantomime, give more frequent breaks.	Decide if oral communication to a scribe or digital recorder is an acceptable accommodation. www.ldinfo.com
Dyslexia	Multisensory, systematic, direct phonetic skill instruction across curriculum areas, e.g., breaking up more difficult multisyllabic vocabulary words, classifying vowel types in literature and text.	Do not embarrass students by asking them to read in front of peers, allow wait time, increase praise for reading progress, use age-appropriate materials.	Increase individual student awareness of letter reversals, e.g., self-corrections and highlighters, allow students to use a ruler, blank paper, or thin overlays as line guides in readings, enlarge smaller text.	Maximize technology for students to ease frustrations, e.g., books on tape, Recording for the Blind and Dyslexic, www.rfbd.org www.interdys.org www.ortonacademy.org

(Continued)

Accommodations and Resources to Embrace DisABILITIES (Continued)

Accommodations for students with . . .	Learning Needs	Emotional/Social/ Behavioral Needs	Physical/Perceptual/ Sensory Needs	Teacher/Student Concerns and Online Resources
Executive Dysfunction	Set up checklists for students to organize, prioritize, and complete assigned learning tasks.	Teacher–student conference to assess, motivate, personalize, and encourage goal setting.	Step-by-step modeling helps students with sequencing, perceptual overload, and memory issues.	Appropriate and realistic accommodations help students to compensate for weaker areas. http://www.tourette syndrome.net/ ef_overview.htm
Intellectual Disabilities/ Mental Retardation	Concrete, step-by-step learning presentations with modeling and repetition of specific requirements.	Circumvent frustrations by rewarding approximations toward learning goals; encourage relationships with peers as mentors and friends.	Ongoing communication with school nurse and families for pertinent medical history and other physical concerns.	Relate learning to individual interests while trying to focus on functional and independent daily living skills. www.thearc.org www.aaidd.org
Obsessive Compulsive Disorder	Channel student concerns for perfection as well as possible ritualistic behavior into appropriate academic/ behavioral tasks, e.g., class sharpener and other productive daily chores.	Appropriate preventive classroom interventions/ strategies, e.g., behavioral monitoring, quiet signals.	Awareness of possible school triggers, physical effects, and emotional stress exhibited as a result of compulsions and obsessions.	Understanding and patient environments that accept and do not ridicule students. www.ocfoundation.org www.adaa.org
Oppositional Defiant Disorder	Empower students with acceptable learning direction/choices, e.g., choose 3 of these 5 listed assignments.	Like the child, but dislike the behavior; try to establish ongoing, nonjudgmental, and trusting relationship.	Be certain students' sensory perceptions are accurate by asking them to paraphrase rules and interactions.	Do not engage in power struggles with students, but be firm, consistent, and fair. www.nmha.org www.mentalhealth.com

Accommodations for students with . . .	Learning Needs	Emotional/Social/ Behavioral Needs	Physical/Perceptual/ Sensory Needs	Teacher/Student Concerns and Online Resources
Physical Impairment	Realize that physical difficulties and learning deficits are not synonymous! Maximize technology options from pencil grips to paper stabilizers, bookstands, word prediction software, and more.	Allow students same access and opportunities to meaningfully participate in all activities with peers.	Coordinate and communicate with physical, occupational, and speech therapists to gain information and strategies to provide and maintain a safe, productive classroom environment.	Ease physical fine and/or gross motor requirements, but do not dilute academic assignments. http://specialed.about.com/od/physicaldisabilities
Sensory Impairment	Informally assess and observe students, and then appeal to stronger modalities.	Comparable emotional/ behavioral/social needs as peers. Recognize and minimize frustrations.	Dependent upon individual sensory needs, e.g., lessen or increase visual/auditory elements.	Use appropriate assistive technology and materials to maximize vision, hearing, and/or Touch. www.devdelay.org
Specific Learning Disability	Use task analysis to determine how to proceed and tailor remediation. Challenge students but do not frustrate. Increase practice, application, and praise.	Vary direct skill instruction with cooperative learning to increase social skills and class cohesiveness.	Address letter reversals, auditory processing issues, and visual and/or fine motor weaknesses that may interfere with reading, writing, and math performance.	Appeal to untapped strengths and interests to motivate students and boost self-esteem. www.ldanatl.org www.ncld.org
Tourette's Syndrome	Give students multiple breaks. Lessen writing requirements. Be sensitive to individual needs.	Educate other students and adults in the school environment about Tourette's, e.g., tics, blinking, grimaces.	Allow students acceptable motoric releases of extra energy, e.g., going on errands or to another temporary private setting without peer ridicule or embarrassment.	Scaffold as needed to address behavioral/ attention issues. www.tsa-usa.org http://www.tourette syndrome.net/

(Continued)

Accommodations and Resources to Embrace DisABILITIES (Continued)

Accommodations for students with . . .	Learning Needs	Emotional/Social/ Behavioral Needs	Physical/Perceptual/ Sensory Needs	Teacher/Student Concerns and Online Resources
Traumatic Brain Disorder	Employ mnemonics and study guides. Use repetitive instruction with a step-by-step approach.	Realize students' learning frustrations; praise approximations.	Utilize memory-strengthening activities that appeal to multiple modalities.	Determine individual students' stamina and daily thresholds. www.biausa.org
Twice Exceptional	Vary types of instruction and assessments, using multiple intelligences and brain-based learning principles.	Reward both growth and accomplishments, honoring unique social/behavioral/ emotional/academic levels.	Address various sensory, physical, and perceptual needs evidenced. Enlist help of school-related services.	Concentrate on growth vs. deficit paradigm. http://content.bvsd.org/ tag/TwiceExceptional.htm
Visual Impairments/ Blindness	Emphasize auditory and kinesthetic-tactile modalities with increased written directions and more learning manipulatives across the subject areas.	Include students in all activities with peer education for classmates about students' visual needs, interests, and strengths.	Eliminate frustrations by removing physical barriers in the classroom environment and school. Work with mobility trainers.	Optimize available technology, e.g., talking Web sites, tactile outlines. www.afb.org www.rfbd.org

Source: Karten, T. (2007d). *More inclusion strategies that work!* Thousand Oaks, CA: Corwin Press.

Multiple Intelligences

I can use _____
Visual-Spatial: clipart, post-its, graphic organizers, illustrations, charts, technology programs such as interactive boards, online museum sites, digital storytelling, content-related art projects that sharpen perceptual needs, and observational skills
Bodily-Kinesthetic: manipulatives such as clay, pipe cleaners, toothpicks, salt, koosh balls, kneaded erasers, content-related movement exercises during classroom instruction, and *brainbreaks* that stretch the body and mind
Interpersonal: cooperative learning, plays, role-playing, committees, stations
Intrapersonal: journals, self-directed learning, tape recorders, candid videos, mirrors, writer's notebooks, diaries, graphing progress, metacognitive reflections
Verbal-Linguistic: books, tapes, debates, poems, essays, videos, magazines, newspapers, weekly readers, illustrative charts and graphs
Logical-Mathematical: computers, thinking activities for deductive and inductive reasoning, life-related learning such as catalogue shopping sprees to improve computational skills, or coupon clipping, classroom consistency with rules and structure outlined
Musical-Rhythmic: songs with content-related lyrics, environmental sounds, instruments, creative expressions and interpretations, background sounds or music while learning, *tapping* to the learning
Naturalistic: organized school and home environments, classification projects, community connections such as beautification projects and more recycling efforts
Existential: Questionnaires, surveys, quotes, infinite sources, those things beyond sensory data, reflective classroom

Source: Karten, T. (2007d). *More Inclusion Strategies That Work! Aligning Student Strengths With the Standards.* Thousand Oaks, CA: Corwin Press.

Valuable and Applicable Things to Do in All Classrooms on a Daily Basis (pictorial version)

establish prior knowledge	pre/inter/post planning and structured environment	proceed from simple to complex
step-by-step	concretize learning	appropriate modifications & accommodations
teach to strengths	multisensory	value inquiry
multiple intelligences	have high expectations	recognize and reward achievements & strides
cooperation & collaboration	reflections & self-advocacy	relate to students' lives

Valuable and Applicable Things to Do in All Classrooms on a Daily Basis

1. Establish prior knowledge.

2. Preplan lessons with structured objectives, allowing for inter/post planning.

3. Proceed from the simple to the complex by using discrete task analysis, which breaks up the learning into its parts, yet still values the whole picture!

4. Use a step-by-step approach, teaching in small bites, with much practice and repetition for those who need it.

5. Reinforce abstract concepts with concrete examples, such as looking at a map while walking around a neighborhood, or reading actual street signs.

6. Think about possible accommodations and modifications that might be needed such as using a digital recorder for notes, or reducing or enhancing an assignment.

7. Incorporate sensory elements: visual, auditory, and kinesthetic-tactile ones.

8. Teach to strengths to help students compensate for weaknesses such as hopping to math facts, if a child loves to move about but hates numbers.

9. Concentrate on individual children, not syndromes, with a growth vs. deficit paradigm.

10. Provide opportunities for success to build self-esteem.

11. Give positives before negatives.

12. Use modeling with both teachers and students' peers.

13. Vary types of instruction and assessment, with multiple intelligences and cooperative learning.

14. Relate learning to children's lives using interest inventories.

15. Remember the basics such as teaching students proper hygiene, respecting others, effectively listening, or reading directions on a worksheet, in addition to the 3R's: *Reading, 'Riting,* and *'Rithmetic.*

16. Establish a pleasant classroom environment that encourages students to ask questions and become actively involved in their learning.

17. Increase students' self-awareness of levels and progress.

18. Effectively communicate and collaborate with parents, students, and colleagues, while smiling—it's contagious!

Source: Adapted from Karten, T. (2005). *Inclusion Strategies That Work!* Thousand Oaks, CA: Corwin Press.

Appendix C

Student Data Documentation

Teachers can keep notes from IEPs read, and monitor how lessons align with modifications and goals listed in the IEP.

Modifications/Accommodations

MBHE—Modified, but high expectations

S—Seating

HW—Homework modified/reduced

P—Preteaching

R—Reteaching/Repetition

A—Assessment varied/simplified

SG—Study Guide

V—Visuals

T—Extra time, or wait time for tasks

BP—Behavior Plan

C/T—Computer/Technology

M—Alternate Materials

OW—Oral/Written presentations

MS—Multisensory techniques

IST—Instructional Support Team

HI—Home Involvement

B—Buddy system

NT—Notetaking system

LOV—Learning Objective Varied

O+—Other modifications

Subject: _____

Teachers: _____

Charting Accommodations and Modifications

Student:	Teachers:
Subject:	Topic/Unit:

Students	Modifications/ Accommodations	Assessments/Dates Mastery Level	Comments
Related Services:			

Source: Karten, T. (2005). *Inclusion strategies that work!* Thousand Oaks, CA: Corwin Press.

Student Data Documentation			
Circle, highlight, add instructional strategies	List Test/Quiz Grades	*Informal Assessments/Observations & Comments— Student Strengths & Interests.* (List specific classroom, small group, or individual interventions)	Dates/ Marking Periods
link to prior knowledge			
preteaching			
reteaching			
multisensory lessons			
concrete presentations			
provide outline/notes			
additional breaks			
family support			
modeling			
step-by-step directions			
study guide			
lessen requirements			
reduce reading			
act out concepts			
self-esteem builders			
cooperative learning			
extra time or wait time			
preferred seating			
homework modified			
more visuals/graphics			
less writing			
peer support			
color code			
more auditory cues			
additional technology			
quiet setting			
student metacognition			
monitor frequently			
coteaching/collaboration			
focus on positives			
manipulatives			
vary assessments			
Alternate task, specify:			
Other, specify:			

ABCD* Quarterly Checklist of Functional Objectives **S**EASONAL **E**LEGANCE *Student:* _____	*Aug./ Sept.*	*Dec.*	*Mar.*	*May/ June*
1. Establishes eye contact with teachers and peers				
2. Uses proper conversational tones				
3. Follows classroom and school rules				
4. Respects authority				
5. Exhibits social reciprocity				
6. Appropriately communicates needs				
7. Demonstrates consistent attention in classroom lessons				
8. Completes all classroom assignments				
9. Finishes all homework and long-range assignments				
10. Able to independently take class notes				
11. Writes legibly				
12. Has an organized work area				
13. Respects the property of others				
14. Works well with groups				
15. Adjusts to changes in routines				
16. Asks for clarification when needed				
17. Takes pride in achievements				
18. Displays enthusiasm about learning				

*Use these codes:	**Other Comments:**
A = Always	
B = Becoming better	
C = Can with reminders	
D or D/R = Doesn't display behavior or doesn't with regression noted	
+, − can be used to note partial improvements.	

Source: Karten, T. (2007d). *More Inclusion Activities That Work! Aligning Student Strengths With the Standards.* Thousand Oaks, CA: Corwin Press.

Word Recognition and Comprehension
Reading Survey for Teachers, Students, and Parents

Circle Reading Patterns	Sentence Read Question/Response	Correct Sentence Correct Response
Insertions +		
Mispronounces −		
Omissions O		
Substitutions S		
Finger Pointing FP		
Reversals R		
Intonation/Fluency I/F		
Self-corrects SC		
Nonpronounciations N		
Hesitations H		
Duplications D		
Vocabulary Issues VI		
Context Clues Weak CCW		
Context Clues Strong CCS		
Comprehension Errors CE	Comments	
Reads for Meaning RFM		

Writing Survey and Documentation

Categories Mastery Codes/Levels: B—Beginning I—Intermediate A—Advanced NE—Not Evidenced	Date ____ 1st Qtr.	Date ____ 2nd Qtr.	Date ____ 3rd Qtr.	Date ____ 4th Qtr.	Comments About Writing a. Effort b. Motivation c. Interest d. Pride e. Progress f. Other comments
Planning					
Stays on Topic					
Organization					
Sentence Fluency					
Vocabulary					
Spelling					
Grammar					
Punctuation					
Writes for Audience					
Holds Interest					
Supporting details					
Introduction					
Conclusion					
Figurative Language					
Accuracy					
Varies sentence types					
Uses transitional words					
Appearance					
Overall Quality					

Math Survey and Documentation for Teachers, Students, and Families

Student: _____ Dates: _____ Color Coded Marking Periods: I green II blue III red IV black	**Comments and Concerns** Observations Math Progress Improvements Noted Applications Behavior Homework Assignments Formal/Informal Test Grades Regressions Future Plans	Codes: S = Strength W = Weakness GB = Getting Better 1–10 Range: 1 = Low Skills 10 = Proficient NI = Not Introduced N/A = Not applicable
Shapes		
Sequencing		
Sorting		
One–One Correspondence		
Counting/Number Recognition		
Patterns/Missing Elements		
Basic + Facts		
Basic − Facts		
Basic × Facts		
Basic ÷ Facts		
Computations		
Time Concepts		
Interpreting Charts & Graphs		
Fractions		
Decimals		
Percents		
Measurement		
Money Understandings		
Multi Digit Addition		
Multi Digit Subtraction		
Complex Multiplication		
Complex Division		
Geometry Principles		
Algebraic Expressions		
Probability		
Solving Word Problems		

Appendix D

Increasing Communication and Collaboration

Teamwork with educational support teams (EST) and related services thwarts miscommunication and includes all staff and teachers in the planning stages.

The Stop and Think Student Planner on page 272 helps all staff and families to collaborate, communicate, and document student levels, possible classroom concerns, and appropriate interventions that are needed to escalate student improvements. Teachers can attach a stapled index card that lists this pertinent information to the planner:

Teacher _____

School _____

Student's Name _____

Primary Language _____

Teacher Contacts: E-Mail _____

Phone _____

Date _____

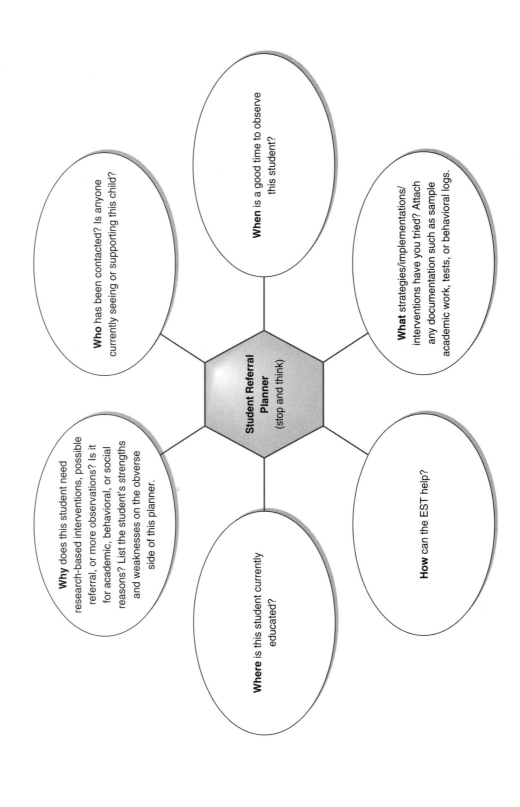

Student Referral Planner
(stop and think)

When is a good time to observe this student?

Who has been contacted? Is anyone currently seeing or supporting this child?

What strategies/implementations/interventions have you tried? Attach any documentation such as sample academic work, tests, or behavioral logs.

Why does this student need research-based interventions, possible referral, or more observations? Is it for academic, behavioral, or social reasons? List the student's strengths and weaknesses on the obverse side of this planner.

Where is this student currently educated?

How can the EST help?

Reflective Inclusive Questions

Check yes or no for these *pedagogically ponderable* questions:

Inclusive Questions	YES	NO
1. Was this student's prior knowledge increased?		
2. If this student did not receive a passing grade, e.g., 50% on an evaluation or test, did he or she master 50% of the material?		
3. Do you think this student will be more proficient when he or she learns about this topic, content area, or skill again?		
4. Is there a way to repeat this learning and somehow individualize instruction within the classroom, e.g., alternate assignment on the same topic, if appropriate support is given, such as a parent, peer coach, or paraeducator?		
5. Would assigning a peer coach be beneficial to both this child and his or her student mentor?		
6. Can the student chart his or her progress to take more ownership and responsibility for his or her learning?		
7. Is the student experiencing more accomplishments than frustrations with his or her inclusion experience in your class?		
8. Has physical inclusion allowed this child to develop a more positive self-image, which has translated to increased self-confidence and motivation?		
9. Are you experiencing personal or professional growth by having this child included in your class?		

Source: Karten, T. (2007d). *More Inclusion Strategies That Work! Aligning Student Strengths With the Standards.* Thousand Oaks, CA: Corwin Press.

Parental/Family Input

Child's Name _____

Parent/Family Member/Guardian's Name _____

1. What does my child think about school?

2. What do I visualize my daughter or son doing in 10 or 15 years?

3. What are my child's needs?

4. Some words I would use to describe my child are _____,
   _____, and _____.

5. What are my child's favorite things to do?

6. What would I change about the school or my child's class?

7. What do I like about my child's class?

8. My areas of expertise are _____
   _____ and I am available to talk to my
   child's class on _____.

9. I'd like to volunteer to help _____.

10. Contact me at
    E-mail _____

    Telephone: Home _____ Work _____

    Cell Phone _____ Home Address _____

Source: Karten, T. (2005). *Inclusion Strategies That Work!* Thousand Oaks, CA: Corwin Press.

Bibliography

Abeel, S. (2003). *My thirteenth winter: A memoir.* New York: Scholastic.

Acrey, C., Johnstone, C., & Milligan, C. (2005, November/December). Using universal design to unlock the potential for academic achievement of at-risk learners. *Teaching Exceptional Children, 38*(2), 22–31.

Anti-Defamation League. 823 United Nations Plaza, New York, NY 10017. Web site: http://www .adl.org; Phone: (800) 343–5540.

Aranda, A., Sanchez-Escobedo, P., &Williams, G. (2002). Classroom behavior: Mexican teachers' perceptions about, management of, and attributions regarding student behavior. *Journal of International Special Needs Education, 5,* 10–18.

The Arc. (n.d.). 1010 Wayne Avenue, Suite 650, Silver Spring, MD 20910. Web site: http://www .thearc.org; Phone: (800) 433–5255.

Back, E., Ropar, D., & Mitchell, P. (2007). Do the eyes have it? Inferring mental states from animated faces in autism. *Child Development, 78*(2), 397–411.

Baker, C. (2000). *A parents' and teachers' guide to bilingualism.* Philadelphia: Multilingual Matters.

Baker, C., & Jones, S. (1998). Encyclopedia of Bilingualism and Bilingual Education. Clevedon, UK: Multilingual Matters Ltd.

Bandler, M. J. (1999, January). Moving people forward: A conversation with Tony Coelho. *U.S. Society & Values, USIA Electronic Journal, 4,* 1. Available at http://usinfo.state.gov/journals/ itsv/0199/ijse/coelho.htm.

Barth, R. (2006). Improving relationships within the school house. *Educational Leadership, 63*(6), 8–13.

Beattie, J., Jordan, L., & Algozzine, B. (2006). *Making inclusion work.* Thousand Oaks, CA: Corwin Press.

Behler, T. (1993). Disability simulations as a teaching tool: Some ethical issues and implications. *Journal on Postsecondary Education and Disability AHEAD, 10*(2), 3–8.

Beland, K. (2007). Boosting social and emotional competence. *Educational Leadership, 64*(7), 68–71.

Bellini, S., Peters, J., Benner, L., & Hopf, A. (2007, May/June). A meta-analysis of school-based social skills interventions for children with autism spectrum disorders. *Remedial and Special Education, 28*(3), 153–162.

Bender, W. (2002). *Differentiating instruction for students with learning disabilities.* Thousand Oaks, CA: Corwin Press & Council for Exceptional Children.

Black, P., Harrison, C., Lee, C., Marshall, B., & Wiliam, D. (2003). *Assessment for learning: Putting it into practice.* Berkshire, UK: Open University Press.

Boggle's World. http://bogglesworld.com. This is a Web site that has teaching resources for TESOL, TEFL, and ESL K–12 students with English skills. There are printable worksheets and lessons.

Brightman, A. (2006). *Connections in the land of disability.* Los Altos, CA: Palo Alto Press.

Brooks, J., & Brooks, M. (1993). *In search of understanding: The case for constructivist classrooms.* Alexandria: VA: Association for Supervision and Curriculum Development.

Bullock, T. (2005, October 5). *Vietnamese lawmakers study U.S. disabilities legislation.* Available at http://usinfo.state.gov.

Bureau of International Information Programs, U.S. Department of State. (2005, August 16). *Fact sheet: Americans with disabilities are achieving real progress.* Retrieved November 15, 2005, from http://usinfo.state.gov.

Burgstahler, S. (2003). The role of technology in preparing youth with disabilities for postsecondary education and employment. *Journal of Special Education Technology, 18,* 4.

Burk, C. (n.d.). *What is applied verbal behavior?* Retrieved June 30, 2007, from http://www .christinaburkaba.com/AVB.htm.

Burke, K., & Sutherland, C. (2004, Winter). Attitudes toward inclusion: Knowledge vs. experience. *Education, 125,* 163.

Carey, B. (2006, December 22). Parenting as therapy for child's mental disorders. *New York Times.* Retrieved January 17, 2007, from http://www.nytimes.com/2006/12/22/health/22KIDS .html.

Carey, B. (2007, June 5). The disorder is sensory; the diagnosis, elusive. *New York Times.* Retrieved June 20, 2007, from http://www.nytimes.com/2007/06/05/health/psychology/05sens.html.

Cavanagh, S. (2007). Math anxiety confuses the equation for students. *Education Week, 26*(24), 12.

Chappuis, J. (2005). Helping students understand assessment. *Educational Leadership, 63*(3), 39–43.

Chen, M. (2007, February 28). Don't weigh the elephant—Feed the elephant. *Edutopia.* Retrieved March 13, 2007, from http://www.edutopia.org/1814.

Christ, T. J., Burns, M. K., & Ysseldyke, J. E. (2005). Conceptual confusion within response-to-intervention vernacular: Clarifying meaningful difference. *Communique, 34,* 1–8.

Christian, N. (2006, November 5). Plea to let doctors kill babies with disabilities. *Scotland on Sunday.* Retrieved from http://scotlandonsunday.scotsman.com/health.cfm?id=1639102006.

Clark, L. (2005). Gifted and growing. *Educational Leadership, 63*(3), 56–60.

Clemetson, L. (2006, December 7). Off to college on their own, shadowed by mental illness. *New York Times.* Retrieved December 10, 2007, from http://news.blogs.nytimes.com/2006/12/07/off-to-college-on-their-own-shadowed-by-mental-illness.

Clymer, J., & Wiliam, D. (2006, December). Improving the way we grade science. *Educational Leadership, 64*(4), 36–42.

Council for Exceptional Children. (n.d.). *A primer on the IDEA 2004 regulations.* Accessed January 7, 2007, from http://www.cec.sped.org.

Cramer, E., & Nevin, A. (2006). A mixed methodology analysis of coteacher assessments. *Teacher Education and Special Education, 29*(4), 261–274.

Cumine, V., Dunlop, J., & Stevenson, G. (1998). *Asperger syndrome: A practical guide for teachers.* Cambridge, UK: David Fulton.

Cummins, J. (1984). Wanted: A theoretical framework for relating language proficiency to academic achievement among bilingual students. In C. Rivera (Ed.), *Language proficiency and academic achievement.* Philadelphia: Multilingual Matters.

Cushing, L., Clark, N., Carter, E., & Kennedy, C. (2005). Access to the general education curriculum for students with significant cognitive disabilities. *Teaching Exceptional Children, 38*(2), 6–13.

Daily, M. (2007, May 31). Inclusion of students with autism spectrum disorders. *New Horizons for Learning.* Retrieved June 1, 2007, from http://www.newhorizons.org/spneeds/autism/daily.htm.

Dardig, J. (2005). The McClurg monthly magazine and 14 more practical ways to involve parents. *Teaching Exceptional Children, 38*(2), 46–51.

DeFord, S. (2006, December 30). In child-care class, dreams trump disability. *The Washington Post,* C04.

Delpit, L. (2006). Foreword. In B. Harry & J. K. Klingner, *Why are so many minority students in special education? Understanding race and disability in schools.* New York: Teachers College Press.

DEMOS. (2002). *Project module: Disability awareness.* Available online at www.jarmin.com/demos/course/awareness/02.html

Disabilities in the Western world. (n.d.). Available at http://www.residentialopportunities.org/html/developmental_disabilities_thr.html.

Disability Social History Project Timeline. (n.d.). Available online at http://www.disabilityhistory .org/timeline_new.html.

Dyslexic pupils to use laptops. (2007, June 12). *PA News,* Science & Technology section. Retrieved June 20, 2007, from http://www.channel4.com/news/articles/science_technology/dyslexic +pupils+to+use+laptops

Dzaldov, B., & Peterson, S. (2005). Book leveling and readers. *The Reading Teacher, 59*(3), 222–229.

The Elementary and Secondary Education Act of 1965. (1965). Available at http://si.unm.edu/si2002/SUSAN_A/TIMELINE/TIM_0015.HTM.

EuroNews on Special Needs Education. (2002). *Issue 9.* Available at http://www.cec.sped.org/intl/progpract.html#inclusive.

Examining family involvement in support of youth with disabilities. (2005). Available online at http://www.nlts2.org/reports/2005_03/nlts2_report_2005_03_ch1.pdf. This document is one in a series of reports from NLTS2 that began in 2003.

Fairbanks, S., Sugai, G., Guardino, D., & Lathrop, M. (2007). Response to intervention: Examining classroom behavior supporting second grade. *Exceptional Children, 73*(3), 288–310.

Field, S., & Hoffman, A. (1994). Development of a model for self-determination. *Career Development for Exceptional Individuals, 17,* 159–169.

Field, S., Sarver, M. D., & Shaw, S. F. (2003, November). Self-determination. *Remedial and Special Education, 24,* 6.

Flynn, S. (2005, October 1). INTO (Irish National Teachers' Organization) to make class size the issue in run-up to general election. *Irish Times*. Available online at http://web24.epnet.com.

Friend, M. (2007). The co-teaching partnership. *Educational Leadership, 64*(5), 48–52.

Furger, R. (2005, November). NCLB confidential. *Edutopia, 1*(8), 40–44.

Garfunkel, S. (1988). *For all practical purposes: Introduction to contemporary mathematics.* New York: W. H. Freeman.

Garrison, C., & Ehringhaus, M. (n.d.). *Formative and summative assessments in the classroom.* Available online at http://www.nmsa.org/Publications/WebExclusive/Assessment/tabid/1120/Default.aspx.

Gitomer, D. H., & Duschl, R. A. (1997). Strategies and challenges to changing the focus of assessment and instruction in science classrooms. *Educational Assessment, 4*(1), 37–73.

Grandin, T., & Johnson, C. (2005). *Animals in translation.* Orlando, FL: Harcourt.

Greenspan, S. (2005, September). Inside the inclusive classroom. *Scholastic Parent and Child, 13,* 1.

Gregory, G., & Chapman, C. (2002). *Differentiated instructional strategies: One size doesn't fit all.* Thousand Oaks, CA: Corwin Press.

Gresham, F. M., Sugai, G., & Horner, R. H. (2001). *Interpreting outcomes of social skills training for students with high-incidence disabilities. Teaching Exceptional Children, 67,* 331–344.

Gustin, G. (2006, December 15). Vocational education is shifting focus. *St. Louis Post-Dispatch.* Accessed at www.stltoday.com.

Gutner, T. (2004, May 31). Special needs, crushing costs. *Business Week,* Issue 3885. Retrieved November 15, 2005, from htttp://web24epnet.com.

Hall, T. (2002). *Differentiated instruction.* Wakefield, MA: National Center on Assessing the General Curriculum. Retrieved December 18, 2006, from http://www.cast.org/publications/ncac/ncac_diffinstruc.html.

Hallahan, D., Keller, C., Martinez, E., Byrd, E., Gellman, J., & Fan, X. (2007). How variable are interstate prevalence rates of learning disabilities and other special education categories? A longitudinal comparison. *Exceptional Children, 73*(2), 136–146.

Halperin, I., & Merrick, J. (2006). Multinational study of attitudes toward individuals with intellectual disabilities. *Journal of Policy and Practice in Intellectual Disabilities, 3*(2), 143–143.

Halpin, T. (2006, May 17). Mainstream schools can't manage special needs pupils, say teachers. *Times Online.* Accessed at http://wwww.timesonline.co.uk.

Harry, B., & Klingner, J. (2007). Discarding the deficit model. *Educational Leadership. 64*(5), 16–21.

Hehir, T. (2007). Confronting ableism. *Educational Leadership, 64*(5), 8–14.

Heng, M., & Tam, K. (2006). Special education in general education programs in Singapore. *Teacher Education and Special Education, 29*(3), 149–156.

Heward, W. L. (2003). Ten faulty notions about teaching and learning that hinder the effectiveness of special education. *Journal of Special Education, 36*(4), 186–206.

Hobbs, T., Szydlowski, S., West, D., & Germava, O. (2002). Special Education and rehabilitation in Georgia: Strengths, weaknesses, opportunities and threats in a newly independent state of the former Soviet Union. *Journal of International Special Needs Education, 5,* 30–35.

Hoopman, K. (2001). *Blue bottle mystery: An Asperger adventure.* London: Jessica Kingsley.

Hoover, J., & Patton, J. (2005). Differentiating instruction for English Language Learners with special needs. *Intervention in School and Clinic, 40,* 231.

Hopkins, J. (2006). *CEC: 2007 brings special education opportunity and challenges.* Available at http://susanohanian.org/show_special_commentaries.html?id=116.

Humphreys, K., Tyne, N., & Gallagher, P. (2003). Teacher education network and special education needs: Creating special opportunities across Europe and America. *Journal of International Special Needs Education, 6,* 28–31.

Hunsberger, M. (2006, Spring). The knot that never goes away. *Families, 15*(1), 23–26.

In Case, the Newsletter for the Council of Administrators of Special Education, a Division of the Council for Exceptional Children. (2005, September/October). Vol. 47, No. 2. Arlington, VA: Council for Exceptional Children.

Karten, T. (2005). *Inclusion strategies that work! Research-based methods for the classroom.* Thousand Oaks, CA: Corwin Press.

Karten, T. (2007a). *Inclusion activities that work! Grades K–2.* Thousand Oaks, CA: Corwin Press.

Karten, T. (2007b). *Inclusion activities that work! Grades 3–5.* Thousand Oaks, CA: Corwin Press.

Karten, T. (2007c). *Inclusion activities that work! Grades 6–8.* Thousand Oaks, CA: Corwin Press.

Karten, T. (2007d). *More inclusion strategies that work! Aligning student strengths with the standards.* Thousand Oaks, CA: Corwin Press.

Kaufman, L. (2006, November 5). *Just a normal girl. New York Times,* Education Life section, 25–27.

Kenney, M., & Bezuszka, S. (1993, November). Implementing the discrete mathematics standards: Focusing on recursion: *Mathematics Teacher, 86*(8), 676–680.

Kenning, C. (2007, March 4). Special educators find the standards stifling. *The Courier Journal* (Louisville, KY). Accessed March 13, 2007, from http://thecourier-journal.com.

Kise, J. (2006). *Differentiated coaching.* Thousand Oaks, CA: Corwin Press.

Konrad, M., & Trela, K. (2007). Go 4 it…now! Extending writing strategies to support all students! *Teaching Exceptional Children, 39*(4), 42–51.

Labon, D. (1999). *Inclusive education at work: students with disabilities in mainstream schools.* Paris: Organisation for Economic Cooperation and Development.

Largest ever search for autism genes reveals new clues. (2007, February 19). *Science Daily.* Accessed online at http://www.sciencedaily.com/releases/2007/02/070218183245.htm

Laurent…A Place of Our Own. (n.d.). *Laurent: FAQs.* Retrieved November 29, 2005, from http://www.laurentsd.com/Newsroom/FAQs.htm.

Lee, Y., & Vail, C. (2003). Understanding culturally diverse families: A case study with Korean mothers. *Journal of International Special Needs Education, 6,* 14–20.

Lynch, S., Taymans, J., Watson, W., Ochsendorf, R., Pyke, C., & Szesze, M. (2007). Effectiveness of a highly rated science curriculum unit for students with disabilities in general education classrooms. *Exceptional Children, 73*(2), 202–223.

Matthews, J. (2006, November 28). Escaping "average." Innovative programs make the case that high-level classes aren't just for the gifted. *The Washington Post,* A08.

McCoun, B. (2006). Case in Point: RTI as a general education initiative and the new role for educational support teams. *Journal of Special Education Leadership, 19*(2), 62–63.

McDermott, R., & Verenne, H. (1995). Culture "as" disability. *Anthropology and Education Quarterly, 26,* 323–348.

McNary, S., Glasgow, N., & Hicks, C. (2005). *What successful teachers do in inclusive classrooms.* Thousand Oaks, CA: Corwin Press.

Michael, J. (1984). Verbal behavior. *Journal of the Experimental Analysis of Behavior, 42*(3), 363–376.

Miller, K. (2004). The law catches up with distance education. *THE Journal, 31,* 7.

Moccia, R. E., Schumaker, J. B., Hazel, J. S., Vernon, D. S., & Deshler, D. (1989). A mentor program for facilitating the life transitions of individuals who have handicapping conditions. *Reading, Writing, and Learning Disabilities, 5,* 177–195.

Montes, S. (2007, June 16). For Fenty's disabilities pick, experience is firsthand. *The Washington Post,* B01. Retrieved June 20, 2007, from http://www.washingtonpost.com.

Morgan, P., & Fuchs, D. (2007). Is there a bidirectional relationship between children's reading skills and reading motivation? *Exceptional Children, 73*(2), 165–183.

Museum of disABILITY History. (n.d.). Available at http://www.museumofdisability.org.

National Association for Bilingual Educators (NABE). (2002). *Determining appropriate referrals of English Language Learners to special education.* Arlington, VA: ILIAD Project, Council for Exceptional Children.

National Center for Education Statistics. (2005). *The condition of education 2005* (NCES 2005–094). Washington, DC: U.S. Government Printing Office. Available at http://nces.ed.gov/fastfacts/display.asp?id=59.

National Center for Education Statistics. (2006). *The condition of education 2006* (NCES 2006–071). Washington, DC: U.S. Government Printing Office.

National Center for Education Statistics. (2007). *The condition of education 2007* (NCES 2007–064). Washington, DC: U.S. Government Printing Office.

National Information Center for Children and Youth with Disabilities. (n.d.). *The education of children and youth with special needs: What do the laws say?* (n.d.). Available at http://www.nichcy.org/pubs/outprint/nd15txt.htm.

National Institute on Disability and Rehabilitation Research: Core Curriculum (Adaptive Environments). (n.d.). Web site available at http://www.dbtac.vcu.edu/whatsada.

National Research Center on Learning Disabilities. (2004). *Core concepts of RTI.* Accessed December 8, 2006, at http://www.nrcld.org.

Newman, L. (2005). *Family involvement in the educational development of youth with disabilities. A Special Topic Report of findings from the National Longitudinal Transition Study-2 (NLTS2).* Menlo Park, CA: SRI International. Available at www.nlts2.org/reports/2005_03/nlts2_report_2005_03_complete.pdf.

Nowicki, E. A. (2006, May). A cross-sectional multivariate analysis of children's attitudes towards disabilities. *Journal of Intellectual Disability Research, 50*(5) 335–348.

Nunley, K. (2003, September). Layered curriculum brings teachers to tiers. *Education Digest, 69*(1), 31-ff.

Nunley, K. (2006). *Differentiating the high school classroom.* Thousand Oaks, CA: Corwin Press.

Obi, F., Mamah, V., & Avoke, K. (2007). Inclusive education in an emerging country: The state of teacher preparedness in Ghana. *Journal of International Special Needs Education, 10,* 33–39.

O'Brien, R. (2004, December 1). Looking for even approach. *Irish Times.* Retrieved November 15, 2005, from http//web24.epnet.com/citation.asp.

PACER, Champions for Children with Disabilities, a parent training and information center. http://www.pacer.org.

Palincsar, A., Magnusson, S., Collins, K., & Cutter, J. (2001). Making science accessible for all: Results of a design experiment in inclusive classrooms. *Learning Disability Quarterly, 24,* 15–32.

Peek, F. (1996). *The real rain man: Kim Peek.* Salt Lake City, UT: Harkness.

Pfeiffer, D. (n.d.). *Two futures of people with disabilities.* Article based on a July 19, 1996, presentation at the Futures Discussion Group. Accessed online at http://www.soc.hawaii.edu/future/j10/disabilities.html.

Philpot, D. J. (2002). *History of federal statutes affecting special education.* Available at http://www.dphilpotlaw.com/html/history_of_federal_statutes.html.

Popham, W. J. (2006, December/2007, January). A test is a test is a test—not! *Educational Leadership, 64*(4), 88–89.

Price, P. (2000, August). *Ethics and inclusion: Diversity and equity.* Keynote paper presented at the 19th RI World Congress, Rio de Janeiro. Quotation retrieved July 2, 2007, from http://www.quotationspage.com/quote/31753.html.

Province digs deeper for disabled. (2005, June 28). *Toronto Star.* Accessed at http://web24.epnet.com.

Rehabilitation International. (2001). *Children with disabilities: Global Priorities.* Available online at http://www.disabilityworld.org/07-08_01/children/global.shtml.

Reid, K., & Valle, J. W. (2004). The discursive practice of learning disability: Implications for instruction and parent–school relations. *Journal of Learning Disabilities, 37*(6), 466–481.

Residential Opportunities, Inc. (n.d.). *Disabilities in the Western world.* Available online at http://www.residentialopportunities.org/html/developmental_disabilities_thr.html.

Rhodes, J. E., Grossman, J. B., & Resch, N. L. (2000). Agents of change: Pathways through which mentoring relationships influence adolescents' academic adjustment. *Child Development, 71,* 1662–1671.

Rivera, C. (2007, June 16). Ending is a beginning for special-needs students. *LA Times.* Retrieved June 20, 2007, from www.latimes.com/newss/local/la-me-graduates.

Rothstein, R., Jacobsen, R., & Wilder, T. (2006, November 29). Proficiency for all. *Education Week, 26,* 13, back page & p. 32.

Rubenstein, G. (2006, September). What's next? *Edutopia. 2*(6), 36–48.

Rustemier, S. (n.d.). Inclusive education: A worldwide movement. *Inclusion Week.* Retrieved from http://inclusion.uwe.ac.uk/inclusionweek/articles/worldwide.htm.

Rycik, J. A. (Ed.). (2005, Summer). [Entire issue]. *American Secondary Education, 33*(3).

Salend, S. (2005). Using technology to teach students about individual differences related to disabilities. *Teaching Exceptional Children, 38*(2), 32–38.

Salend, S., & Sylvestre, S. (2005). Understanding and addressing oppositional and defiant classroom behaviors. *Teaching Exceptional Children, 37*(6), 32–39.

Samuels, C. (2006, November 29). Special education directors hope to sway federal policy. *Education Week, 26,* 13, 8.

Samuels, C. (2007a, January 31). IDEA imposes hefty data burden on states. *Education Week, 26*(21), 23–24.

Samuels, C. (2007b, June 21). Ed. Dept. evaluates states' records on students with disabilities. *Education Week, 26.* Retrieved June 27, 2007, from http://www.edweek.org/ew/articles/2007/06/21/43plan_web.h26.html?print=1.

Schiller, E., Burnaska, K., Cohen, G., Douglas, Z., Fiore, T., Glazier, R., et al. (2003). *The study of state and local implementation and impact of the Individuals with Disabilities Education Act: Final interim report* (1999–2000 school year). Bethesda, MD: Abt Associates.

Sebald, A., & Luckner, J. (2007). Successful partnerships with families of children who are deaf. *Educational Leadership, 39*(3), 54–59.

Shreve, J. (2005). No train, no gain. *Edutopia, 1*(8) 40–44.

Skinner, B. F. (1957). *Verbal behavior.* New York: Appleton-Century-Crofts.

Smith, J. D. (2003). *Stories of disability in the human family: In search of better angels.* Thousand Oaks, CA: Corwin Press.

Sotto, T. (n.d.). *ArtsEdge: Five easy drama games for the early elementary classroom.* Retrieved December 4, 2006, from http://artsedge.kennedy-center.org/content/3917.

Sousa, D. (2007). *How the special needs brain learns.* Thousand Oaks, CA: Corwin Press.

Southern Poverty Law Center, Teaching Tolerance. 400 Washington Avenue, Montgomery, AL 36104. Web site: http://www.tolerance.org.

Special Olympics. (n.d.). *Attitude research: Multinational study of attitudes toward individuals with intellectual disabilities.* Retrieved June 28, 2007, from http://www.specialolympics.org/Special+Olympics+Public+Website/English/Initiatives/Research/Attitude_Research/Multinational+Study.htm.

Spitz, K. (2005, September 9). Support, advice available among parents of disabled children through group. *Akron Beacon Journal.*

Sproul, R. (2006, November 27). Handling of AD/HD students criticized. *The Australian.*

Standen, A. (2006, November 28). Inside the teenage brain. An interview with Raleigh Philip. *Edutopia.* Available at http://www.edutopia.org/1720.

Steedman, W. (2005). *10 tips: How to use IDEA 2004 to improve education for children with disabilities.* Accessed June 15, 2006, from http://www.wrightslaw.com/idea/art/10.tips.steedman.pdf.

Sternberg, R. (2006). Recognizing neglected strengths. *Educational Leadership. 64*(1), 30–35.

Stewart, E. (2007, March 6). Classrooms go high-tech. *Desert Morning News,* Retrieved March 8, 2007, from http://desertnews.com.

Sundberg, M., & Michael, J. (1998). *A collection of reprints on verbal behavior.* Pleasant Hill, CA: Behavior Analysts.

Switzer, R. (2007, June 10). *Relief in sight as brain secrets unlocked.* Retrieved June 20, 2007, from http://www.theage.com.au/news/national/relief-in-sight-as-brain-secrets-unlocked.

Sword, C., & Hill, K. (2002). Creating mentoring opportunities for youth with disabilities: Issues and suggested strategies [Issue Brief]. *Examining Current Challenges in Secondary Education and Transition, 1,* 4. Retrieved June 28, 2007, from http://www.ncset.org/publications/viewdesc.asp?id=704.

Szalavitz, M. (2007, February 27). Gifted? Autistic? Or just quirky? *The Washington Post,* HE01.

Tanner, L. (2007, May 15). Autism, other disorders diagnosed earlier and earlier. *Associated Press.* Retrieved May 17, 2007, from http://www.courant.com/news/health.

TASH. Organization offering more opportunities and inclusion to people with disabilities. 1025 Vermont Ave., Floor 7, Washington, DC 20005. Web site: http://www.tash.org; Phone: (202) 263–5600; Fax: (202) 637–0138.

TESOL. (n.d.). Teachers of English to Speakers of Other Languages. 700 South Washington Street, Suite 200, Alexandria, VA 22314. Web site: http://www.tesol.org; Phone: (888) 547–3369.

Theroux, P. (2004). *Differentiated instruction.* Retrieved December 7, 2006, from http://members.shaw.ca/priscillatheroux/differentiating.html.

Tomlinson, C., & McTighe, J. (2006). *Integrating differentiated instruction & understanding by design.* Alexandria, VA: Association of Supervision and Curriculum Development.

Tories put Blair's challenger on special needs in spotlight. (2005, March 8). *The Times* (UK). Retrieved November 16, 2005, from http://web24.epnet.com/citation.

UN Enable. (2005, December 3). *Secretary-General's message on International Day of Disabled Persons.* Retrieved June 27, 2007, from http://www.un.org/esa/socdev/enable/iddp2006.htm.

UN News Centre (2007, May 15). *UN experts examine disability issues, family support.* Retrieved July 2, 2007, from http://www.un.org/apps/news/story.asp?NewsID=22557&Cr=disabilities&Cr1

Unger, L. (2006, December 10). New teaching method may aid autistic students. *Courier Journal.* Retrieved December 18, 2006, from http://www.courier-journal.com.

Urquhart, I. (2005, November 9). Special ed debate returns to haunt Ontario. *Toronto Star.* Retrieved November 16, 2005, from http://www.thestar.com.

U.S. Department of Education. (2002). *The Carl D. Perkins Vocational and Technical Education Act, P.L. 105-332.* Available at http://www.ed.gov/offices/OVAE/CTE/perkins.html.

U.S. Department of Education. (2007). *Welcome! About the Institute of Education Services.* Available at http://www.ed.gov/about/offices/list/ies/index.html.

U.S. Department of Education. (n.d.). *History: Twenty-five years of progress in educating children with disabilities through IDEA.* Retrieved November 29, 2005, from http://www.ed.gov/print/policy/speced/leg/idea/history.html.

U.S. Department of Education. (n.d.). *A reading checklist—Helping your child become a reader.* Retrieved December 4, 2006, from http://www.ed.gov/print/parents/academic/help/reader/part8.html.

U.S. Department of Labor, Office of Disability Employment Policy. (2007, July 7). *Cultivating leadership: Mentoring youth with disabilities.* Available online at http://www.dol.gov/odep/pubs/fact/cultivate.htm.

Villa, R., & Thousand, J. (2003). Making inclusive education work. *Educational Leadership, 61,* 19.

Villegas, A., & Lucas, T. (2007). The culturally responsive teacher. *Educational Leadership, 64*(6), 28–33.

Ward, M. J. (1996). Coming of age in the age of self-determination. A historical and personal perspective. In D. J. Sands & M. L. Wehmeyer (Eds.), *Self-determination across the lifespan: Independence and choice for people with disabilities* (pp. 1–14). Baltimore: Brookes.

How should the disabled be described? (2006, March 30). *The Washington Post.* DZ01.

Wedl, R. (2005, July). *Response to intervention: An alternative to traditional eligibility criteria for students with disabilities.* St. Paul, MN: Education/Evolving. Available at http://education evolving.org/pdf/Response_to_Intervention.pdf.

Weir, L. (2005, May). Raising the awareness of online accessibility. *THE Journal, 32,* 10.

Whitbread, K., Bruder, M., Fleming, G., & Park, H. (2007). Collaboration in special education: Parent–professional training. *Teaching Exceptional Children, 39*(4), 6–14.

Zimmerman, E. (Dec. 17, 2006, December 17). On the job, learning disabilities can often hide in plain sight. *New York Times,* Section 10, pp. 1, 3.

Index

CORWIN PRESS

The Corwin Press logo—a raven striding across an open book—represents the union of courage and learning. Corwin Press is committed to improving education for all learners by publishing books and other professional development resources for those serving the field of PreK–12 education. By providing practical, hands-on materials, Corwin Press continues to carry out the promise of its motto: **"Helping Educators Do Their Work Better."**